Anthea Lawson has fought for many issues over three decades including controls on the arms trade and an end to the financial secrecy offered by tax havens. She helped launch a campaign for transparency over company ownership which resulted in changes to the law in dozens of countries. After training as a journalist at *The Times*, she worked for campaign groups including Global Witness and Amnesty International. She is the author of *The Entangled Activist*.

Praise for *How Not to Save the World*

'A wise, rich and crucial book, which is helping me to do better, and will help many others.'

George Monbiot

'Read it and weep, laugh, cringe… It might bring more compassion and togetherness in a broken world.'

Dr Gail Bradbrook, co-founder of Extinction Rebellion

'Anthea Lawson's provocative book provides us with deep insights into the tactical, emotional and ethical complexities of campaigning – and, in particular, of how best to set about saving the world.'

Sir Jonathon Porritt

'An urgent book, a scintillating call to match our outer activism with inner self-awareness. And this, not just to win campaigns, but towards the deeper transformation of the world.'

Professor Alastair McIntosh,
author of *Soil and Soul* and *Spiritual Activism*

'A vital intervention. Even with the best intentions, organisations and individuals can inadvertently makes things worse. This book points a way forward that invites us all into our agency as citizens, so we can build the world we want together.'

Jon Alexander, author of *Citizens*

'Deeply researched and refreshingly honest, this book is for activists – and the activism-weary. It helps readers interrogate their own protest practices, mindsets, and intentions, cultivating kinder, more reflective campaigning rooted in connection and community.'

Sarah P. Corbett,
author of *The Craftivist Collective Handbook*

'Highly readable… Lawson's book provides a map of the possible pitfalls of working towards a better world. A realistic, funny assessment of what to do if you worry about the cringe parts of activist culture but can't stand to watch the world burn.'

Sarah Stein Lubrano,
author of *Don't Talk About Politics*

'Provides concrete storytelling and strategy about many different forms of social justice work while speaking directly to some of the ways that justice-oriented folk get in the way of the work we want to build. Anthea tells these stories with a mix of directness and compassion. This is humility and it is part of how we become the world we want to see.'

Susan Raffo,
author of *Liberated to the Bone*

'Lawson invites us to critically reflect on our own assumptions, shortcomings and strengths, whilst offering hope that change is possible. An outstanding book and essential reading for every activist, practitioner and thinker concerned about the future of our planet.'

Emma River-Roberts,
Founder and Director of the
Working Class Climate Alliance

'Anthea Lawson's book is a searing self-examination of her work as a climate activist. Her brutally honest account of her experience moved me in unexpected ways, especially as she came to realize the class divides that climate protestors have had such difficulty overcoming.'

Professor Catherine Liu,
author of *Virtue Hoarders*

'This is a must read for anyone working in the NGO sector! A brilliant reflection on how the very systems that we are attempting to dismantle are recreated in our movements when we approach activism as a quest to "save the world".'

Martha Awojobi,
creator of Uncharitable Political Education

'Anthea Lawson is one of the world's most serious thinkers on the limits of "activism". Her thinking has been and continues to be very influential on vital efforts to create a new moderate flank to the most attention-grabbing environmental campaigners.'

Rupert Read,
co-director of the Climate Majority Project
and author of *Why Climate Breakdown Matters*

Also by Anthea Lawson

The Entangled Activist

HOW NOT TO
SAVE THE WORLD

*Doing Good Without
Annoying Everyone*

Anthea Lawson

A Oneworld Book

First published by Oneworld Publications Ltd in 2026

Copyright © Anthea Lawson, 2026

ISBN 978-1-83643-175-6
eISBN 978-1-83643-176-3

Typeset by Geethik Technologies
Printed and bound in Great Britain by Clays Ltd, Elcograf S.p.A.

The authorised representative in the EEA is eucomply OU,
Pärnu mnt 139b–14, 11317 Tallinn, Estonia
(email: hello@eucompliancepartner.com / phone: +33757690241)

Oneworld Publications Ltd
10 Bloomsbury Street
London WC1B 3SR
England

Stay up to date with the latest books,
special offers, and exclusive content from
Oneworld with our newsletter

Sign up on our website
oneworld.co.uk

MIX
Paper | Supporting
responsible forestry
FSC® C018072

CONTENTS

To everyone working in service to life

INTRODUCTION

THE SAVE-THE-WORLD SCRIPT

I have been trying to save the world for more than twenty-five years and – spoiler alert – I have not yet succeeded. This book will not tell you how to start a petition, devise a campaign plan or avoid getting arrested at a protest. It will not teach you how to organise, raise funds, get TikTok famous or persuade old media to care. You may pick up tips along the way because I will be sharing some stories; a few of my own and plenty from other campaigners. But I am here instead to invite us to pause for a moment, even though it's all very pressing, and think together – whether you are a change-maker already, or might consider it if only change-makers weren't so weird sometimes – about *how* we try to save the world. About how we show up.

Those of us striving for positive change can create problems for ourselves, the people we hope to help, and the causes we are working for. We can become inflamed with righteousness, blocking real communication and preventing the formation of more powerful coalitions. We can go at our tasks like a firestorm and quickly burn out. We can unconsciously internalise stories about being a hero and end up trampling on the people we want to help. And we are so intent, so passionate about saving the world that we rarely scrutinise the shadow side of our actions.

For those already involved, these problems are familiar: we all know that while working for change can be joyful, energising and rewarding, it can also be fractious and exhausting. Discussing the shortcomings of the 'activist' is hardly new within left-wing and progressive circles,[1] and it only escalated once social media showed us what everyone else was up to. From the outside, righteousness and saviour heroics sound like the usual stereotype of the tiresome do-gooder. Righteousness in particular remains a staple criticism, whether from divide-and-rule culture warriors on the right, or from pro-democracy and centrist voices who'd like us to *dial it down a little* so as not to exacerbate polarisation. If only the left weren't so *annoying* perhaps we'd have got rid of the fascists by now. Maybe it's the activists' fault that the liberal dream is sliding away?

Meanwhile, the police have been given sweeping new powers to surveil and arrest protesters and decide if a demonstration is too loud or annoying.[2] A young woman is arrested for protesting a policeman murdering another young woman; climate protestors are jailed for taking part in a video call; pensioners face terror charges for holding up signs in support of Palestine. When there's so much that's stacked against us and so much at stake, dare we even ask the question… are *we* sometimes part of the problem?

It's true that we don't always help ourselves. I will come to that. But I'm not going to lecture from the outside. Firstly, I am not on the outside – I have skin in the game. I am writing about what I've been doing for much of my adult life. Secondly, because my intention is to offer some deeper psychological, cultural and philosophical explorations into the desire to save the world. And while I'm going to suggest that we can and should do things differently, I'm not saying that what's now happening in the world is all our fault. Also, let's remember, the state of things is rarely caused by individuals – just as it cannot be resolved by individuals acting alone. The forces of big money pitted against a thriving biosphere and a just society are colossal. Faced with all this, it can be tempting to turn away. I don't think that's the answer. But neither is it always right to just keep trying the same thing.

After more than two decades of seeking to improve things, I see a repeated narrative. It runs under the surface, whatever the issue. This *save-the-world script* is laid out on the contents page. It tells us we must be heroes and that we must make things pure. It tells us that we are good, that we know better than others, that *we* are okay, that others are not and so *we* must save *them*, and that it's so urgent we cannot rest. I have seen fragments of this script in community groups, grassroots campaigns, big charities, climate protest, within both non-governmental organisations (NGOs) and among people who hate NGOs, within the Labour Party and on the wider left, among human rights lawyers, among people who love calling themselves 'activists' and among those who resist that label and try to act simply as citizens – the script plays out wherever people are working towards a better world. Not everyone adheres to the entire script. But many of us find ourselves acting out parts of it. I have grappled with all of these pitfalls myself – and continue to do so.

This inherited script is culturally transmitted and can be picked up at any stage of life, whenever we turn to change-making. In its British incarnation, the focus of this book, we find elements of the UK's Christian heritage and its histories of class and empire. 'Religious' behaviour is a typical criticism of activists, especially when we appear to be pursuing dogma, or descending into Puritan or Inquisition mode and

demanding conformity of thought; there has been speculation that activism can fulfil some of the roles that organised
religion used to play in people's lives.[3]

It's true that religion can be a positive motivating force
for careful, considered campaigning for justice: I've learned
much from protesting and advocating alongside Buddhists
and Quakers, for example, and their influence permeates
some of the insights in this book. On the other hand, observations about dogmatic behaviour are not entirely wrong.
There is even more to it, I think: I look at how the entire
frame of 'saving' emerges from Christian thought structures
that we no longer recognise as Christian in our secular age.
There are roots, too, in ancient myths and in the psychology
of the unconscious that psychoanalytic thinking has opened
up to us in the last 125 years.[4]

The script is far older than the current culture wars and
did not create them, but it ratchets up progressive people's
participation in them. It doesn't prescribe specific words
or actions, but guides us towards the kind of roles we
think we should be playing, and shapes a way of being,
speaking and approaching problems that feels so instinctive
we do not realise we are being influenced. And while we
are happy to spend time debating theories of change and
analysing the political situation, we are often less willing
to examine these infectious and subterranean habits that
guide our thinking and behaviour in the task of trying to
make change.

The save-the-world script not only impedes our effectiveness, preventing us from being heard by those we want
to influence. It also turns off those who might otherwise
like to help, who can read – often better than self-identified
change-makers – the script's implicit message: that if you
are not like this, you cannot take part. That if you have

flown recently or eat meat, you cannot speak about the climate catastrophe. That if you don't know the answer, you shouldn't try to name the problem. That if you are aware of your privilege, there is nothing for you to say. That if you feel broken, you can't help anyone else.

I do not assume any participation or prior knowledge of how change-making works. Maybe you are a veteran campaigner. Maybe you picked up this book because you are worried about the way things are going and want to contribute in a way that doesn't look like standard-issue activism. Perhaps you feel so overwhelmed by the enormity of the problems that you are not sure where to begin, and want to take a step back to think about how to effect real change. Perhaps you would like to understand why your recently politicised family members are engaging in open combat at the dinner table. Or maybe you are irritated to hell by people gluing themselves to trains, even when you support the same causes, and wish there was a better way to do it.

Pointing out problems with the status quo will always provoke defensiveness and discomfort, yet there are alternatives to the save-the-world script, and antidotes to the old saviour patterns. I have spent two years interviewing campaigners, charity workers, grassroots organisers, political activists, union organisers, humanitarian workers and volunteers in their communities who are finding ways to subvert the script, and who have generously shared their stories and experiences. You will hear from them about new experiments, and old wisdom that is easily forgotten in the heat of urgency.

I came of age to the repetitive beats of the early 1990s, sat my finals as Tony Blair was elected in May 1997 and learned how to influence policy, laws and treaties in what felt like a stable political and international order. I trained and worked as a news reporter at *The Times*, but as the century ended, I was also out on marches with the global justice movement, protesting against corporate power and the IMF and World Bank's stranglehold over indebted countries. I became a full-time campaigner for human rights groups: Amnesty International, where I researched weapons sales to regimes violating human rights, and Global Witness, where I ran teams investigating how banks, oil companies and tax havens contributed to poverty, corruption and environmental destruction. I worked in coalitions that later won the 2010 ban on cluster munitions and the 2013 Arms Trade Treaty, and launched a campaign to lobby for mandatory disclosure of the owners of companies – so that tax evaders, profit-shifters and the corrupt cannot hide their identities – that resulted in changes to the law in the UK and, subsequently, dozens of other countries. (These were rolled back under Trump in the US in March 2025).[5] This work won the TED Prize in 2014 for Global Witness, and I was subsequently interviewed by academics studying what makes a policy campaign successful.

That world in which I first began fighting for change has gone. This became obvious when the MP Jo Cox, whom some of my friends and colleagues knew from her years at Oxfam, was murdered in the street by a far-right extremist a week before the Brexit referendum in 2016. As the poison from Brexit and Trump's first victory spread, the issues we had been plugging away at for years – human rights, economic and social justice, protection of the living world and a safe climate – were being weaponised and derided in the right-wing press and by culture-warring conservative politicians as 'woke'. (Remarkable really that we persist in calling these things 'issues' when they are the foundations of life.) We had always wanted more mainstream recognition as we strategised how to win public attention, but this was not the kind of attention we were after. By summer 2024, as British citizens stood in the streets against far-right-provoked riots, and by early 2025, as Trump took aim at the post-1945 transatlantic alliance and a Labour prime minister in the UK echoed the far-right talking points on immigration that have been relentlessly pushed in mainstream media, it felt like we were being overtaken.

Support for the far right's scare tactics and scapegoating only grows as societies are hollowed out by inequality and their social safety nets shredded, as in the UK now. We are a country where one in six workers say they are skipping meals[6] and even by the government's own reckoning 31% of children – 4.5 million – are living in poverty.[7] Artificial intelligence is destroying jobs, while housing, health, social care, education and environmental protection are in crisis after years of austerity, privatisation and financialisation.

Meanwhile climate breakdown continues to threaten the biological systems on which we depend for food. The increase in average global temperatures went past 1.5C in 2024, as emissions continued to rise.[8] In 2023, oil and gas extraction were at a historic high, and during 2024, the warmest year on record, forty-eight major banks increased their financing for fossil fuel extraction, bringing total oil and gas funding from the world's sixty-five largest banks to $7.9 trillion since 2016, the year after the Paris Agreement.[9] Mainstream political parties and commentators still refuse to discuss what many of us can see are compulsory alternatives to endless economic growth on a finite planet, even as we move closer to climate tipping points whose consequences we can barely imagine.[10]

It's now much harder to down tools and go on strike than in previous generations, and non-violent protest has recently been criminalised to an extent unprecedented in this country, so that it is now treated more seriously than many forms of violence. During 2025, as the state of Israel was bombing and starving the people of Gaza, a non-violent organisation protesting the UK's support for Israel was banned under terrorism legislation. While I've been writing this book, peaceful protesters have been serving sentences or are being held on remand in British prisons. This is especially striking at a time when prisons are over-crowded and convictions for sexual violence are rare.

These are some key elements of the current juncture. Now, it's true that we don't always reflect on past action to absorb its lessons because we are battling the next crisis. Conversely, we can hark back to mythic glory days – battles that won legal change like the fights for civil rights or women's suffrage, or epic instances of togetherness such as Greenham Common or the 1990s roads protests – and take insufficient account of what it actually took to win change, or what is different now. But even if I wanted to write a book for my younger self to share what I have learned over my years of experience, does a campaigner who cut their teeth in those pre-2016 decades have anything to say about fighting for shared values now?

Yes, because while politics since 2016 feels unprecedented (and the open alliance between tech and authoritarian power is new), the triumph of authoritarians like Trump is a feature, not an anomaly, of neoliberal capitalism and the inequality it generates. I had been trying to show the holes in neoliberalism's 'normal' for years. Trump is the expected outcome of a system that deifies profit for the few, gives far too much power over politics to the extremely wealthy, encourages the brightest graduates to turn over their passion and energy to the wealth-defence industries[11] of banking, consultancy and corporate lawyering, and reports on politics as an entertaining spectacle. Those of us who were following the money have been warning for years that the offshore financial system will facilitate the kind of wealth accumulation that undermines democracy.[12] We have been arguing that the neoliberal ideology of deregulation and the practice of financialisation will gut the state and its ability to offer protection, leaving us all vulnerable to corporate predation.[13] The kind of campaigning I have done has given me a pretty clear-eyed view of the consequences we are witnessing now. And our societies are not going to resist the siren call of polarising messages from the radical right until far more of us are calling clearly for economic justice for us all.[14]

Another reason why my pre-2016 experience remains relevant is that the human psychology I was observing through those years is perennial. Our learned patterns are remarkably persistent. Some of the behaviours encoded in the save-the-world script are risks recognised by ancient wisdom traditions and myths as well as by modern psychology: the purity-seeking, the quest to be the hero, the desire to identify with the good while projecting our darker side onto others. Others are a hangover from centuries of rigid class structure, empire and white supremacy, like relating to people from a saviour position rather than joining in solidarity, and elevating our own knowledge and ways of knowing over other people's lived experience. The habit of urgency, meanwhile, is at the heart of modernity, driving the accumulation narratives and insistence on economic growth that have got us into this mess.

Of course, the threats we face are urgent. Yet while diving in to 'save the world' according to the classic script may make us *feel* better, it may not have the impact we want. If we hold our own knowledge dearly and think that we alone are right, we may assume that it is sufficient to protest or lobby to make our point known, rather than doing the hard yards to build people power with those who do not share all of our views. If we have not questioned the assumptions that come with our own position, we may think that 'saving the world' means returning things to that illusory – and, history is likely to show, very temporary – state of complacency in which some of us did not have to think about the impact of our own way of life.

I mentioned that the stable world in which I started campaigning has vanished, but had I spent the early 1990s in the nations of the former Yugoslavia, or in Angola, Sierra Leone, or Liberia, where wars were tearing holes in homes and lives, it might have been more obvious that the whole Western end-of-history idea[15] was partial. Within the UK, if I had grown up not in a middle-class family within a suburb in the South East, but instead in a working-class family in an industrial town whose economy was shattered by Thatcher, I might not have had such a confident sense that the world was mine to change.

I tend to be upfront about being white and middle-class. We can all sniff out inauthenticity, and it pisses us off when someone casts too wide a net with their 'we'. To someone with more experience of hardship or marginalisation than me, my ongoing blind spots in this book may be obvious. Yet it does seem that some of the instructions in the script – the knowing-better and the saviour-relations – appear deeply encoded in particular middle-class ways of being in the UK, ones that I'm very familiar with. (Of course, 'middle-class' can mean different things to different people.[16]) It is fantastic that well-resourced people may have time, skills and resources to offer to their communities and to working towards the common good. And there are exceptions to what follows: if this is not you, you don't need to wear it. But I do observe a pattern: that middle-class folk can be better at information provision and declarations of position and protest than we are at getting out there and connecting with people. Indeed, I suspect that some of us can be more comfortable with a diversity of ideas than being with a diversity of actual people. And for any of us, our behaviour and assumptions also feed our emotional needs – for status, meaning, and to avoid feeling our own vulnerability. To do things differently, we need to be willing to look below the surface at ourselves – though this turning inwards cannot be our only focus.

There is an old polarity between inner attention and outer action. Relentless action with insufficient reflection may keep us on a seesaw between saviour heroics and burnout. But too restricted a diet of individualised psychology or abstracted metaphysics and we may forget the hard reality of politics and power. Actually, we need both. It is helpful to ask nuanced philosophical questions and prepare ourselves psychospiritually to fight together for a different future. The obstacles to a sane and just society living within planetary boundaries are, still, unfettered corporate power and the vested interests of a small and very rich proportion of the world's population. The long-standing Labour MP Tony Benn was right: every generation has to fight for its rights.[17]

The save-the-world script is an artefact of individualism, which is hard to see when it is the water we swim in. What most of the antidotes to the script that I am sharing have in common is that they take us out of our individual selves and into better communication with others. So often the reason that we don't try to change anything is because we don't think we alone can make a difference. If we think, as the script tells us, that the job is to act on our own and our goal is to save the world, such an assessment might seem logical. But the alternatives to the script help us to see that the job is about finding others, and that the next step might be right in front of us.

'I AM GOOD'

The line separating good and evil passes not through states, nor between classes, nor between political parties either — but right through every human heart.
    Aleksandr Solzhenitsyn, *The Gulag Archipelago*[1]

The end justifies the means. But what if there never is an end? All we have is means.
    Ursula K. Le Guin, *The Lathe of Heaven*[2]

GOOD PEOPLE DOING GOOD THINGS

Bushra Ahmed had spent two decades raising kids, caring for family members and running her family's launderette business in Croydon, South London before her community work took off. She was prompted by necessity. Their launderette was burned down in the riots of August 2011 after the police shot dead Mark Duggan, a 29-year-old Black man in Tottenham on the other side of the city. The police stood by as her family's property, livelihood, and the rest of the terrace — nine businesses in total — were destroyed.[3] It took Ahmed and her neighbours more than three years to get the promised compensation: 'hundreds of meetings, hundreds of rooms, hundreds of strategy conversations and community-regeneration conversations, year after year being told your compensation has been paid. Well, no, it hasn't, and we're here to say it hasn't,' she told me. 'Finally we got the payments, but in that time I was thinking, what do I do with all of this?'

'This' was the realisation that she was enjoying speaking her mind in public. Ahmed discovered she could put her prodigious energy and networking flair to good use. She thought about electoral politics, but had observed how the politicians she lobbied were bound by their parties. 'I was finding my voice at that point and didn't want it clipped,' she said. She was involved with projects working on youth violence, and someone suggested she should become a charity trustee. She was offered positions on the boards of local organisations, was picked for a civic leaders' mentoring programme run by the Mayor of London's office, mentored younger campaigners, and started to be recommended as a trustee for national-level charities. She has held several board positions since then. This was a political awakening and a personal and professional growth trajectory for Ahmed, but something else was happening along the way: a series of encounters with racist charity leaders.

Doors would close when she showed up. A board would decide to meet its 'diversity requirement' via the finance position. She would turn up for interviews and encounter pillars of the not-for-profit establishment with impressive CVs full of public service – who made denigrating assumptions about her abilities, or about her Muslim community's attitude to her work. They must have opposed her speaking out as a woman, the interviewers assumed. Actually, no, she replied, they supported her; in the particular story about urban regeneration she was telling, the real opposition came from local UKIP supporters who were spontaneously combusting at a hijab-wearing Muslim woman speaking up for the local area, not just her community. In one meeting with charity leaders, the response to her suggestion that they make their trustee boards substantially more diverse was 'but would that open the floodgates?', an unwitting re-statement of one of the far right's favourite metaphors about ethnic minorities. 'Do you realise what that means?' she later asked the person who said this. They responded with a barrage of flummery about how such a move would bring in lots of skills.

Perhaps it had always been this way, like sexual assault and harassment were ever-present in the decades (and millennia) before #MeToo went viral in 2017. But from 2018, influenced by #MeToo and Black Lives Matter, stories of discrimination, harassment, bullying and abuse in UK charities began to hit the news. It was revealed that Oxfam aid workers had paid survivors of the 2010 Haiti earthquake, some of them underage, for sex. Two senior managers at Save the Children's office in London had sexually harassed female staff. Both organisations already knew, and neither had investigated the allegations properly.[4]

Amnesty International's toxic culture of pressured martyrdom was laid bare in a 2019 report after two staff suicides;[5] a separate review found that 'a serious failure of management' at Amnesty had contributed to one of them.[6] Following the global anti-racist uprisings after George Floyd was murdered in Minneapolis in 2020, another two investigations found overt racism in Amnesty's London offices, and a culture of systemic institutional racism in both the global headquarters and the separately run offices of Amnesty's UK section across town, where complaints of racist bullying had not been followed up.[7]

Meanwhile in 2020 the Alzheimer's Society was alleged to have paid off staff who signed non-disclosure agreements amid claims of a bullying culture emanating from its CEO and other senior staff; the CEO, it was reported, was dropped by the Samaritans where he'd been about to take the helm.[8] The Charity Commission later found no evidence that confidentiality clauses were used to suppress whistle-blowing,[9] but according to a media report, they did not interview staff and were accused of a whitewash.[10] The following year, the Chartered Institute of Fundraisers was criticised for failing to act on complaints of sexual harassment.[11] At the National Lottery Community Fund – which distributes hundreds of millions of pounds of cash from the UK's National Lottery each year – whistle-blower accounts of bullying led to a government investigation. Of the nearly half the staff body who offered evidence, a third had witnessed or experienced instances of bullying, harassment or discriminatory behaviour.[12]

And there was little help to be found from one of the key industry bodies in the UK, the century-old National Council for Voluntary Organisations (NCVO), because it was in the same mess. In 2021 a leaked report revealed that overt, pervasive and systematic bullying and harassment based on race, gender, sexual orientation and disability occurred at all levels of the organisation.[13] Complaints of harassment and race discrimination made against the CEO and his deputy would be upheld by another independent investigation the following year.[14]

A charity worker in London called Sophia Moreau was one of the first to tweet the hashtag #NotJustNCVO. 'It was the hypocrisy. And knowing, even if we all comment on this, it's not just one organisation. It's happening everywhere,' she told me. The resulting wave of allegations of abusive behaviour across the UK's charities was modest next to the global #MeToo tsunami, but it rattled the sector.

When I spoke to Moreau eighteen months later, the stories were still coming in, now to a steering group that convened around the hashtag to offer support and advice, and she was running information and support clinics for people who were disclosing. When she first tweeted it, Moreau was campaigning for maternity rights for students with a pressure group called Pregnant Then Screwed. She was also part of an informal network of charity staff who had been sharing stories in response to the 'CharitySoWhite' hashtag a couple of years earlier, that, she said, 'was a real awakening moment. It lifted the lid on something we'd been talking about. If we draw a parallel to the #MeToo movement, it was yes, that happened to me; it's not just you. And we'd see that the exact same steps had systematically occurred.'

Bushra Ahmed had also noticed how hard it was to speak out. 'If you are employed in the sector, whatever level you're at, it's hard to say anything because first of all you don't want to lose your job, secondly you don't want to be seen as a troublemaker, and thirdly, it is very cliquey. I've had trustees say to me, "Oh well, if they say anything, don't worry, I know that person and we'll go talk to them." Something goes wrong in one charity, there'll be a little review, silence, no accountability, and two minutes later you find this person has hopped over to another job having taken a really cushy settlement or redundancy. That's why the problems keep going.' Finally, the silence about such arrangements seemed to be lifting.

Is it news, though, if there's something rotten at the heart of some of the UK's charities? 'There was some criticism,' Moreau said, 'about whether it's bad PR for the charity sector when these issues aren't unique to it.' Misogyny, racism and bullying occur in the public and private sectors too, because they are endemic in the wider culture. Before

I worked in charities, I was a journalist, and had seen plenty of vile behaviour in my short few years in Fleet Street newsrooms. But the press gets hot for charity scandals because hypocrisy sells. Whether we're working in them, volunteering with them, donating to them or receiving their support, we expect congruence between what charities do and how they do it. It's disturbing (or, to cynics, inevitable) when they fail. When my agent and I first pitched this book to publishers, one wanted it to be a juicy tell-all about the misdeeds of do-gooders. After more than two decades in this work I have many such stories, but I'm not here to point fingers; that's not the story I want to tell.

These examples are here as illustrations of the story that lies underneath the bullying scandals, a story that reveals itself through the defensive responses they provoke. Moreau volunteers at employment tribunals, supporting victims of discrimination, and notices that charities and other nonprofit organisations are far more defensive than companies. In the private sector, she notes, there are more standard responses to being held accountable. 'When you raise concerns, you are a complainant, or you're challenging something, but you're not automatically perceived to be raising something systemic that is against the organisation's mission and so has broader implications. But in the charity sector, the affected person who raises concerns instantly becomes a whistle-blower. So you're often treated worse, because you're attacking whether they're fit for purpose.' Defensive moves against whistle-blowers betray the strong investment in being *good* that the whistle-blower threatens to undermine – for both individuals and organisations who are trying to make the world better.

'I am good' is the foundational instruction on the save-the-world script. It obstructs self-reflection because it carries the message, 'we are not the problem'. 'Good people doing good things, who cannot do bad things' was the title of the 2022 inquiry into institutional racism at Amnesty UK. 'I am good' prevents us seeing the rest of the save-the-world script, because we think it doesn't apply to us or, if it does, our behaviour is outweighed by the concrete good we are trying to achieve. That's why this book begins here, because if we cannot get past the obstacle of thinking we're 'good', we cannot look at what else we are doing that may be unhelpful.

When these organisations hit crisis, 'we are good' plays out differently depending on the stage of the allegations. Early on, the charity tries not to lose their 'good' status. That means fighting: defending a tribunal claim, or denial, avoidance and turning the objection back onto the complainant.[15] Once it's gone public and there are independent reviews that cannot be disputed, the approach changes. Now they are trying to *reclaim* their good status as quickly as possible by apologising and offering hasty plans for change. I noticed this as I reviewed the statements from these organisations following the reports into their failings. They apologise, and note that apologies are insufficient. They promise to strengthen procedures, make action plans, improve their culture. These apologies and acknowledgements are necessary – their reputation and brand are at stake and funding is in question too, from the public and, in Oxfam and Save the Children's cases, from the government.[16] But reading these statements, one after another, I felt uneasy. Having been on a senior management team at a nonprofit campaigning organisation, I know just how hard it is to implement such declarations, let alone to truly change organisational cultures. But I was also hearing the dissonance between 'we acknowledge the problem and we're truly sorry' and the unspoken eagerness to reclaim their status as 'good'.

Deep in the Covid winter of early 2021, I was following these stories online as they unfolded. I was remembering the sexism I had experienced, told I was being 'too aggressive' when I protested about being paid less than a man for the same work. I was realising, too, that it was unlikely that I had never acted from the assumptions of whiteness,[17] or expressed any racist bias in a workplace. There was also a grim sense of recognition. I had encountered bullies, and the poor management that enabled them, since I first started working in human rights campaigning organisations nearly twenty years prior. I couldn't understand it: people campaigning for human rights and dignity, being horrible to each other! It made no sense.

After another decade and more in which I kept seeing this strange dissonance, my curiosity got the better of me and I started to investigate. And so as these charity scandals were breaking, I was just finishing writing my first book, *The Entangled Activist*. It was my search for an answer to this question: why do people trying to make the world better end up recreating the problems they are trying to solve? I had interviewed many other campaigners, from different backgrounds, working on diverse issues, to find out whether they were asking the same question, and if so, whether they had any answers. They did, though those with less access to power often had a better handle on how and why systems of power replicate themselves through the behaviour of those trying to dismantle them. I started to see how enmeshed we are in what we are trying to change. We can kid ourselves that we are better than everyone else, that we are separate from the problems we work on, because we don't want to see ourselves as part of them. It is often counterintuitive to activist culture to admit that we might not be the good ones; that we might be part of the problem.

Now, here was institution after institution doing just this: reluctant to recognise their involvement in inequality and injustice, because they wanted to identify with the good. And I knew how easy it is to become attached to that image. I experienced profound relief and enjoyment at being on the unequivocally 'good' side when I started working for campaign groups in my late twenties. My first paid role was at Amnesty International's secretariat in Farringdon, as a junior researcher on a team investigating weapons sales to human rights-abusing governments. The papers, books and reports cascading from desks in my corner of the ground floor were familiar from newsroom life, but in every other respect the atmosphere of the office was thrillingly different. The joy of conversations with colleagues who were like-minded. No longer needing to censor myself. I had been a business news reporter at a corporate-owned newspaper, where I struggled with the focus on share prices to the exclusion of the human and environmental impact behind those upticks and downturns of the markets. At last, my work felt aligned with my observations about what was wrong with the world: ongoing colonial economic relations, even after the end of empire, and the UK's role in the global arms trade as part of it.

That feeling of congruence is filed, in my mind, inseparably from the memory of those messy offices, windows bracingly open to the London air in contrast to the sterile air con of the corporate newsroom I'd left behind. The pleasurable feeling, however, slid into a slight superiority towards anyone not doing such work. The intrinsic pleasure of doing good work merged with the satisfaction of feeling better than *others*. Here is one of the consequences of considering ourselves 'good' – it puts us on a road to seeing others as not-good. This is one of several consequences of 'I am good' for how we go about trying to make change.

'IF YOU BELIEVE YOU REPRESENT THE FORCES OF GOOD...'

Attachment to being good in the face of evidence to the contrary isn't limited to charities and pressure groups. 'The fundamental problem,' said an independent inquiry into the culture of the Labour Party under Jeremy Corbyn's troubled leadership, 'is that people who are committed to progressive politics find it difficult if not impossible to accept that they might have acted in a way which was discriminatory. There seems to us to be a tendency among Party staff to believe that they are insulated from the ills of their society.' It added, 'There is a tendency on the Left in general, and in the Party (irrespective of tradition) to a specific type of self-righteousness.'[18]

Led by Martin Forde KC, the inquiry was commissioned by Keir Starmer when he became Labour Party leader in April 2020,[19] and received 'overwhelming' evidence of discrimination in thousands of pages of submissions. The Forde report set out evidence of a 'toxic culture in Party workplaces', antisemitism and factional weaponisation of antisemitism complaints that failed 'to recognise the seriousness of antisemitism [and] its effect on Jewish communities', serious problems with racism and bullying, a 'hierarchy of racism' with antisemitism taken more seriously than other forms of racism, and discriminatory attitudes among senior staff.[20] It detailed paralysing factionalism, systematic efforts against Corbyn's leadership and secret resourcing of anti-Corbyn MPs at the 2017 election.

Both sides of the pro- and anti-Corbyn divide within Labour felt somewhat vindicated by Forde's criticisms of the opposing faction, though Forde and his panel were taken to task on the left for being too 'both-sides': failing to acknowledge the power struggles in the party.[21] The UK's first-past-the-post voting system has forced the different political visions of socialists and centrists to cohabit within Labour. The criticism here was of political naivety: that Forde had worked so hard to be even-handed, the asymmetry of the situation was flattened. The reality, in this view, was that Labour's left isn't only up against the 'establishment' in the UK as a whole – the wealthy, finance, big business, the media – but the right of their own party. For Forde to focus on culture sounded to some ears like he was plaintively asking 'why can't everyone just get along?'

In a different sense, however, Forde was suggesting something profound. He was arguing for a radical change of culture among people who profess to want the UK to be a more caring place, and pointing out that the obstacle to it is their attachment to an idea about themselves as good. A roundtable participant in the inquiry put it like this: 'if you believe you represent the forces of good and if you believe your struggle is by definition morally superior to anyone else's... you may allow yourself to behave in ways that might otherwise shame you.' Forde warned of 'a culture of intellectual smugness' at the extremes of both Labour's left and right flanks which 'has led to the dismissal of valid, albeit sometimes uncomfortable' views.[22]

There's no need to relitigate the problems of Corbyn's leadership here.[23] Labour said it had implemented most of the report's recommendations, but Forde expressed concerns in an interview with Al Jazeera that the wider implications of his findings had not been taken up. In response, Labour's lawyers sent him a strongly worded letter trying to stop him speaking about it. He responded with a letter of his own and heard nothing further.[24]

I find Forde's analysis (and Labour's response) interesting because it's not often that the dynamics arising from 'we are good' get named, especially in a big institution like Labour. As scholars of the psychology of misconduct point out, researching unethical behaviour by organisations is challenging because the organisations usually try to hide it.[25] I saw parallels with the charity and NGO scandals – though there are differences. In the third sector, denial and cover for bad actions derive from an equation that goes something like: 'we're doing good work and therefore we are good; the power we exert must therefore be good and cannot possibly be bad.' People involved in charities and campaigning can disavow our will to power entirely. Because our work involves grappling with hegemonic power we can forget that this is only one kind of power, and that there is also the more generative power to make things happen, power of the sort that we need to cultivate. Wary of how power is used by those in charge, we can push our own desires for controlling power further into shadow and, like anything we suppress, they can emerge in unexpected and damaging ways.

In electoral politics, however, the conflict is open. The brutal calculus of building power, winning or losing at whatever scale – whether the internal argument for your policies or the next election – means that 'we are good' operates something like this: 'we need to get into power to do our good work, therefore anything is justified to achieve that.' The ends justify the means. Treating people well and winning can come to be seen as mutually exclusive. 'It's about being the tough activist, or the tough person in the bureaucracy who is making things happen,' said a former Labour staffer, preferring to speak anonymously.

I spoke to people on both the left and right of Labour: people who have worked in the party's head office, the leader's office and in constituency parties, and in various locations on the extra-parliamentary left. They all recognised Forde's observation that the conviction of moral superiority was used as an excuse for terrible behaviour.[26] 'There's great store put on being a proper radical and that means not caring too much about who you trample on,' the ex-staffer continued. 'Your interpersonal relationships are secondary, because you're serving a higher purpose. Some people are quite explicit about it and play up to it. Treating people as completely instrumental, and setting up a series of instrumental relationships... which big bureaucracies tend to do anyway, right? There are other models: I mean, most union organisers don't behave like this at all. If you're on the ground, actually trying to organise people, you can't do this. It's once you're sitting somewhere else in an institution that it starts to become more of a problem. Then you say, 'Well, here we are, all supposed to be on the progressive side of the spectrum. And this big machine is set up to do good things and I'm serving the machine so I must be doing good things, and it doesn't matter what I do – it's a bit of a cliché, but as a means to an end.'

Isabel de Bruin Cardoso recently coined the term 'NGO halo effect' to describe the 'glorified perception of moral integrity within NGOs' which 'can create blind spots for unethical behaviour.'[27] She's a lecturer in organisational ethics at Erasmus University in Rotterdam, and saw a paradox: that unethical behaviour occurs *because* of the perception of moral integrity, not just in spite of it. As an adviser for nonprofits and UN agencies on their safeguarding systems to prevent sexual abuse, De Bruin Cardoso had seen their policies were failing to prevent abuse. And while there was a long-standing academic literature on safeguarding in business, there was little research on safeguarding in NGOs. 'I wondered if it had to do with the perception that NGOs are generally considered as "good" organizations, and thus whether there was a perception in NGOs that they don't need any structures to manage safeguarding,' she wrote. NGO staff she interviewed would describe their colleagues as 'heroes' or 'angels'.[28]

The halo effect was first theorised in psychology more than a century ago. It describes how a general positive impression can create overly positive distortions in our perception of a person or thing.[29] People in NGOs perceiving their work as morally good was not, in itself, the issue, De Bruin Cardoso found. It was the glorification of moral goodness – the addition of the halo, in effect – that was the problem; it was a factor in 92% of the cases of unethical behaviour (discrimination, abuse, financial mismanagement, corruption and abuse of power) that she analysed.[30] These findings cast additional light on the UK charity scandals and what Bushra Ahmed had been telling me. Reading De Bruin Cardoso's research papers with the Forde report and the Labour Party in mind, her findings made an intuitive sense in that context too.

'But do you think there are any kind of institutions in which people don't treat each other in sub-optimal ways?' one interviewee asked me. Anyway, he reminded me, this is hardly new on the left: arguments have been going on about the relevance of personal conduct since the beginnings of socialism.[31] He was wondering if I might be getting stuck on something that is a normal and inevitable part of people getting together to achieve something. Why does it matter, then?

It's a good question. Let me suspend, for a moment, my make-things-better impulse. Let's assume as that interviewee did that treating people badly is inevitable, and in a still-misogynist and still-racist society, ill-treatment may often take misogynist and racist forms. Let's recognise that while congruence between organisational aims and personal behaviour is important for charities that need their reputation to fundraise,[32] it might be less important for more combative forms of change-making like politics or protest.

Let's also acknowledge that being 'good' is hardly a requirement for changing the world. Those we're up against are rarely bothered about being seen as good, which is one reason why they can come across as more relatable. They reserve for their work all that energy that we spend trying to be good. The neoliberal right hasn't cared about being good; for decades they have felt free to get on with their projects of taking power to change society into their market-based, individualised image of what it is to be human. Now the radical right are busy crafting and wielding populist messages that gravely harm immigrants and other scapegoated groups, and want to unleash further deregulation that will worsen poverty and condemn the ecosystems we depend on for life. Nobody doing any of this is worried about being 'good'.

So let's assume for a moment that *being a good person, or being on the good side*, is certainly not enough. But this attachment to the idea that *we are good* is a problem. One reason, as we've seen, is that wanting to be 'good' makes us less likely to admit we haven't behaved well. It gets in the way of building organisational systems with the necessary governance and cultures of growth that might lead to less racism, sexism and bullying. A second reason is, as De Bruin Cardoso argues, that glorifying our goodness increases the likelihood of harmful behaviour. Thirdly, it impedes our awareness of other unhelpful habits encouraged by the save-the-world script. We're more likely to assume we know best how to make change – even if we have not experienced the issue in question (see Chapter 4), or have little idea of the growing body of research, some of it counter-intuitive, on what it takes to influence people's views (see Chapter 2). We're more likely to approach our interactions with the old class and imperial habits of thinking that we can 'save,' and have the best solutions; this brings the racism and white saviour problems that Bushra Ahmed and Sophia Moreau were describing, and has huge opportunity costs (see Chapter 5).

Finally, being attached to the idea that we are good is a problem because it makes us sound righteous and moralising. I've been talking about this for years with people who are *not* trying to save the world, and it's the sanctimoniousness that's most likely to piss them off. Psychology research into the phenomenon of 'do-gooder derogation' backs up my anecdotal observations. In one study, the lifestyle choices made by 'morally-motivated others' – like cycling or veganism, for example – are likely to be perceived as less attractive when others perceive a moral superiority in connection with them. Doing something on a moral basis – in these examples, because it is better for the environment – 'is an implicit indictment of anyone taking a different path.' This 'stings because people are particularly sensitive to criticism about their moral standing', which 'motivates resentment against do-gooders', say the researchers. (It is a robust social psychology finding that threats to self-image are countered by disparaging others.) This occurs irrespective of whether or not the vegan or cyclist in question is actually judging the non-cyclist or meat eater.[33] On this basis, it's bad enough that we are even trying to do the right thing. The last thing we should do is to start explicitly moralising.

I was interested to see that one of the principles in which De Bruin Cardoso grounded her research on the NGO halo effect was that 'the same general organizational characteristics that explain the good side of organizations can also explain their unethical side.' The dark and the light are, in effect, inseparable. This insight has solid theoretical foundations in the study of organisations.[34] It also touches on the ancient truth – and the insight from psychoanalysis – that it is at our peril that we disavow the dark side in ourselves.

BASTARDS

Halfway through the afternoon of an averagely fractious family Saturday in September 2022, my dearly beloved and I hatched a last-minute plan to spend the night up on Dartmoor, the elevated granite wilderness in Devon whose rounded edge appears sharp in silhouette against the sky from our window a few miles away. We are practised at this; it takes half an hour to assemble two rucksacks containing sleeping bags and mats, two little tents, a tiny gas burner nicknamed the pocket rocket, a saucepan, a pack of pasta and jar of sauce, a bag of porridge oats with sugar and raisins thrown in, plus water bottles, apples and chocolate, teabags and mugs. The kids can carry their own pyjamas, jumper, woolly hat, waterproofs, torch and toothbrush in their school backpacks. Twenty minutes' drive, less than an hour's walk, and we're onto the open tops.

I'm a third-generation hillwalker on my mother's side and have loved Britain's often bleak hills since my early teens, when family holidays were walk-all-day-every-day trips to a spartan mountaineering club bunkhouse in North Wales or a leaky cottage in the Lakes. I've learned since then that the scoured uplands in these islands are the creation of enclosure and sheep farming. Left alone without ovine depredation, the hills would revert to richly diverse temperate rainforest of which only fragments remain in the western reaches.[35] Yet this doesn't stop me loving them. I still feel, walking with anticipation over grassy tussocks and heather onto a high moor or mountain shoulder, the respite from suburbia that I first felt at thirteen, a peace that I learned to associate with that great emptiness.

I know now that those sweeping unbroken horizons are the product of modernity's war on nature. Yet, I confess, I still find in them the closest echo that we children of modernity can experience of the primal scene: a view without many of our own kind. The kids capered in the sunset and leapt between granite outcrops; eerie tendrils of ground fog crept closer as we wriggled into sleeping bags to tell stories. I dozed, elbowed by the restless child with whom I was sharing my digs, and opened my eyes sometime after midnight to a glow almost as bright as morning, insistently calling me outside. The thin fog was lit up as if from within by a huge harvest moon, pale behind its cloudy gauze. The eldritch light had drawn my husband from the other tent, and he wandered to the edge of the high land to observe the gleam playing across the farmland and sea down below. Back in my cocoon, I drifted through waking dreams about the Bronze Age woman found buried in a bearskin on Whitehorse Hill to the north.

Barely three months later, Alexander Darwall, a hedge fund manager who owns four thousand acres of the southern moor – including the place we rested that night, leaving no trace – took the Dartmoor National Park Authority to the High Court. His lawyers persuaded the judge that the right to wild camp on the moor, the last remaining such right in England, had never existed. One of the arguments they ran was that being asleep didn't constitute a 'leisure activity', a casuistry that betrayed their desk-bound lives – or, perhaps, cynicism. Some outdoor enthusiasts said never mind, we'll continue surreptitiously to camp overnight up there, as we already do on other high land in England and Wales. Others responded that this doesn't help the organisers of children's and young people's activities who must stay within the law; or those who already feel unwelcome in rural areas because they are not racialised as white.

There was plenty to discuss in all this. And I'd had no previous dealings with Darwall nor any idea what he was actually like. But my first reaction to his move was: what an absolute fucking *bastard*. Many of the responses to an angry thread I posted on Twitter included the word 'bastard', as did some of the signs carried up onto the moor in the huge protest I joined the following week. It was like a script playing out, the Norman Yoke once again made visible. Here was an access-denying landowner, that mythically resonant figure against whom so much social history and folklore has been generated. We were drawing on ancient wells of antagonism and resentment and he'd willingly cast himself as the archetypal villain.

'Let's get the bastards,' my former colleagues and I would say when we were investigating hedge funds, bankers, oil companies and tax havens for their facilitation of corruption, poverty and environmental destruction around the globe. Righteous anger is motivating. The bankers, lawyers and oilmen do bear great responsibility for those problems. But after I'd left that job, I started to see that this emphasis had carried risks. By focusing on what we viewed as individual 'bastards' or evil companies, we can indulge in a psychological projection. This means we see, in others, what we cannot bear in ourselves. Squashing what we cannot acknowledge within is an unconscious habit, learned young to make ourselves safe and acceptable in the families and societies we come from. The psychic material we repress does not disappear, however. It comes to tap on our window, in the form of people who embody all that what we cannot bear in ourselves.[36]

Projection helps us to create a sense of belonging in groups, and to maintain our own status as 'good'. Any politics that focuses resentment on scapegoated groups like immigrants or trans people is weaponising this human tendency. But those of us opposing that kind of politics can do it too. Reading psychoanalytic thinking about how we project onto others, I saw how we construct our identities as the 'good activist' by locating all of the 'bad' in the people we're opposing.[37] And when we see all the bad 'over there', in someone else, we can avoid looking at our own complicity in the problems we are exposing or talking about.

In that investigative campaigning I was doing, 'getting the bastards' made it easier to avoid our own carbon emissions, or our consumption of goods manufactured with the minerals whose supply chains we were investigating. Here, in agitating about land-access rights, we're grappling with the British class system: its feudal estates, some handed down through families, some bought, as Darwall did his, with big money. But what kind of behaviours can we sidestep when we focus on the big bastard with his money and acreage? The part of south Devon where Darwall's estate lies, for example, has the highest rate of second home ownership in the country, contributing to its housing crisis.[38]

Focusing on the bastards, we can also divert attention from systemic problems. The people we like to call bastards are the product of bad systems. They're enabled, incentivised and emboldened by those systems, and it's the systems that we want to dismantle. Darwall is the symptom of a system that rewards wealth over the common good, that recognises only certain upper-class forms of land stewardship, and that gives the wealthy a sense of entitlement that they can try to make laws benefitting only themselves. I knew all this, yet, still, my anger was drawn to him magnetically. I also noticed how much faster and further the algorithms shared this personally targeted rage than they did any of my nuanced musings about the psychology of change-making.

Canny campaigners work hard to benefit from the motivational gathering-power of 'let's get the bastard(s)', while making sure their analysis also takes account of deep structural roots. As Darwall instructed his lawyers in 2022, the Right to Roam campaign was just getting going. Founded in 2020, it's the latest incarnation of the generational struggle for access to the countryside, and for the right to roam to be enshrined in law in England as it now is in Scotland. Its organisers can sometimes be heard thanking Darwall, tongue-in-cheek, for the vim, energy and funds his legal action unleashed. But, beyond the court cases he initiated, they deliberately chose not to focus much attention on him. Several of Right to Roam's founders have come from more antagonistic forms of activism. (Some might argue that their trespassing tactic is inherently antagonistic, so yes, this is relative.) They were politicised by the student protests after tuition fees were introduced in 2010 and had spent time in leftwing groups that had fallen apart; now they wanted to try something different.

'From the start we wanted to actually win something,' Jon Moses, one of the co-founders, told me. 'People are not just going to get to look cool and say radical things and set up a scene. We realised that when you define your politics by confrontation – when it's antagonistic – it's a binary framing. It's class war and class conflict. And that's all well and good. There's truth in that. It *is* how society is structured. And yet at the same time, if you *front* that, and if that's the core of what you're about and how you act and behave, how you define your strategy, then it will eat you in the end. You put all that negative energy out into the world, and it's a boomerang. It will come back and be corrosive and make the things you're doing less joyful. You'll be souring the pot of social discourse, and in the end, all that corrosive energy, when things aren't going well, will end up getting internalised in your movement.'

He was speaking, here, about how righteous 'getting the bastards' can turn into hunting the bastards on your own side, who are rather more accessible. Some of this involves purity desires, to which I'll turn in Chapter 3. But it also stems from the hunter's wish to bolster their own 'goodness'.

Moses continued: 'So even though we've got our antagonistic enemy, which is a thousand years of feudal land ownership, we're not going to make it personal, as much as we can. It's quite hard with feudalism, but we're going to focus on the structural issues. We do obviously care about access, but it's also a weak chink in the armour. It's an easy way to talk into these profound and uncomfortable issues in English politics. You're inevitably also talking about land ownership, the ecological crisis – bigger themes that come out of this quite simple ask, which is, can I exist in this place, please, without being shouted at? We're not going to have our events as protests. They're going to be joyful, they're

going to be celebrations, they're going to forefront recon-
nection. That's why we bring botanists and birdwatchers on
the trespasses. We just do what we want to do: we act as if
we're already free, rather than fixating on waving banners
and singing songs.'

When they plan a trespass, they're choosing an estate
and a landowner to target. 'So you *could* invent a bad guy:
you could go down that road, but actually it behoves you
to avoid that as much as possible,' Moses said. The Darwall
situation was a bit different to Right to Roam's other trespasses because he chose it. 'We didn't force it on him, and
that creates a different framing. When it's happening to you
and you're having to defend something and so you're in
protest mode, it asks different ethical questions of how you
relate to the person who's coming for you.' But even when
an opportunity arose to directly draw attention to Darwall
– following an encounter with the man himself while trespassing on his estate – they chose not to.

'We'd found out that he was over-stocking pheasants next
to a Site of Special Scientific Interest, so we went back to
see what was going on.[39] Just a nice day out, kids and sand-
wiches, very relaxed affair.' (They were walking on his land
at this point.) 'I spotted this guy in the distance and raised
a hand, and the quad bike goes round then the guy appears
over the prow of the hill and it was like, "Oh fuck, it's
Alexander Darwall!" He was way more nervous and anxious
and het up than I was, which is not normally the case –
landowners often come in all guns blazing. We teach people
how to manage these situations, it's all about how to bring it
back to a more equal footing so you can have a calm, polite
conversation. But I didn't need to do any of that because
instantly, he was the nervous one. It made me weirdly sorry
for him; it felt there was this deeper hinterland. He maybe

wasn't someone very at ease with himself; maybe there's some deeper reach to his antisocial nature. It was a very odd exchange. We wondered what to make of it afterwards, whether we should post about it, and we thought, there's something weird going on there, and just flogging this guy's name all the time isn't productive, let's just not mention it.'

In July 2023 the Court of Appeal overturned the High Court ruling, restoring wild-camping rights. Darwall made another attempt to appeal but in May 2025 the Supreme Court upheld the decision in favour of camping.[40] It's a constant tension, Moses observes. 'Sometimes you get fed up with the whole damn injustice and go more spiky; sometimes you have more grace and the latitude to be more cosmic. Sometimes your "opponents" have handed you an open goal, and it'd be a dereliction of duty not to shoot at it. It's just about being mindful when, and why, you're doing it.' Strategic morality, he calls these deliberations.

All that said, it can be harder to communicate our stories without identifying baddies. Yes, we need to draw attention to the underlying systems that enable their machinations. Most people, however – unlike full-time campaigners and political wonks – don't see 'systems' in the abstract. They see, and hear, stories. And stories, as any screenwriter knows, have protagonists and antagonists. An organiser who works on housing told me that one of the reasons it's such a good issue to organise around is 'because there's a shit-bag landlord, or agent, or developer on every street.' One of the messages found in the US to be most effective on climate puts the oil companies squarely in the frame, a climate campaigner told me: 'they knew; they lied; now they need to pay.'

'Pick the target, freeze it, personalize it, and polarize it,' said Saul Alinsky, the influential US organiser. By 'freeze it,' Alinsky meant being clear who is responsible, since in a complex bureaucratic society it's easy for the buck to be passed. By 'polarize it', he meant be clear that this person or organisation is in the wrong. 'One acts decisively only in the conviction that all the angels are on one side and all the devils on the other,' he said.[41] Alinsky's book *Rules for Radicals*, written later in his career, abounds in such rough wisdom, learned in action through organising Chicago meatpackers to fight for better conditions from the late 1930s, and later with Black communities in the civil rights struggle.[42]

With the landowners being targeted by Right to Roam, the identity of the 'devils' was so obvious that they hardly needed to emphasise it. Still, I found it interesting that they chose not to make more of the central-casting 'bastard' that Darwall presented them with. I didn't learn to campaign in an organising tradition,* didn't have *Rules for Radicals* in my back pocket as I started out. Yet I had absorbed, from those I learned from, that you inevitably have to go hard when you're up against power.

I was also thinking, listening to Moses, about another campaign close to home that was choosing neither to 'personalise' nor 'polarise'. I already knew Hannah Pearson from a local community of year-round swimmers in the river Dart, arguably the most outrageously lovely of the bosky Devon rivers that rise from the bogs up on the high moor. Pearson had moved into action following a disturbing period in the summer of 2022 when more than 250 people reported sickness after swimming in the river. I was away that week else I might have been in the same difficulties.

---

* See Chapter 4 for more on how organising works.

Across the country, the old wastewater infrastructure, designed to release untreated sewage into rivers only rarely, was now doing so all the time thanks to increasing housing, greater rainfall due to climate change – and a failure by the privatised water companies to upgrade infrastructure while continuing to pay out massive bonuses and dividends to their executives and shareholders. Nationally, as of 2023, the water companies were loaded up with debt that was costing an average of twenty percent of their revenue to service,[43] having borrowed £65 billion to pay dividends.[44]

With shit in the rivers and on the beaches, public rage was growing and water companies were responding with disinformation and greenwash.[45] Starting with a Facebook post, Pearson found herself in a group of five or six people, discussing how they might respond. Within months they were running a community-interest company called Friends of the Dart that was marshalling local volunteers to test the water quality, applying for bathing water status, and talking to South West Water about stopping the spills.

I wanted to talk to Pearson because I'd heard on the bush telegraph that despite public anger at the profiteering, she was pursuing a non-confrontational route. 'When we started, it was like, "We're going to talk to the water company,"' she told me. She has an unflappable, calm demeanour and breaks easily into peals of laughter. 'And a lot of people were saying to me, "No, you can't do that, they're a big company, there won't be any space for negotiation or discussion."' And that just didn't feel true to me. Also, what was coming back from them was, "We want to engage with the community, we're interested in hearing from you."' Within a few months Pearson had met Susan Davy, the then CEO of Pennon, which owns South West Water and several other water companies.

It's true that you don't always get to meet a CEO that quickly. The big banks tried to fob me off with their 'compliance' or 'corporate responsibility' suits for years. But then the battle-hardened campaigner in me says, *Hang on, they met Davy in April 2023* – the same month in which South West Water was fined £2.15 million by the Environment Agency for sewage spills between 2016 and 2020.[46] A few weeks later the parent company reported a dividend payout of £112 million to shareholders, up ten percent despite a loss-making year.[47] Of course they were keen to talk to communities! They engage when they're in trouble and trying to restore their reputation.

In May 2023, Davy was reported to have 'given up' her £450,000 bonus.[48] Her salary that year was £543,000, and her total remuneration the previous year, including a 'long-term incentive plan', came to £1.527 million.[49] She waived her bonus for 2024 too,[50] as a pathogen in the drinking water poisoned half of the fishing port of Brixham, hammering tourism and leaving some people still horribly ill weeks later. Yet the shareholder dividend still went up, by 3.8%.[51] If we are in getting-bastards mode, Davy and South West Water look like classic targets.

But another one of my internal voices chipped in: *Shut up, Lawson, and listen.* Susan Davy came to meet Pearson and her crew by the Dart, in one of the meadows popular for bucolic picnics and teenage waterside larking on summer evenings. 'For me,' said Pearson, 'it was about simple connection, building relationships. These are people who are in that work because they're interested in water. And so finding that point of "everybody loves the river and wants the best for it" and assuming that, I think there's something in showing up with that openness. There were so many people on the fringes of what we were doing saying, "We need to shout at them and get them to apologise." Our focus has kept coming back to, what's actually going to serve? Really paying attention to where we're investing energy, and what we're investing it in, and how we're investing it.'

'Can I make a confession?' I asked. 'I think I've stayed back from what you're doing because I know how much aggro energy I've got. And I could see right from the start you weren't doing that. I just don't think I can find it in myself.'

'And I think the reason I have been able to, is because I've seen it,' Pearson replied. 'I've seen people move from one state to another so many different times, in so many fields, and I know it's possible.' In her day job Pearson works as a coach, 'supporting leaders to move from being in a "survival state" where you're reactive, you've got blinkers on, you're looking very short term, and you lose perspective of the whole picture.'

By 'survival' she means a fight-or-flight state of nervous system activation that shuts down our wider capacity to relate or take in information. She applies this thinking to those of us working for change. 'Because when you get into "survival" you get into pushing. And even in simple connection or communication, the response people have to that is shut down, or self-protection.' Angrily denouncing the bastards, in other words, will not lead to the conversations you might need.

'It's really genuine: I care about the people I'm having discussions with,' Pearson says. 'Because if I don't, then what am I doing? What I'm interested in is what drives the individual – what do they actually care about? I want to know that before I even know their job title. When you peel everything away and come back to it, everybody wants a cleaner river. Whoever they are. Everybody loves the river.'

When we first spoke about this in early 2024, I asked Pearson if she thought the nature of her approach had made a difference to South West Water's response. 'They've said that clearly: it's one of the reasons they're willing to engage with us. Our approach is why they've begun work on updating three of the combined sewage overflows,' she said.

I was intrigued by this. She did agree that legislation governing the water companies has to change, and discusses that with other groups around the country. But the focus of Friends of the Dart's work with South West Water at that point was to minimise harm to the river by building the personal relationships that might lead to the company prioritising the necessary repair works. And by not moralising about the water companies, which would potentially let the rest of us off the hook, she said she was also changing how residents think about the river, so that everyone works together towards its long-term health. 'I'm not just asking South West Water to take responsibility, I'm asking everyone in our community. There are still people putting nappies down the loo, and wet wipes. There's no point people jumping up and down when at home they're using bleach.'

I checked in with Pearson a year later, in January 2025. Upgrading those three overflows had not yet happened, but they were included on a list of fourteen outflows into the Dart that South West Water had committed with DEFRA (Department for Environment Food and Rural Affairs) to upgrade by 2030. They were all upstream from or near the four designated bathing water areas that Friends of the Dart had been granted during 2024.[52] This was a win for their approach.

I noticed, however, that Pearson was seeing the causality slightly differently from a year earlier. It wasn't *how*

Friends of the Dart communicated with the company; it was their tactic of applying for bathing water designations that had worked, she said. It was a lever. The relationship and communication with South West Water was still there, but Pearson and her team were no longer pursuing some of the routes they had first tried. The company had backed away from discussions, for example, about making a binding agreement about water quality when they saw that 'we knew what we were talking about'. Meanwhile Pearson stopped asking for things, and instead used freedom-of-information requests to obtain documentation about the company's permits relating to the river.

I asked her if she'd shifted her view on how to engage with them. 'We've realised that whatever they might want to do as individuals, as an organisation the structure is flawed while it's still just focused on shareholders – and abstract shareholders who have no relationship with the river,' she said.

Many of us, after spending time trying to influence companies, come to similar understandings. While it is undoubtedly true that being in a calm rather than fight-or-flight state produces better interactions, and however well-intentioned the individuals we are dealing with, it also remains true that without a change to the law (and, in the view of many of us, renationalisation) there are structural blocks to these institutions being able to prioritise other goals alongside their bottom line. The senior executives of water companies are humans who can acknowledge their love for the river and we can engage with them in ways that encourage them to reveal that – and also, they are still actors who are choosing to remain tied in by huge financial incentives to a system that will put profit over life until there is no life left.

In my getting-bastards mode, it would be easy to tell this story as 'Campaigner realises after a while that you have to stop being good and hit the bastards round the head'. But that's not quite right, and it's not that simple.

'Do you think you were naive in how you first approached the company?' I asked.

'No, it was the right way to do it,' Pearson said.

'Do you think you've toughened up a bit?' I wondered.

'I've made a point of not doing that, because that's not our intention,' she said. 'It causes part of the problem, being hard. The focus on connection hasn't gone away, we're just honing the focus of our attention to what we have learned works.'

The way Pearson sees it now is that you *do* need to hit them with the legal stuff, and yet at the same time, she is not disconnecting. She sees the way Friends of the Dart works as a contribution to the world that she wants to create. 'When you've got connection, when you're in right relationship – with the other people, with the river – you've got health. I enjoy the way that we're focused on connection and collaboration, and the challenges of that. Campaigners will come to us and say "Yeah, we've got to get them!" How do you bring someone into the fold so they feel they're taking positive action and moving out of this aggressive place that's only going to get met with aggression, and not going to move things forward?'

I sometimes feel a great divide between the part of me that knows the depth of the truth that Pearson is trying to embody – that nothing will really change until we all start behaving differently – and the other part of me, that knows we also have to dig where we stand. And we are standing, in the mid-2020s – to broaden the lens – not only in a world where profit still rules, but on the brink of a slide

into far-right authoritarianism, which would be a catastrophe for the rest of nature as well as for humans. Resisting
it may take more than open-hearted engagement. I think
Pearson's approach, of balancing legal manoeuvrings with
non-moralising connection, has merit for direct engagement with a company. But there will be situations where it
is not enough on its own.

A typical criticism of campaigning that tries to be 'nice'
to people, or to behave in a 'good' way, is that it's the respectability politics of middle-class liberals who've never had to
fight for survival. 'If you are able to distance yourself from
the brutality of a system because you have not been affected
by it, you will seek an objective position. If you are simply
brutalised by the system then that system will become your
enemy,' writes Dom Hunter, a community organiser in
Sheffield, who appears in Chapter 4.[53] I was noticing that
the progressive-liberal version of the desire to be 'good' is
endlessly adaptable. Instead of bolstering our 'good' self-
image by projecting and fixating on the bastards, we can
end up bolstering it by avoiding going for the bastards at all.
Our fervent desire for oneness and connection can bring
delusions about what it takes to truly create it, which may
inevitably – because we are in opposition to the status quo
– have to involve some hard-nosed strategy and politicking.
To be clear, I don't think either Moses or Pearson are doing
this. But it could be a risk in other settings.

Even if we can acknowledge our own shadow and
tame our tendency to project onto the other side, we are
increasingly up against leaders, funders and spokespeople
of far-right movements – and their enablers in mainstream
politics, business and media – who appear to be manifesting
the full force of their darkness. There may be good strategic
reasons to treat them as the bad guys; I'm not saying we

shouldn't. But it's easy to forget that while our 'we're good and they're bad' discourse feels enjoyable and reassuring, it changes nothing on its own. It's tempting to moralise about how bad they all are in lieu of actually doing something. Focusing on our own being 'good', in such situations, can blind us in at least two ways. It keeps us in a frame of thinking that what we are like, as individuals, is the most important thing: keeps us in the individualist frame, which is where the political developments and market forces of the last forty-five years have wanted to keep us, less likely to join together to fight back. All of the observations in this book, in fact, are made in a context in which the very possibility of collective action has been removed from many people's view. And by creating a divide between those of us who get it and those who don't, being 'good' puts up additional barriers to our coming together, without which no serious change has ever happened. It blinds us to the work of communication that needs to be done with those who don't already agree with us, which I turn to in the next chapter.

2

'I PROTEST'

Layla believed in the improvability of human character, which made her the only real idealist Maryam knew. Zahra didn't fall into that category because Zahra didn't believe people could become better; she just thought she could change the world by the force of her arguments.

Kamila Shamsie, *Best of Friends*[1]

ONE OF THOSE BUMS

It's rare that my phone is off for thirty-six hours, but I was at a farm-turned-retreat centre in Kent and my mother couldn't get hold of me. It was a slightly scruffy place in a wide valley in the North Downs, chosen, perhaps, for its lack of mobile reception, which might enable attendees to concentrate on the intensive strategy meeting being convened for a potential new campaign. My kids were little and I was appreciating the prospect of a respite from family life even if short and work-related, so I checked out of responsibility for the night and didn't bother seeking out the wi-fi password. It wasn't until I was cutting across a golf course on my way back to the station the next day that I picked up my mum's voice messages. She sounded frantic, convinced, it seemed, that I had been arrested. I dialled her number as I

strode at a brisk clip across the neat weed-killed grass, keen
not to miss the next train back to London.

'Darling!' she exclaimed.

'I'm fine, I'm fine. I was in a meeting for two days. Are
you okay–'

'She looked like you… I thought it was you!'

'You thought who was me?'

'The picture in the paper. I thought one of those bums
was yours–'

'*What* are you talking about?'

It was early April 2019, and while I was out of phone range,
Extinction Rebellion (XR) was warming up for the protests
that would shut down parts of central London a fortnight
later. Eleven people, women and men, stripped to their pants
in the public gallery of the House of Commons, interrupting
a Brexit debate in the chamber below. They stood, arses to
the glass, slogans and hourglass symbols painted across breasts,
stomachs and backs, until the police cleared the gallery of
citizens observing democracy in action and then, one by one,
removed them. Videos circulated showing the Labour MP
Ed Miliband's comic double take, eyes huge; his colleagues
competed to include a double entendre in their speeches.

I'd vaguely mentioned to Mum that I was regularly
attending meetings for a new climate campaign. That was
all she knew – her imagination did the rest. This was before
most of Extinction Rebellion's big road blocks, before
Just Stop Oil, before complaining about climate activists
became a staple of the right-wing press. With her copy of
the *Evening Standard* on the kitchen counter, she and her
friend Mark had been peering at the row of rear ends, trying
to work out if one of them was mine. Mark, I was relieved
to learn, had been appropriately reluctant to opine on the
similarity of my arse to the one that Mum was focused on.

Fear clouds the vision, and as a mother, she was afraid. In the difficult conversation that followed, I said it wasn't me in the picture, and I hadn't been arrested. However, I added – rashly – I probably would be arrested at the next action. Her reaction was strong, and, in the heat of it, I forgot what I've learned over many years about how best to communicate when we disagree. Instead, I went into an instinctive 'fight-persuade' mode: I repeatedly spit out facts, argue louder and faster, take no account of how far the other person's starting-place is from mine or, as was the case here, that they are someone I love. In this case – as I remembered once I'd calmed down – Mum is averse to rule-breaking. She tends to identify with the establishment and tradition. The prospect of her daughter – even a middle-aged one – deliberately breaking the law was a shocking and profound threat. Her response was an atavistic distress, and there was no strategy logic, of the type I would later present to the judge when I was prosecuted ('I've been lobbying governments for years about the environment, and it's not worked…') that she could have heard in that moment, let alone the heavy-handed attempt to change her mind that I was embarking on.

Needless to say, the conversation did not go well. You might have thought that I'd already have known this by this point. Thinking about it later, I saw that I'd reverted rapidly to my old mode: trying to persuade, forcefully, from a position of opposition. We all know the likelihood of slipping back into old patterns with family members, and this is one of mine: loud protest.

I became curious, thinking back on that conversation, about the links between our domestic protest habits and our political ones. Linda Doyle, two decades younger than me, also took part in Extinction Rebellion in 2019, getting much more involved than I had. She'd recently moved to London from Ireland after a master's degree and had worked just three months in a new job for an education charity before packing it in and moving into a squat so she could afford to volunteer full-time for Extinction Rebellion. She didn't tell her dad or aunt back home (her mother had died when she was twenty) 'for a long time'.

'But then I exploded in a kind of *you don't understand* moment and said "I've been arrested five times!" It wasn't in a really angry way. But it was very charged. It was a sense of wanting to be in connection with them, wanting to be honest and truthful and tell them about what I'm doing and hope that they're joyful about that – or at least that they'd understand me a bit better.

'That's not what I got. Everybody's reaction was a sharp indrawn breath and the conversation stopped.' She has a sense of some of the reasons why. They were in a long family habit of 'hiding and minimising' views, not talking about politics. A cultural and class shift had taken place after she attended university, which her father had worked so hard to enable but had never done himself, and it had opened up a gap in mutual understanding. 'There were the questions like, "But are you making money? Why are you not working five days a week, you're young and healthy and you can, so why not?" And I get that from his working-class perspective, that is crazy. He's worked so hard all his life to give us a good life.'

By the time I met Doyle in 2024, she was working as a trainer for social enterprises and campaign groups. The fact that she was in paid work, running a business she'd set up herself with two colleagues, was making things a little easier with her father – perhaps, she wondered, because the outlines of her working and living arrangements were now more legible. But she still tries to persuade him of her views, like buying organic vegetables, for example.

'They can afford to do that, but for them, why? Why would you do that? It's like a nonsense thing. And even though I can do this with other people in my life, it somehow doesn't work that way to do it with my dad: to just try to explain things! I feel I can take a more calm approach with other people. In my head, I have a picture of older people that I meet, perhaps my partner's parents or something, where it feels that I don't have so many stories about them. And so I can start from a place of assuming that the bridge to cross is a lot shorter. With my dad, it just feels like it's an ocean to cross. And I'm almost overwhelmed, or confused about how to do it. So I'm like, let's just run and jump and see how far we get, then.'

This launching of ourselves at interpersonal communication when it feels like it's going to be difficult feels familiar. The climate psychologist Renée Lertzman talks about the problems of 'telling, selling and yelling'.[2] It's what I did to my mum in that conversation when she thought I'd been arrested. The initial reaction was hers – but the drama that followed was all me. And it's what I used to do all the time with my dad, who died a decade ago. In one sense it was easier to argue with him because he didn't get emotionally hooked in like my mum and I do, but it was also harder because he was largely unmoveable from his unfettered-free-market views. I would just go on at him, not really listening, keen to land my next point. I'd realised, when I was writing *The Entangled Activist* a few years ago, that some of the drive behind our arguments was about approval. If I could get him to agree with my political views, that would be a kind of approval of me. If I could persuade the men who ran the finance industry to adopt the regulation of banks and tax havens that I was advocating for, that might serve as approval by proxy.

But other things clicked, hearing Linda speak. I asked her how it feels in those moments where she throws something out at her dad and aunt – like her five arrests – which just shuts down the conversation, especially when some other part of her knows how unstrategic this sort of communication is. 'I think it's coming from a place of frustration,' she said. 'Maybe it's the cognitive dissonance of living in these two worlds: this world that I've built for myself with my activist friends, and then going home to Ireland and it's just a different world and I feel like a different person. But I want to be the same person. I do want my dad to know about what I'm doing, because I want to be a unified whole of a person!'

Approval, then, might be part of the dynamic with families. But so is the quest to be seen as we really are by those who raised us. And from the perspective of the rattled family member, I was hearing something else, that wasn't just about their political objection or their being 'conservative', as progressive and activist types often assume when someone disagrees with us. In both of our situations, I wondered if, beyond parental fear for our well-being, there was a kind of identity threat relating to hard-won class and economic position feeling threatened by a child choosing to break the law.[3] This was mixed with concerned care: that by criminal activity we might be imperilling for ourselves whatever security had been achieved – in Linda's family by her father's graft since childhood; in my mother's family, since their shift into the middle classes two generations earlier. I've heard from several other participants in environmental direct action whose families' difficult reactions to their lawbreaking were rooted in a fear of losing their recently claimed position among the middle class. This adds a little depth to the criticism – often true – of Extinction Rebellion as a bunch of white, middle-class folk who could risk encounters with the police and take paid leave or afford not to work for a few days.

At first, when I joined Extinction Rebellion in the first half of 2019, desperate to try out its theory of public disruption after years of policy advocacy, I thought the public anger was a necessary part of the process. Later, however, I questioned whether we should be targeting fossil fuel companies instead. I began to see the public anger as, yes, whipped up by the plutocrat-owned right-wing press, but also as a useful feedback mechanism that should help refine our tactics. But at neither stage did I think about these many difficult conversations that were going on in some of the families of the 3,004 people[4] who were arrested on Extinction Rebellion protests that year, and that were part of the process of changing how people think about climate risk.

Generational conflict over radical politics is not new. The Bloomsbury group reacted against stuffy Victorians; the baby boomers against the war generation. But what I want to think about is this: in our desperation to reach our families, Linda and I were adopting what I've come to think of as the 'protest voice'. By 'voice', I mean a whole mode of communication – what we say, and how we say it. The protest voice that failed to work with our families is the voice of objection. The protest voice is, most obviously, what we use when we are on an actual protest, march or picket – to express our 'no': to loss of work, or low pay. To war and genocide. To the destruction of nature. To racism, misogyny, homophobia. Protest is part of the change-making repertoire (although it's not the only option: there's organising in communities, lobbying policy-makers, working through charities or NGOs, or businesses, or social enterprises; there's storytelling, memes and making cultural interventions).[5]

Protests can demonstrate numbers; forge solidarity; wake people up to the existence of different views; very occasionally, ignite revolutions and bring down governments. Protests can involve marches, sit-ins, strikes and civil disobedience, which is deliberate lawbreaking. Arguments rage about whether civil disobedience 'works' and whether the inconvenience caused is 'worth' it – arguments of the reactive variety, on radio phone-ins; the academic kind, among sociologists and psychologists who study the impact of protest; and the strategic kind, among those who are discussing whether actually to do it. What is less controversial is that protests can make us feel better. They are a candle held in the dark; a form of bearing witness; a way of preserving our own humanity when something awful is happening.

But the protest *voice*, which is what I want to think about in this chapter, isn't just a way of presenting ourselves when we're out on an actual protest. It is also a way of speaking and writing. It's the voice we might use when we're in broadcast mode on social media, when we address a meeting of fellow campaigners, when we're on a political rant at friends or colleagues, when we're calling out people who we think should do better – and, indeed, when we're berating our families. It carries the weight of all our emotions, but does not necessarily consider those of the person we're talking to (or, more likely, at). Afraid that we'll convey weakness by allowing any nuance or shade, we press our point so hard that we leave no space to engage with any counterarguments, even those that might strengthen our position.

So this chapter is not saying don't go out and protest. You might need to. We all might need to. It's about the difficulties that arise when we continue to use protest speech and its vibes once we've left the march. And it's about the other options that exist for spreading the word.

COMMUNICATION OR CONVERSION?

Cognitive psychology research – the study of how our thinking and emotions work together – is clear that first we need to make a connection for our words to land. Jonathan Haidt, an American psychologist, used the image of an elephant and a rider to illustrate how the strength of the arguments we throw at each other are secondary to our intuitive view of the person behind them. We think we've got a handle on the 'elephant' of our intuition because we can use our thinking mind (our 'rider') to justify and provide reasons for our intuitions. But just as an elephant can quickly evade its rider's control and crash off on its own path, our emotions do the same. Much of our decision-making comes from an instinctive response, overlaid with subsequent rationalisation.

Haidt's message, to anyone trying to persuade others of their view, is therefore that we should speak to the other person's 'elephant' first. We should form a human connection so that people's instinctive impression of us is positive, before we begin to share our view.[6] When progressives and people on the left focus on facts first, we go against this advice. The political right are often better at making people feel seen and understood before bringing arguments to the table. At this point, the messages are more likely to land.

Others are less confident that we can – or indeed, should – change people's minds. 'You cannot transmit wisdom and insight to another person. The seed is already there. A good teacher touches the seed, allowing it to wake up, to sprout, and to grow,' said Thich Nhat Hanh, the Vietnamese Buddhist monk, teacher and peace campaigner who died in 2022.[7] Wisdom traditions might suggest that we can never really influence directly. But so also do behaviourist accounts that decline, on principle, to go beneath the surface since it is only observable behaviour that can be measured. The idea, popular in the 2010s, that governments could 'nudge' people into new behaviours by changing the 'architecture' of the choices they are given – lowering the price of the healthier options in a canteen, for example – emerged from behavioural economists' recognition that people will consistently make irrational choices or be guided by unconscious routines, and that changing people's minds and habits is actually very hard.[8]

'This is why I'm an analyst and not a self-help guru!' said Vanessa Sinclair, a psychoanalyst, when I asked her if it was possible to change people. 'If I take the position where I have the knowledge, and the person is coming for information, and I dole that out – "You'll feel less depressed if you think in this way, or if you exercise three times a week" – then even to their own detriment they will act out and get worse just to thwart you and your authority. But I'm not going to tell you what to do, and probably I will be the only person in your life who doesn't. So when you come into a space where someone's not telling you what to do, you finally have room to actually think "What do I want to do?" instead of constantly reacting to other people's demands, or projections, or what they think you should be or not be. It comes back to the defence against parents and the authority figure.'

I had long noticed a type of campaigner, unwavering in their use of the 'protest voice' regardless of context, who usually experienced strong authority figures earlier in life – at home, at school and, for some upper and upper middle-class types, at boarding school – who may have evoked their fighting stance in reaction. (Conversely, there's also something of that in how we 'ask' governments for things, 'Like asking Dad,' as one interviewee put it.) But hearing Sinclair speak, I started to see that this dynamic extends beyond the those 'NO!'-driven characters. It's in all of us, the desire not to be told what to do. Psychology researchers call it 'reactance': the desire to regain autonomy when being told what to do, by refusing the advice. It's why using the 'protest voice' interpersonally doesn't work: people feel hectored; they resist.

Protesters, especially, resist accepting what they are told is right: we're busy saying 'no' to the world as it is. So why do we still do it to others? In *On Wanting to Change*, a short meditative book about the possibility of changing ourselves and each other, the psychoanalyst and author Adam Phillips shapes his thinking around the word 'conversion'. For a long time, conversion in its religious sense was revered as one of the deepest forms of personal or cultural change. These days, he writes, whether we're talking about conversion to 'religious fundamentalism, communism, profiteering or gender identity', people often view conversion with wariness.[9] Psychoanalysts are interested in conversions because in Freud's specific use of the word, we unconsciously convert our unacceptable thoughts and shameful desires into bodily symptoms. We do this to survive or just get by in family or social environments where some of our thoughts or desires are not acceptable. The job of the analyst is to 'reconvert' the symptoms, these confusing somatic messengers from our uncomfortable bodies, back into desires that we are now conscious of.[10] By doing this we rob them of their power over our behaviour. Reading Phillips, I saw a connection between my own fierce desires to convert others to my point of view – using, invariably, the full-power setting of my protest voice – and my own resistance to being converted. It was that word 'conversion' that did it, igniting something previously out of reach.

I had studied Christian missionaries in the context of European empires during my history degree. I was intrigued by conversion stories, and how they sometimes weren't really conversions at all. People might convert pragmatically under duress, like some of the Jews of Castile after 1492, given the choice between conversion and expulsion or death.[11] Or they might adopt Christianity on their own terms, so it merged with or offered cover for their ongoing practice of old rites and beliefs, like the Aztecs and other Mexican peoples facing the Catholic missionaries who arrived with the Spanish conquest. I was fascinated by the Mayan elites who were discovered employing, quite logically, I thought, the vessels of the mass for their cosmos-maintaining traditions of animal and human sacrifice. This did not end well for them.[12] In other locations the missionaries largely failed, like evangelical Protestant attempts to attract mass converts from Hinduism during British rule in India in the nineteenth century. The crowds usually preferred their existing rites and cosmologies, while at the elite level, the Hindu pandits put up a sophisticated theological defence, posing awkward questions about the Trinity and engaging the missionaries in long, distracting arguments.[13]

Such cross-cultural encounters offered plenty to analyse in those formative years when I was sharpening up my mind and my views. But I was also taken by them as stories of resistance to conversion. I thought this was because these were political resistance narratives: examples of resistance to colonisation, which chimed with my own developing politics as I learned how empire had shaped the world and continued to do so. This was the mid- to late-1990s, a time of growing protests against impoverished countries' debt burdens and the post-imperial empire of the World Bank, International Monetary Fund and the multinational corporate power that they served. This would be enough in itself to explain the draw. But *why* are we interested in what we're interested in? What happens if we keep asking 'why'? It's a technique I've found useful when excavating my subterranean attachments to the save-the-world script.

At the point when Adam Phillips switched his narrative from Christian conversions back to the psychodynamic variety, something landed, thirty years after leaving home. It was about my own resistance to being 'converted', moulded into something that my parents wanted me to be: an eldest child who could fulfil their ambitions, for myself and perhaps, indirectly, for them. The heat of my instinctive resistance couldn't be targeted directly. I turned the refusal outwards, into political and ideological resistance. My argumentative objection was not, then, just a generic response to 'authority'. It was a specific response of equal and opposite reaction: I refuse the conversion of me; I try to convert others. I wondered if I had converted, in the psychoanalytic sense Phillips was describing, my inexpressible resistance to being shaped into a determined effort to try to shape others. If so, no wonder my 'protest voice' has been so charged.

But we are not only shaped by our personal histories. The world continues to exist outside our heads. Our motivations for becoming political are also, and usually primarily, the just causes that trouble us and that we want to fight for. 'Just because [your change-making work] is a re-enactment of your family dynamic doesn't mean it doesn't actually make social change. I would argue that everything everyone is doing is a product of how we grew up, and that's just how people are,' said Vanessa Sinclair, the psychoanalyst. Furthermore, there could be material reasons – beyond the fact that we may be overdoing our 'protest voice' in reaction to our own history – why we are failing to change someone's position.

I spoke to one woman, Sofia, who had split with her partner, the father of her young child, over their divergent views. Her environmental campaigning had activated latent problems stemming from their class difference; she came from a middle-class family, he from a working-class one. It wasn't her campaigning that was the problem: she was going on protests, and organising parents to gather locally and plan kid-friendly actions about climate change. The issue, as so often with relationships, was what came up when they talked about it. Listening to her speak, I heard something of the immovability of her 'protest voice' as it was used in the home, together with his defensive reactions, rooted in his experiences.

'I'd tell him,' she said, 'we shouldn't have a car or fly as much, and he'd say, "But you've flown fifty times more in your life than me, and your family always had a car, and now you're telling me I can't have a car when my family never had one, or I can't fly, and I never did that till I was an adult. You can't tell me that. You come from this privileged background and that's why you think you can change the world. All I want to do is create financial security for myself and support my family." And that's totally valid,' she told me. 'But it was just impossible to maintain those two intentions in one house. I sometimes wonder if I hadn't got a bit extreme, because I panicked. Perhaps he'd have come round in a different way.' Several years after their split, she said, 'I'm still trying to convince him. I just can't stop. But it will never work, just trying to say the same things for five years.'

So, we can't change other people, force them to agree with us, or get them to 'see' something they don't want to. Approaching them with criticism or hostility will result only in defensive reactions. That's not to say that we can't influence people, but we can only be a catalyst for them to change their own minds. Almost every possible precept in the realm of psychological good health and effective communication runs counter to use of the critical protest voice interpersonally. Vanessa Sinclair says – inevitably, perhaps, given her job – 'Work on yourself. Find the external structures that you have been socialised into – whether it's capitalism, racism, gender, transphobia, ableism, things that you've grown up within, then interrogate those systems in your own psyche, within yourself, and try to dismantle them on an individual level. I feel that ends up resonating with people more. When they see people doing that work for themselves, it might help other people to start questioning their own belief systems. The only way it will actually stick in the long run is if people come to that view on their own.'

I agree that we need to examine ourselves in these directions. But the do-your-own-work perspective is connected to the shout-loud-to-convert people approach; in a way, it is its inverse. And both are individualised perspectives. (Indeed, the very foundation of almost all Western psychology – as with liberalism more broadly, from which it emerged – is to think in units of the individual.[14]) It can be easy, looking at public discourse, to think that the protest voice that makes our own moral position known *is* change-making, and that we must either press every other individual to sort them-selves out – or retreat from it all to sort ourselves out. But there are other forms of influence.

ATTRACTING OR PERSUADING?

In my early twenties I made a few short trips to the dry hills of Andalucía on the recommendation of a badly pho-tocopied leaflet I'd found in a vacation work file at the university careers office, featuring a line drawing of trees and houses under a rocky skyline. Sunseed Desert Technology was (and still is) an hour's bus ride north of the sea of plastic polytunnels around Almería that are used to grow year-round salad for northern Europeans, at high cost to the health of the water table and the migrant workers who spray the pesticides.

Set up by English environmentalists and researchers a decade earlier in the mid-1980s Sunseed occupied a few thick-walled whitewashed houses in a village that had been largely abandoned over the twentieth century. Its vol-unteers were reclaiming the overgrown terraces to grow organic fruit and vegetables and to research techniques for dryland horticulture and tree planting. The river that made possible this magic enclave of verdancy ran in the bottom of the valley and was dammed into a pool, the scene of after-hours naked swimming, loafing and other wholesome debauchery. (The river is currently threatened by extraction for nearby olive plantations.[15])

We were off grid, with a little solar and wind power, and compost toilets. There were a few permanent staff, some year-long researchers from universities, and a revolving gang of volunteers like myself, who could stay a few weeks if we contributed four hours of labour a day and a modest weekly sum towards subsistence. I baked bread, wielded mattocks, watered trees, painted walls and wheelbarrowed huge containers of piss about the place with someone who was setting up a hydroponics experiment to grow tomatoes using urine filtered through reed beds. It's not everyone's idea of a holiday, but I returned three times in as many years.

There are many debates within activism and among those who write about it, over the merits and demerits of such 'prefigurative' activities. That word means projects that 'prefigure' or demonstrate-by-doing the world that we want, rather than protesting against the world that we don't want. Those against prefiguration argue that it leaves existing power structures untouched. It's true that Sunseed's organic-self-sufficiency denizens were not making a dent in the supermarket and consumer demands, agro-industrial power, and inequalities facing migrants that combined to produce the polytunnels of *el mar de plástico* just to the south. But on the positive side, inasmuch as these things are weighable at all, prefigurative politics introduce their participants to new ideas about how the world could work at an affective level that doesn't only rely on the transmission of facts or on being 'told' something.

Sunseed opened a door to me and many others over the years. When I arrived aged twenty-one, I hadn't been exposed to low-impact living, organic growing, veganism, nor to people long involved in collective environmental and leftist political action. There was a small but fascinating library in the main house, and there were back copies of *New Internationalist* and *Red Pepper* lying around that added detailed reporting to the understanding I was building of a

world run by and for only a tiny proportion of its population. I subscribed when I got home, and began to educate
myself about the movements that were resisting corporate
power on capitalism's frontlines. That led to taking part in
the global justice protests against the IMF and World Bank a
couple of years later, and from there, to working for human
rights organisations.

'Is it more "We must change things!", using our power in
that way? Or is it more, "We must cultivate a way of living
that feels attractive, that draws people in?"' This was Mark
Vernon, a psychotherapist, author and former Anglican
clergyman. I told him that I'd been thinking about the
subterranean influences on activist culture, including
Christianity, with its emphasis on proselytisation and history
of missionary activity.

'It's the thought that we've got a better view of life than
you, which we want to tell you about... I think that it's
very widespread in western Christianity,' Vernon said. 'That
maybe even the main role of the Christian after they've
become a Christian is to tell others. It's interesting, because
I think there's more to it than that. The only missionary
person in the Bible, as in, someone who actually deliberately went out to try and persuade people, was St Paul;
none of the other so-called apostles actually ever did that.
They seemed to have returned to a quite settled way of life.
And then, you know, hoping the new way of life radiated
out. The kind of power that attracts rather than persuades.
And I think that was lost in western Christianity and certainly in English Christianity since the colonial period.'

The kind of power that attracts rather than persuades.
That's what Sunseed was for me. Look, hippyish projects
aren't everyone's bag. Nor are they the only answer: kinder
and more mutually supportive ways of living shouldn't have

to require wearing felt or living in the woods. Others will have had transformative experiences of their own. But we all know that transfiguring excitement of something that speaks directly to us when we observe or experience it. It rarely comes when someone is striving too hard to communicate it directly. More likely the electricity is transmitted when people are in their flow, doing what they most want to do, what gives them joy.

'It'll be interesting, where you ultimately feel you stand on this, in your stance towards change,' Vernon said, later in the conversation. We must change things! Or: let's draw people in by living as we want the world to be. I understand what he's saying: they can be very different things. Sometimes, in order to prevent current harm, we do have to apply our energies very clearly at the point where the problem is manifesting, rather than only embodying the world that we want to create. But I'm not sure I want to have to choose between them. And I think that there are ways of actively trying to make change, while simultaneously enacting and articulating a way of being and doing that has attractor power.

THE POWER OF CURIOSITY

Professor Corinne Fowler was teaching colonial and postcolonial literature and heritage at the University of Leicester when she was invited by the National Trust to help investigate its properties' links to empire and slavery. She led an audit of existing peer-reviewed research that found a third of National Trust houses had imperial connections,[16] and ran a collaborative project called Colonial Countryside inviting primary schoolchildren, historians and writers to tell the stories of the Indian, Caribbean and

African links at eleven of these properties. They included Speke Hall in Liverpool, one of three properties bought in 1795 by a slave trader, Richard Watt, and Penrhyn Castle in North Wales, built with sugar profits from the Caribbean. Unlike any of the formerly enslaved, Penrhyn's owners received compensation when slavery was outlawed. Some of this money paid for paintings at the castle.

Historic England had already reported, separately, on the links between slavery and some of English Heritage's properties.[17] 'All of this work had been commissioned well before the Black Lives Matter protests, but the reports were released at a time of intense debate about how we, as a nation, commemorate, represent or deny our colonial past,' Fowler later wrote.[18] Her project was made public in 2020, shortly after George Floyd was murdered, igniting the biggest anti-racist protests in a generation and, in the UK, the toppling of a slave trader's statue into Bristol harbour.[19] There was a backlash from the right-wing press and the self-described 'Common Sense Group' of Conservative MPs, who tried to use the National Trust report to raise fears of an attack on 'British values'. It was culture war stuff; whipping up fury for political ends. But it had personal consequences for Fowler. Every time an article was published – and they appeared each week for about four months – she received a torrent of hate mail and threats.

Many of the articles were inflammatory, she told me. 'I did have my eyes open when I was working on the National Trust report, but I didn't quite realise how massive a story it was going to be. I wasn't given any right of reply for ninety-eight percent of the articles. I wasn't interviewed, or asked about my work. So a lot of people got very angry and sent me emails, letters and threats. Though I did also get equal amounts of support, saying keep going; solidarity.'

I wanted to speak to Fowler because I'd heard from someone who knew her about what she did next. She wrote back. 'I thought if people are going to send me angry emails and call me names, maybe they can help me to understand what has upset them, and this could be really informative for me. And it might help them, as well, to understand my actual words and what the actual evidence I'm working with is, rather than how it had been reported. So it might be more productive just to reply. I couldn't do this all the time because I was bombarded every time there was an article. But each time I did pick, almost at random, a number of emails and I'd reply. I wouldn't say "Thank you for your email" because that would sound sarcastic, which I didn't want to be. I would just say, "I read your email copied below, and I'd like to respond to some of the points that you made," and I would start a dialogue with them.

'Then, if they responded – which nearly always they did, the second time much more politely because I think they were taken aback that I'd respond to an angry email from a stranger calling me names – they would respond with further questions, less hostile but often still in opposition to what I was trying to do.'

When people replied like that, I wanted to know, were they engaging with her response? 'Often, they were,' she said. 'It was imperative that I spoke to them without assuming any knowledge on their part, but without being patronising and assuming that they were ignorant about whatever point they'd raised. We'd have an exchange, usually of three or four emails, and nine times out of ten – perhaps more – they'd wish me well and apologise. But I didn't want an apology and I wasn't looking for one. I was trying to understand why they were upset, and provide more resources for them to think through the topic with further information, because I didn't feel that was something that had been offered by any of the newspaper articles. I think that was appreciated – that I took the time to engage. I sometimes got quite effusive responses: "Wow, respect to you for answering!"'

She also got into a long dialogue with someone from a landed family who lived in one of the National Trust houses, who wanted something that they didn't like taken out of the report. It didn't come out, and she wanted to talk this person through the bigger picture of the slavery system of which the house's history is part. 'But actually,' Fowler said, 'we had a much more finely grained discussion about her family's own roots, and how her husband had been a miner, and this conversation really influenced me quite a lot over time. It fed into something which people often said, both in those emails and in public gatherings: "Why don't you talk about the oppression of working people? Child labourers in the factories, agricultural labourers in poverty?"'

'What about *us* and *our* ancestors?' they were asking. It's the kind of question that can be used defensively when the listener doesn't want to hear the information that is disturbing their world view (in this case, about Britain's active role in slavery). Mobilising our own counter-defences, we might call such questions 'whataboutery'; we might dismiss them as ignorant or racist. And it's true that there *is* often racism in the objections to talking about imperial histories: the journalist and author Sathnam Sanghera received extensive racist abuse after writing his book *Empireland* about the after-effects of empire on Britain. He describes the fact that historian and TV presenter David Olusoga has required police protection as a 'national disgrace.'[20]

Fowler took this question not as whataboutery, but at face value. It prompted her next book, *Our Island Stories*,

which weaves together histories of colonial extraction with
working-class histories in Britain.[21] 'Maybe on one level
you could say that people might be asking that question to
shut the conversation down about colonial history,' she said.
'But what if you take that question seriously: how does
the history of British labour intersect with the history of
colonialism? How do toolmaking, copper, mining, tobacco
imports – how does all that connect with the history of
empire? They have given me something, posing a challenge
to me intellectually to go away and answer that challenge.
So I did listen to them too, you know. They really helped
me produce something that could be much more helpful
to them, and to anybody who's coming from the same
position in relation to colonial history.'

I was struck by Fowler's story: that she responded at all;
that people returned to civility over just a short exchange
of emails; by her openness to let these dialogues inform her
research. She let the conversations change *her*. As Octavia
Butler put it in her speculative fiction *Parable of the Sower*,
'Everything you touch, you change / Everything you
change, changes you.'[22] A few years earlier John Ashton,
formerly the UK's climate envoy spanning the Blair, Brown
and Cameron years, had told me about the anti-fracking
protests he had been attending near Blackpool. Something
he said lodged in my mind. 'If you are trying to change
something external, you have to be open to being changed
yourself. Otherwise, the lever you're trying to hold will
snap.' I kept coming back to this, feeling the resonance of
his words and intuiting that they were profoundly true
while not quite being able to land what he was saying with
a concrete example.

What Fowler was saying lit something up here for me.
She engaged with people who had been vile to her and

who held opposing views, but in doing so, she was open to whatever might happen – hopefully to their views changing, but also to her own work changing tack. The potential for relationship, and everything that then flowed from it is – coming back to John Ashton's words – the 'lever' that would have broken if she had not been open to and curious about what her correspondents were saying; if she had, as I might have been tempted to, replied with a dose of protest-y attitude. 'I definitely don't think of myself as an activist, but that obviously doesn't mean I'm not interested in helping to resource change,' she said.

Was she scared when these emails arrived, or when she was sending her replies? 'No. It was just curiosity. I think it gave me a degree of control over being the recipient of that toxic kind of communication. By answering calmly, managing my own emotions and responding in a digni-fied way, it gave me more courage and composure,' she said. 'But also I realised that if I do anything public-facing, it's really important to explain that I haven't always known what I know now; to give a sense of the journey, which is something other people can embark on in their own ways. Because we don't know everything. We don't start from a position of knowledge, we start from a position of igno-rance. I make an effort to explain that I didn't learn about any of this at school, and I think that immediately estab-lishes the point that it's not something that everyone should automatically be expected to know.'

What I was hearing in Fowler was a genuine – and genu-inely humble – curiosity about *why* the people haranguing her didn't know what they didn't know. The answer to that question includes a failure of education, rooted in our national blind spots about empire. It's a vicious circle unless the conversation can be widened. But what so often happens in public discourse is scorn, perhaps the opposite of curiosity. Scorn is often deeply embedded in the 'protest voice'. The curtain was drawn back on this kind of contempt by the Brexit vote, when Remain voters were reeling and could often only see in Leave voters an ignorance of the European cultures that they were privileged enough to have had access to, and not the many material reasons why so many people were keen to kick the establishment. But the contempt is older and wider than that, and it produces something familiar in supposedly progressive circles: a kind of scorn about and towards people who don't get it.

I'm curious about the factors that might produce that scorn. The left has always been a necessary coalition of the working class and progressives within the middle class. I can sometimes discern a difference in tone between the scorn that is dished out by those whose life experience means they *do get it* (and sometimes I think, fair enough), and the scorn that emanates from those who don't have that life experience, which comes across as more of an intellectual or academic superiority.

There is also the question of whether people share their political outlooks with their families of origin. Those who do can inherit a whole set of understandings that others must find out for themselves, in journeys that are sometimes winding. In my twenties I was in awe of people my age who could confidently express their political views. I had instincts – about what was wrong with the world, and what needed to change. After a while, I could talk about the specific issues I was working on. But I couldn't always articulate them as part of wider socialist, or feminist, or green traditions. I didn't grow up hearing any of this at home and I didn't learn it at school: I had to start from scratch. It took me years of campaigning, reading and learning from others to get clear on what I think is wrong with the world and what needs doing – and my views continue to develop.

I could see that some of those who grew up experiencing marginalisation could articulate their political demands confidently; that made sense, though it took me longer to understand that their analysis might still be hard won. It also took me longer to notice that many of those with an authoritative progressive analysis in their relative youth, even if they didn't have personal experience of poverty or marginalisation, had nonetheless grown up breathing those views because they were common currency in their families. When our protest voice is scornful of people who don't already know, we're buttressing our own confidence while cutting off the possibility that they might still be growing. We're pulling up a ladder that was there for us – and cutting off our own growth, too.

IT'S NOT ABOUT PERSUADING

So, let's say we have realised that banging on at people in our protesting voice rarely works. We have seen the possibility that engaging carefully can have positive effects. Let's say we can calm down and have a conversation. Does that mean we are winning? There is a bit more to it than that. I turned to some campaigners I know who are well-versed in the research into what works. They were concerned that the very idea of persuading people is a red herring.

'Some issues aren't really about reasoning at all,' said Sarah Stein Lubrano, a political theorist who uses cognitive psychology to make sense of politics and to train activists. We met in 2017 while helping to organise a gathering of people interested in new approaches to politics; since then she's written a PhD at Oxford on the psychology of political reasoning and a book, *Don't Talk About Politics*, about why debate doesn't work to change people's minds.[23] We interrogate one another's ideas from time to time, and enjoy comparing perspectives. I'm a Gen Xer, she's a millennial; there is usually some grist for our discussions.

Her point here was that when there are real inequalities of power, you can debate all you like, but you're unlikely to move people away from their material realities: communities without decent jobs or affordable housing, versus – for example – private-equity-fund managers or property developers with the ear of usefully placed MPs.

I confessed that I used to fantasise about what it would take to bring round to my point of view the tax lawyers who service multinational companies and plutocrats by running the offshore financial system and the profit-shifting, tax dodges and dark money that it enables: activities that aren't illegal because they're arbitraging the spaces between the laws of different jurisdictions, but whose effect is ultimately to hollow out the public realm and to undermine democracy by offering cover for political donations and support to think tanks.

Stein Lubrano laughed and reminded me of the cold reality underneath that fantasy. 'You couldn't persuade them, not because you can't tell them good things, but because they're already corporate lawyers! Think about what it would take for them to change their mind – they'd have to quit their jobs!'

I did know at the time that we might all burn in hell before they agreed with me (indeed, climate-wise, that's probably the road we're on), and would remind myself of the American political writer Upton Sinclair's words: 'It is difficult to get a man to understand something, when his salary depends on his not understanding it.'

When I was doing that work on financial transparency at Global Witness, our actual theory of change was to lobby governments and international standard-setting bodies into creating new mandatory transparency standards and regulating the hell out of corporate lawyers; the lawyers' own opinions were immaterial. But that little fantasy that I might one day personally convert some of them to my view is a useful reminder of the dangers of thinking about the problem in terms of debate rather than a straightforward struggle for power.

One of the reasons it was easy to think like this was because our policy-advocacy model of change relied on persuasion – on convincing people inside government who might be able to pull the levers of power. A decade on, as the limitations of policy persuasion when faced with right-populist or authoritarian governments become more apparent, some of the NGOs seeking to change laws and policies are starting to think in terms of developing strength in numbers (more on this in Chapter 4). But even when we recognise that the job is also about building wider movements of support, many of the underlying assumptions about the use of argument to change people's minds (to get them to join our movements, for example) persist.

'Liberals are obsessed with persuasion because they think it makes their model of democracy work,' Stein Lubrano says. 'Culturally, much of liberalism relies on the idea that "debate" or a "marketplace of ideas" will mean the best ideas win. But we can't have a public sphere that's only about this kind of persuasion. That's ridiculous, because all the best evidence suggests political views are not primarily determined by, or indeed much changed by, being given abstract reasons.'

When it comes to changing people's views in the long run, there seem to be two things that have the most profound effects, she says. One is who we spend time with. 'People who end up belonging in new groups do change their views,' she says. Especially when it comes to issues of prejudice. 'So people who go to university, and people who work in the military, become less racist. If people are placed in your social world as equals, you will eventually come to see them as equals, and universities and the military do this really well.[24] More generally, our friends are very good predictors of our views, and when we are able to make new friends, they do change our views on some issues, and also help us clarify them, while motivating us to care about politics.'

The other factor most likely to change people's views is their own actions. One of the impacts of protest for which there is the most robust evidence, says Stein Lubrano,[25] is not its impact on observers but its effect on participants, who are far more likely than observers to shift their actions and lifestyles in line with what they have been demonstrating about.[26] Some studies have shown that those who join protest movements have their views and lifestyle changed permanently, from higher divorce rates to lifelong changes in their political views. The pressure felt from cognitive dissonance can cause participants to align their beliefs with their new actions; new groups of friends within the movement can open up the sense of what kinds of lives are possible.[27]

Furthermore, the action taken doesn't have to be protest-related in order to change the person doing it. A study by behavioural researchers across sixty-three countries and nearly sixty thousand participants, testing which kinds of interventions are more likely to change beliefs and behaviours on climate change, found that the most successful move in increasing support for new climate policies was asking participants to write a letter to a child they knew, twenty-five years in the future.[28]

We could also ask what exactly we think people need persuading of. 'When people see this quite disruptive, radical [protest] they tend not to like the activists, but they do still agree with the cause. And so it doesn't shift people away from the cause, but nor does it shift people towards it. People paint that to mean this kind of protest is pointless – but that's not the point.' This is Colin Davis, a professor of psychology at Bristol University who studies the psychological factors that affect the impact of protest on observers.[29] He does some protesting himself; he's racked up a few arrests with Extinction Rebellion. 'While I'm pessimistic about the possibility of changing people, we don't need to change people, because actually – they're already on board,' he said. 'If we're talking about climate change, people are very concerned. They agree there's an emergency, they're aware the government is lagging behind.'

In the light of this, there are two jobs, Davis suggests. One is getting people to realise that the concerns they already have are shared. He is talking here about 'pluralistic ignorance', a social psychology term that describes our failure to realise that others actually share our opinions.[30] A survey of nearly 130,000 people across 125 countries during 2023 found significant support for action on climate change: 69% globally were willing to give 1% of their income for climate action, 86% endorsed 'pro-climate norms' and 89% demanded greater political action. Yet in each country surveyed, the majority of people also underestimated the proportion of *other people* who are willing to contribute to the common good.[31] The authors speculate that the reasons for the gap might include the media 'disproportionately emphasizing climate-sceptical minority opinions' and the effect of the fossil fuel lobby.[32]

But there can be social norms that go against expressing our opinions. And sometimes it's because we are just not talking enough. The only way out of pluralistic ignorance is many more conversations, of the sort that happen between family and friends. A number of efforts have been underway over the last few years trying to train people to talk about the climate with those they know; one person working in this field told me during 2024 that they knew of thirty-six such projects in the UK. All of them are proceeding on the basis that the conversations have got to be on 'normal' social turf, and not in a situation where somebody is being the protester, campaigner or lecturer. An organisation that has been running one of these projects, Larger Us, draws inspiration from the success of 'deep canvassing' doorstep conversations in the US that softened opposition towards undocumented immigrants and trans people,[33] and from research suggesting that children's conversations with their parents can change the adults' views on climate.[34]

And if we're not actually having to persuade people to change their minds, the other job, for Davis, is 'getting them talking about it, getting the issue up the agenda to put more pressure on politicians. I like to think about the pipeline leading from concern about the issue, through to the people actually taking action, introducing policies. There's a blockage, but where is it? Much of the time, people talk as if it's with the general public: scientists are saying these things, activists are doing these things, but the public aren't listening.'

Davis thinks that is wrong. 'If you look at what people are saying in polls, they agree that climate is an imminent and serious threat. So the block is between the general public and the policymakers. And it reflects regulatory capture, which is a polite way of saying that fossil capital has bought politicians. So as well as asking whose mind it is we need to change, we also need to ask, what aspect of their beliefs needs to be changed? It's not about the importance of climate. The thing that needs to be changed is we need the UK public to come to the realisation that we don't live in a democracy, and that maybe they should try to do something about that.'

If it sounds like Davis is changing the subject, he's not. He is talking here about the amount of corporate money and lobbying influence in politics, and that it will take sustained collective pressure to change that. We'll have to be working together, and there's more on that coming up in the next two chapters.

Still, if the job isn't always persuading individual people directly, are there, nonetheless, ways that we can communicate better?

SET OUT THE VISION YOU WANT

My concern with the messaging was not the reason that I stayed at home on the day of the 'anti-austerity' protest in Westminster in June 2015, after the Conservatives were re-elected the previous month. I was sick as a pike from a rough pregnancy and did little extracurricular activity – beyond growing another human – for several months that year. But I was worried about the messaging, even though I strongly agreed with the feeling behind the march.

Carrying a protest sign saying 'end austerity', as many did that day, would have helped to strengthen, in anyone who saw that sign, the frame of 'austerity' that the Conservatives had carefully chosen when they took power in 2010 and began the next stage in their assault on the functions of the state and the public realm. In the wake of a financial crisis created by an unregulated banking sector, that word cleverly conjured ideas about sensible household economies (even though a national economy bears little relation to the household version), tightening of belts, wartime rationing and Blitz spirit. It thus activated the deeper frames of battle, good-against-evil and righteousness. The Conservatives claimed that heroic moral ground for more than a decade, helping lead us to where we are now, and as of 2025 a version of that story still underpinned some of Labour's moves.

'Don't think of an elephant!' said George Lakoff, the cognitive linguist. 'Seriously, try it for a moment,' he would tell his students at Berkeley. His political communication book of that name was published in 2004, the year that the Democrats lost again to George W. Bush.[35] This elephant was a different one to Jonathan Haidt's, although both men are invoking a force too large to control. Lakoff's purpose was to help progressives get better at using stories and language. His elephant is saying: If you repeat your opponents' message in order to negate it, you will reinforce it. People will remember the word 'austerity' more than the 'no' that you put in front of it. That hard-to-dismiss elephant relates to an important cognitive psychology finding about the difficulty of suppressing thoughts, although the illustration originally took the form of a white bear.[36]

Lakoff's political-communication advice grew out of his and colleagues' decades of work on 'embodied cognition', which is about how our understanding and meaning-making is rooted in the physical experience of our bodies moving and interacting with our environment. Metaphor, in this view, is not just a 'rhetorical flourish' or a matter of the intellect[37] but an embodied system for understanding and thinking ('I'm feeling *down* today'). His framing theory, which built on this understanding, suggests that the words we hear activate 'frames' – like 'austerity' – which are stories or underlying complexes of ideas, held in metaphor, that structure how we see the world, and are connected to our values.[38] The image of the frame in photography, determining what we see and don't, is helpful to understand how these linguistic frames work by shaping the sense we make of what we hear.

I was introduced to this set of ideas in 2013 by a change strategist who was helping us sharpen up our campaign messaging at Global Witness. I stayed up late reading the social psychology findings on values, whose implications were being brought together with Lakoff's theories about framing by a former policy campaigner at WWF (World Wide Fund for Nature), Tom Crompton. Like me, Crompton was increasingly unconvinced about NGOs' assumptions that their access to people in power was going to be enough.[39] He argues that people's values have a greater effect on their actions and views than facts do, and so campaigners need to pay attention to values. Empirical research finds that people hold related values in clusters, and that this is consistent across cultures. What are those clusters? 'Self-enhancement' or extrinsic values, like achievement and power, are about how we're seen from the outside. 'Self-transcendent' or intrinsic values, like universalism and benevolence, include tolerance and care for nature and matter to us for themselves. These are not character profiles; we all hold something of all of these values, in varying strengths.

There are two robust findings in this body of research. One is that it's hard to hold opposing values strongly at the same time. The other is that different values can be strengthened in us by what we hear and experience: by the messages we are exposed to. Activating one value strengthens those similar to it, and suppresses those that are opposed. This is where Lakoff's thinking comes in: the words we hear activate deep frames and thus influence the kind of values we hold.[40] That's why the experience of living in neoliberal societies has made people more individualistic over four decades, and why 'austerity' was such a powerful frame. It activated a set of ancient images – responsibility, security – that were already established, and that made spending on libraries or Sure Start Centres for new parents start to sound like something we couldn't afford.

When the deep frames aren't already strong in the culture, we have to build them. If politics is a contest between different value systems (authority versus empathy, for example),[41] then it is also a contest to build the frames that activate those values in our shared culture. Conservatives, Lakoff argues, have done this more effectively than progressives, so they can 'communicate easily in a few words,' rather than needing paragraphs. Conservatives 'have spent decades, day after day building up frames in people's brains' to promote their ideas. Think about what the expression 'tax relief' is doing, for example: it reinforces the libertarian idea of tax as theft by the state of what should rightfully be ours, rather than what makes civilised society with clean and lit streets, healthcare, schools and emergency services available at all. There are many possible frames for tax as a positive, like referring to taxpayers as 'contributors' to society – but new frames cannot be established overnight against such deliberately established ones. Progressives, say Lakoff, 'have a hard time building up the appropriate system of frames from scratch. And if they make the mistake of thinking that words are frames, they will assume that all they need are the right words or slogans.'[42]

Lakoff could also be describing here how neoliberalism and its project to make everything subservient to 'the market' has been made to feel like common sense, and attempts to articulate the need to put care for life at the heart of society sometimes feel like they just bounce off. Or how, over the last decade or more, Conservative and Labour governments' parroting of hard-right views on immigration only strengthens support for hard-right parties.[43]

These insights about framing are landing on an ancient mythic truth: that to name things – whether good or bad – has transformative power. In practice, it can be hard to avoid naming the bad frame.* One reason is because it's easier to critique than create, especially when our minds are shaped by the world as it is. Another is that movements of people can be grown relatively quickly in opposition to a hated policy;[45] but it takes longer to settle on what to call for *instead* when there are competing views. So this is not just about those no-to-austerity signs being carried on that protest in 2015, and nor am I having a go at anyone who held one. It is about getting away from yelling against 'what is', so we don't strengthen that false perception, assiduously cultivated by those in power, that there is no alternative to

---

* Debunking misinformation needs slightly different advice, because a brief mention of the lie or myth, so long as it doesn't restate it, helps connect the new data to the previously held false information. But don't repeat the myth in its usual form; warn that you're about to state it, and sandwich the correction between two mentions of the truth.[44]

'what is'. The point is to be clear about the world that we want and offer solutions.

Discovering all of this rearranged my mind, primed, as I was, by my disquiet with tactics reliant on the presentation of facts. Learning about values and frames was a gateway to the psychology behind our assumptions about rational decision-making. It led, eventually, to my interest in the 'inner' and interrelational aspects of change-making that I've written about here and in my first book. There's been greater attention paid in the last ten years to 'narrative change', and frames and messages based on these theories have been tested. A project called Framing the Economy, for example, was run by campaigners frustrated at the dominance and resilience of that 'austerity' frame. They analysed how the British public thinks about the economy, then tested how best to communicate a progressive vision. They found that people hold pervasive existing stories – that the 'economy' is a mysterious black box, that people are inherently greedy – creating fatalism.

Two new approaches worked in the focus groups. One was a 'resisting corporate power' story that said: 'We need to reprogram our economy so that it works in the interests of society rather than just in the interest of corporate elites'. The other was a 'meeting our needs' story: 'A good society makes it possible for everyone to lead a meaningful and fulfilling life. Yet, our society is currently focused solely on profit, and people are forced to chase money rather than happiness. The laws and policies that we make lay down tracks that determine where the economy takes people. Right now, our economy is built around profit rather than being built to get people to their true needs.'[46]

You can see how this message begins with a positive statement, yet works with people's current grasp of the issue. But this is not the same as 'meet people where they are'. 'Where people are *sucks!*'[47] says Anat Shenker-Osorio, a communications expert in the US who has made a name providing pithily blunt advice to the Democrats and to progressive causes. We can do better than meeting people where they are, on turf already defined by the other side. But it's better not to think about it as changing people from hardened views, she advises. A minority at the other end of the spectrum from us may be firm in their opposition, but for the majority of people it is much more likely that they are being swayed all the time by what they are exposed to – as Corinne Fowler's story showed. We can become part of that influence, including by staying in the conversation.

Increasingly, communications folk working in the UK recognise this need to set out our own vision and frame. But before we move on, I sometimes wonder if we have, any of us, *really* got the other memo which arises from values and framing theory: the one about repetition. The one that the populists and demagogues do so well when they parrot 'MAGA' and 'Brexit'. Framing theory tells us that repetition of well-chosen phrases would be important to strengthen the frames that we want to cultivate, even if we were just up against common-or-garden neoliberal, consumerist, market-based stuff, and not the new techno-authoritarianism shouting far-right messages onto devices in everyone's pockets. This is not to chuck out of the window everything I've just said in this chapter. I think repetition can potentially be compatible with varying our protest voice. But – and with noble exceptions – some of us tend to have a bunch of problems with repetition, whether on social media or in real life. Intellectually, it can feel crass, dogmatic, foghornish, dare I say it, *populist*, to keep making the same point. Relatedly, those of us with university degrees, where it was all about the data, abstractions and debate, can be bound by norms of intellectualism and get focused on facts and arguments as ends in themselves. We spend longer honing the argument than actually taking it out there.

Another academic-ish habit comes from having to label which ideas belong to whom. Citational practice is a cornerstone of intellectual endeavour and the building of knowledge – and we definitely need to give each other credit; sometimes in our hustle there isn't enough of that. But we can take it a step further: wanting to be considerate, wanting not to duplicate labour when we are so few, we say 'that's so-and-so's work so we can't touch it' – and leave it to that organisation or person to talk about 'their' issue. Nonprofit funding practice is a problem here, as organisations have to elbow each other to make clear which space in the public sphere is theirs so as to justify their funding. 'You wouldn't hear the Heritage Foundation saying that!' laughed a fellow troublemaker during a pub strategy session, when someone demurred from a potential tactic because another group they knew were already onto it.

We can also be bound by norms of politeness, that make us squeamish about picking up the phone repeatedly. Yes, I know, that's a generational thing, too… but dialling versus messaging is not what I mean. People who have worked as researchers in MPs' Westminster offices will tell you that corporate lobbyists call a dozen times before lunch to remind the MP about voting on something they have previously discussed, and that for every one normal person who comes in to meet their MP, there are ten people in suits telling the MP to do the opposite thing. Meanwhile the NGO and charity lobbyists can be delighted if we have scored just one conversation or meeting.

*

The protest voice has limitations in many circumstances and, crucially, there are alternatives. They can be found in curiosity, connection and shared experiences, conversations that overcome pluralistic ignorance, and the power of setting out our own vision. In some situations we can meet people where they are, and allow them the grace to not know what we already know. In other settings, we will be more effective by *not* meeting people where they are, so as not to strengthen our opponents' framings, and instead we should communicate the ground where we want to be in an inclusive way so that people can see themselves there.

But changing the world isn't just about how to reach the people we want to influence. It's also about getting enough of us involved, and keeping us together once we've started. Growing movements and working together bring challenges. The save-the-world script has some unhelpful things to say about how we campaign together ('I'm pure!' 'I know better than you!') but there are also people finding positive ways to subvert it.

3

'I AM PURE'

Coalitions are necessary.
Timothy Snyder, 'How to Stop Fascism'[1]

IT'S NOT A PURITY QUEST

In May 2024, hundreds of writers, editors and other workers in the publishing industry sent a letter demanding that Baillie Gifford, an investment management company that sponsored several book festivals, divest its holdings in fossil fuels and companies 'that profit from Israeli apartheid, occupation and genocide'. An author friend had signed this letter, which was organised by a collective called Fossil Free Books. He received a swift phone call from the owner of his publisher, an independent, expressing grave concerns about the potential fallout. 'He said he wasn't opposed to the aims behind it at all, but thought the organisers didn't know how effective this was going to be. He thought it would escalate really quickly, and given a choice between divesting from billions of pounds worth of finance and dropping their cultural affiliations, they will drop literary culture. And then exactly all of that happened.' As authors withdrew from their events, the Hay and Edinburgh literary festivals cut ties with Baillie Gifford, and in response to that, the company pulled all its funding from the other seven book festivals it sponsored across the UK.

During the hour or so in which I was reading some of the press coverage, a discussion was underway on one of the WhatsApp groups of climate activists that I lurk in. It was about whether and when the Atlantic Meridional Overturning Circulation (AMOC) – that drives the Gulf Stream and maintains Britain's climate – will break down. This decade? This century? Sometime thereafter? There were arguments for each of these views. Harvests will collapse; anyone under forty should have a passport and a useful skill to offer as a migrant, posted someone who follows the academic research on changes deep in the Southern Ocean and thinks it could be the first of those possibilities. The truth, another contributor pointed out, is that we don't know when the AMOC will break down as temperatures rise, and that's bad enough.

The point that climate-focused people tend to make is that even if we were to halt greenhouse emissions now (though in reality they are still rising), the coming disruption already baked in is of an order of magnitude that might render book festivals irrelevant, thus any difficulty caused by protests is justified. But publishers thinking about the viability of book festivals train their attention on more immediate time horizons.

Commentators and columnists, also operating within the bounds of a current-normality frame, were furious. This was an activist incursion onto their own turf and they had strong words: 'desecration of literature', 'narcissists', 'thuggery', 'coercion'. Authors were split: more than sixty Scottish writers, responding to the threat to the Edinburgh International Book Festival, issued a counter-protest against the 'deeply retrograde' impact and 'Pyrrhic victory'. Literary festivals offer a precious space for free and intelligent debate, they argued; this intervention did nothing to change how the fossil fuel industry operates, yet risked the spaces where writers can gather with their audiences, share their ideas and promote their books.

It was also hypocritical, the critics said. Tech companies with links to Israel include Amazon and Meta, yet authors are happy to sell their books on the former and promote themselves on Instagram. How dare they pull down shared goods like literary festivals in pursuit of a purity they can't achieve themselves?

That purity criticism is often wielded against us. 'How did you travel to the protest?' 'Where are your trainers from?' 'When did you last fly?' I've done media interviews where my personal consumption credentials were the main topic and it was an effort to get the conversation onto what we collectively need to do to stop the fossil fuel industry destroying our shared home. Focusing on the activist's failed purity status is a long-standing tool to distract attention from the terrible truths of more systemic failures around climate breakdown. But when the purity criticism is made in the context of boycotts, shareholder divestment or campaigning against cultural sponsorship it can also illustrate a misunderstanding about tactics and strategy.

Perhaps that's because the activists are not always communicating it effectively… and perhaps we sometimes carry this misunderstanding too. The strategic goal is not to make *ourselves* pure of contamination by ensuring we have no connection with any of the companies implicated in human rights abuses or destruction of the biosphere. Breaking connections with them is a *tactic*. The strategic goal is either to render them non-viable investments, or to destroy their 'social licence' to operate – the reputation that makes them an acceptable part of public life. That can be targeted at companies or countries. It's the purpose of the Boycott, Divestment, Sanctions movement against the Israeli government's oppression of Palestinians, as it was for the boycott of apartheid South Africa. It's what Liberate Tate, a collective of artists who successfully ended BP's sponsorship of the Tate in 2017, were doing when they staged a series of performance pieces over five years, including manoeuvring a 16.5-metre wind turbine blade into Tate Modern's Turbine Hall.

My purpose in thinking about the Baillie Gifford imbroglio is not to lecture activists on what they should have done: plenty of others have done that. My interest here – and as many of the responses to Fossil Fuel Books showed – is the way that we're trained to read such activist spectacles as quests for moral purity. This is the save-the-world script in action again. This time it's telling us, whether we're the activist or the observer, that the job is to make or to keep things pure – including ourselves. It's easy to fall in with the script because nobody wants to be seen as the hypocrite – the frequent flyer climate campaigner, the 'vegan' in leather shoes.

Where is this purity directive coming from, what happens when we act from it in our change-making, and how can we avoid it?

That misunderstanding about the purity task would come up in reactions to the work I used to do campaigning against cluster munitions and for stronger controls on arms exports. In these situations, it would be part of the justification for not getting involved. I would be told that this work was impossible, utopian. 'You're not going to be able to make the world perfect,' people would say, shaking their heads. But these were the same people who would also say things like 'What's the point?' or 'How on earth do you find the motivation for that?' I would file them in my category of 'doesn't care enough' and carry on. My diaries for those pre-smartphone years (a pile of black Moleskins: pretentious but beautiful) are scribbled thick with flights, trains, meetings and long stays in friends' and colleagues' apartments in Geneva and New York while lobbying United Nations conferences. I would meet diplomats, bureaucrats, academic researchers, film-makers, photographers, journalists, soldiers, public health workers, and communities torn apart by armed violence.

Our aims were ambitious: curbing the sales of weapons to human rights-abusing governments; imposing restrictions on the tidal surges of second-hand arms from one conflict zone to the next; and banning a weapon, cluster munitions, that was used by armies across the world. It is also true that in a broad sense, underlying the very nature of progressivism is a view that societies can be improved, perhaps even perfected, as opposed to the more pessimistic assessment of human nature that underlies conservatism. There is a necessary streak of wild thinking in trying to get anything changed, whatever the method or theory of change.[2]

We made steps towards some of these aims. My colleagues who continued working on these issues (after I moved to investigating the predatory behaviour of the financial sector) won a global ban on cluster bombs in 2008, and a treaty preventing the sale of weapons to governments using them against civilians in 2013. Both treaties have proven in reality to have manifest limits, either when countries don't all sign up, or find ways round them, most recently evidenced in the UK's arming of Israel.[3] Yet none of us were aiming for *perfection* by working towards those treaties. We were trying to make things less awful.

While outsiders often misunderstand our tasks as an attempt at purity, however, actual perfectionism and purity politics can sneak into our actions because of change-makers' own adoption of the save-the-world script.

One manifestation of campaigner purity involves lifestyle and behaviour. 'If someone ever takes a flight, if they eat meat, if they don't take time off work to go to a protest, they're not committed enough. I've done a fair bit of environmental campaigning and there are some really unhealthy examples within the culture of those organisations. You get a hierarchy over who is the purest – and it put me off.' Lucy Hawthorne has been working for change for two decades, both as a volunteer and professionally. She helped to get fracking banned in the UK in 2019, and now facilitates conversations about climate breakdown. Like so many experienced change-makers, she found it hard to be in groups where the purity script was running the show.

'I hated feeling like I was being judged for not being good enough at being good,' she said. 'A lot of energy ends up being directed towards the internal culture and having a completely perfect formation of how people are supposed to behave. It gets a bit self-obsessed.' She has seen organisations doing important work where things were 'just so purist that it was difficult to agree anything. The internal culture was so specific and their standards were so high it was just impossible to make any progress.'

When people working for change get very particular about how they do things it can be with the intention to – as Gandhi gets misquoted – *be* the change they want to see in the world. Emma River-Roberts, founder of the Working Class Climate Alliance, an international network, thinks that lifestyle-focused purity policing 'has a lot to do with middle-class lives, where the lifestyle, the physical things you own act as markers of morality and showing people "I'm living a virtuous life."' In environmental groups she has been asked why she doesn't make her own clothes. 'Because middle-class lives are heralded in mainstream society as the types of lives everyone should aspire to, it means they can take over and position themselves as exemplary citizens and say that consumption is this really important way of doing things,' she says.

This has many negative effects. One is that working-class people perennially feel they don't belong; it's why she was motivated to set up a network promoting working-class perspectives on climate action. Another is that for a long time the instinctive consumption focus encouraged parts of the environmental movement to play into the hands of fossil fuel-funded efforts to divert ecological and climate concern into guilt-driven individual consumer action – recycling, solar panels, electric vehicles – rather than pressure for wider system change.[4]

Tactics is another arena for purity battles. In environmental and climate groups this often comes over as a hierarchy where the 'hardest' approaches are the most valid. 'It's this judgement that you're not activist-y enough unless you're doing direct action,' says Lucy Hawthorne. Direct action means putting your body in the way. It can be done to prevent something from happening, like an eviction or deportation, or to make a media-worthy scene, as Greenpeace have long done by scaling power stations and oil rigs. Or it can be blocking public space or events to get arrested, with its sense of sacrifice, as Extinction Rebellion and Just Stop Oil have done in recent years.

'But I don't want to D-lock my face to Downing Street,' Hawthorne says. 'Those aren't my tactics. I'm good at understanding what different kinds of approaches work best to influence different kinds of people, and how the different approaches need to fit together like a jigsaw. And what the direct-action people are doing is great… but what I'm doing is needed too. They're not going to win without me. And I'm not going to win without them. I'm okay with that – but some of them are not! We won the ban on fracking in 2019 because we looked at it as a system: a coalition of organisations played different parts to different people, and that's what tipped it over the edge.' Local communities in Lancashire and Sussex had been resisting fracking attempts for several years, alongside big groups like Friends of the Earth. There were people willing to talk to the Conservative MPs who were critical in swinging it with their own party, working alongside people who wouldn't dream of working with a Tory.

What Hawthorne is alluding to here is 'movement ecology' – the idea that there are many niches in the complex ecosystem of people and forces that might end up creating change. It's extraordinary, really, for any of us to think that just one intervention (coincidentally, our intervention!) is going to be *the* thing that will swing it. If you put that proposition to many campaigners, they'd say 'Come off it, obviously I don't think that.' In practice, however, the judgement continues. When campaign groups have to raise funds, the need to claim responsibility for particular impacts can drive the criticism of other approaches. And the judgements can be about goals, too, not just tactics and methods.

Achieving plurality is often a problem for those wanting to change the status quo, because we don't all hold the same vision of 'what-instead'. It can be easier to permit a diversity of approaches (as the tech- and fossil fuel-funded libertarian right in the US has been doing) if it's really clear that we have a shared goal. But we are not united behind the goal of profit or power for its own sake, as our opponents often are. We are often split by the differences between centrist and socialist visions. 'My current life but renewably powered' might seem a great target if we are living relatively comfortably, but such a goal might be incomprehensible or a continued betrayal if we are not. There might be good reasons we find it difficult to contemplate compromise.

HARD ON OURSELVES, HARD ON THE WORLD

These conversations were making me think of the mid-twentieth-century psychoanalyst Donald Winnicott's concept – that beloved gift to exhausted parents – of the 'good enough' mother, and whether we should start talking about the good-enough campaigner. For some of us, however, 'good enough' is anything but. While writing an early draft of this chapter I got stuck for a few days. Feeling guilty for not being productive in those swift hours while the kids are at school, I went out in the February grey to meet a friend for coffee and a grumble. Steamed-up windows, dogs, the friendly hiss of the espresso machine: much better.

I confessed that I was spiralling. 'What are you writing about?' she asked. I looked down, running my finger over the worn grain of the table, realising what was about to happen. 'Purity and perfectionism,' I said quietly. Her shout of laughter quieted the noisy room. But then she got serious. We had previously discussed the parallels in how we were raised to get it right, to please, to do it properly. 'It just stops you dead,' she said.

The psychoanalyst Karen Horney, who died in 1952, called this 'the tyranny of the "should"'.[5] I have known many change-makers run by that tyrant. They rarely let themselves stop even though the list of potential tasks is without end. Then there are the people (in my experience, mostly women) who hold back on going public with their message, campaign, blog, because they want to get everything lined up, backed up, completely prepared before they say a thing. The 'tyranny of the should' is a good description, then; it conjures the burnout-inducing list of tasks that will never be complete, and how we can hold back from getting out and doing what's needed. But 'the deadly perfect,' the Jungian analyst Marion Woodman's name for it, lands more squarely in my heart. Woodman, who died in 2018, explored the connections between perfectionism and addictions. 'If you think you have to be the perfect son or daughter, you will drive yourself relentlessly to achieve,' she said. 'This actually is a desire for death not life. It means making life into a perfect and lifeless structure.'[6]

One of perfectionism's many ill-effects is to deaden our own creativity. It does this in the voice of judgement, a voice that dons the black cap and passes a sentence of mortal shame before we have allowed forth a word, brushstroke, movement or note. My voice of judgement did this for two decades of adult life. If I was writing for an employer – a newspaper, when I was a reporter, or, later, a human rights group – I could quell it. But to reveal myself and my ideas without institutional cover? To use my judgement capacity merely for discernment, quality control and strategy, and not to give myself a hard time? Forget it. I had to learn to see that critical voice for what it was and, as this conversation in the café was reminding me, it still takes the daily application of a careful kind of mindful attentiveness in order not to be felled by it.

The judgements we make of ourselves and the judge-ments and demands we make of others are often related. We are more likely to find others wanting when we cannot accept something in ourselves: our critical eye and voice have been sharpened. Accepting others' flaws would open the possibility of accepting our own. Will our inner critic allow that? Its long years of pointing out our own failings may be an outdated safety strategy that we no longer need, but all of this – both the need for a safety strategy ('Be good or there'll be trouble!') and the rough form it has taken ('That's not good enough!') – can be painful to contem-plate. No wonder it's easier to keep up the judgement of others.

Is this one of the reasons why so many campaigners are inclined to perfectionism? In its positive aspect, our critical voice can act as our conscience – with ourselves, and for the world. But our habit of demanding better from the world, of noticing what's wrong and needs to be improved, has developed together with that tough-on-self inner voice. Critical thought, with its potential for nuance and appeal to a common good, can distort into a need for pure thought, with its inevitable exclusions and polarities.[7] In some of us, furthermore, any expectation or goal that things in the outside world can be made perfect might also have been something of a liberal progress-fantasy; a delusion from a position of comfort. If we have grown up in poverty or experienced discrimination, we may be less likely to have ever believed that the world can actually be made perfect. And if we have to fight to secure the conditions of our own or our community's existence, perfectionist demands are likely to be less of a driver. 'Chat to people who are economic migrants or refugees,' one organiser told me. 'Their idea of perfectionism looks different: why do you lot talk so much without getting stuff done? What is the point of all these meetings?'

There may be another specific class effect too. When I first got to know Gail Bradbrook in early 2018, she and her fellow co-founders were cooking up what was about to become Extinction Rebellion. In our first conversation we talked about class: her working-class and my middle-class background. She could see in me something that I was coming to recognise, but had not yet attributed to class: a striver's worry about how I was being perceived, and whether I was getting things 'right'. That is my memory of the vibe generated by my grandmother, born in 1909: having to get it right; showing that you knew how to do things 'properly'. Through marriage to my grandfather, an accountant, she continued a class shift begun by her own mother, who grew up in poverty before marrying a butcher. These moves generated none of that upper-middle-class or upper-class insouciance. You showed where you had got to by not putting a foot wrong; that required control, much of which is physically held in the body, a structure like an internal corset. I was interested to learn, after years of migraines emerging from tense shoulders and neck, that my grandmother suffered them too.

Gail felt much freer of all that, she told me. She'd noticed how often shame and fear of getting things wrong could hinder action in groups running on middle-class norms. I thought about that conversation a few times over the following years, watching her launch a movement that helped, in its moment, to shift public awareness of climate breakdown, and that has grown to more than a thousand groups in more than eighty countries.

The negative appraisal of ourselves is ultimately that we are not enough as we are; that we must make ourselves acceptable through our achievements and our doings. Psychotherapists might look through a lens of parental approval-seeking, but working hard to make ourselves good-enough also echoes what the Protestant Reformation brought in the sixteenth and seventeenth centuries: the necessity of showing through your good and active works that God's grace had been bestowed. You could no longer confess and do penance to obtain salvation, as Catholics still do. Nor could you work directly *for* it – the new doctrine taught that salvation would be by grace and not by effort; by faith and not by prayer. Yet you could strive to demonstrate that you were *already* the recipient of grace. You could still show that you were good enough.* The effect, ironically, was the same as if you did have to work for it. Hard work was lionised. Not-enough-ness was normalised. 'Your right to belong, to feel attached, we body-believe, at a cellular level, is based on how good a person you are,' writes Susan Raffo, a bodyworker and writer about intergenerational transmission of culture.[8]

The Puritans took things further, wanting to purify the Church of England, created over the preceding century after Henry VIII's break with Rome, of its remaining Catholic practices. You might say that they took a perfectionist approach to their project of reforming their world. One explanation for their zeal is that it arose from the intense individual encounter with God that so characterised their religious feeling: 'Once he experienced the redemptive love of God in the new birth, the Puritan was possessed of a spirit that would not let him rest,' wrote Jerald Brauer, an American scholar of Puritanism in the 1950s.[9] As he peered into the hearts of people three hundred years earlier, I hear something of what I have seen among people trying

---

* There is more on the long tail of the Reformation in Chapter 5.

to change our current world. We have an experience, or something happens in the world, that makes clear what needs doing and what our task is, and we throw ourselves into it like the convert with new purpose in life. But our earnest intention does not always reach its target. Some of its energy is turned on our peers. They draw the fire that we might perhaps direct towards those in power if we had better access to them.

The Puritans offer useful reminders about what can drive us on the road from purity to intolerance. One way of looking at purity politics is as they did: a way to draw a line between the sacred and the profane. Certainly, a kind of religious feeling can be observed in the policing of literalist boundaries between what's in and what's out, what's correct and what's not.[10] In a different view, purity distinctions are less about the sacred, than a way of creating symbolic order in a culture.[11] On this basis we're giving ourselves a meaningful sense of order and control in a world – and perhaps in our own lives – where that feels lacking.[12] But there's little chance of us actually living a pure life, however hard we try. We are inevitably implicated in non-purity, consuming goods from globalised supply chains rooted in abuse, extraction and inequality; we are constantly making ethical compromises.[13] Perhaps we can distract ourselves from this discomfort by creating a sense of order based on judgements about the choices of others.

'THERE'S SOMETHING WRONG WITH THE ACTIVISTS'

When the Labour MP Jo Cox was murdered by a white supremacist on a busy high street in her constituency during the Brexit referendum campaign in 2016, the shock registered on many levels, though I was too disturbed to disaggregate them at the time. There was the physical roiling felt by each of us at such a violent disturbance to the shared body politic. There was the horror of realising how quickly the dogs of division and hate had been unleashed by David Cameron's daft decision to project the Conservative party's internal crisis over Europe onto a country where so many people were struggling with his party's cuts to public services on top of decades of post-industrial decline. And there was a personal horror at how close this poison had suddenly come to us, a small group of people working for charities, campaign groups and aid agencies, some of whom had shacked up with each other and were now having kids.

Because Cox, a mother of two, was one of us. She was a campaigner at Oxfam before running for public office. A colleague at Global Witness used to swing into the office after his monthly gathering of campaign directors from the big UK charities full of admiration: 'Well, Jo thinks we should…' I didn't know her, but we had friends and colleagues in common. I was at home, in bits, with a new baby, as they all gathered in grief for a vigil in Trafalgar Square, sharing her message of love and connection with thousands who hadn't known her.

The following year, with Brexit and the culture wars underway, Cox's widower and a few of her friends set up More in Common, a think tank to push back against extremism and counter polarisation in public opinion, including against migration. The organisation's name came from Cox's maiden speech as an MP, in which she said 'we are far more united and have far more in common than that which divides us.'

In 2020 More in Common published a ground-breaking piece of social psychology research, based on surveys and interviews across the UK, segmenting the population not according to the left–right political spectrum or the decades-old occupation-based demographic classifications used by pollsters, but by values and identity. The seven segments they labelled included 'progressive activists' (for whom politics is at the core of their identity), 'civic pragmatists' (also socially liberal, but more likely to take action through community or charity), 'disengaged battlers' (disillusioned, struggling, socially liberal), 'established liberals' (comfortable, cosmopolitan, trusting), 'loyal nationals' (anxious about threats to Britain, proud, patriotic, leftish on inequality, right-wing on immigration), 'disengaged traditionalists' (patriotic, self-reliant, keen on strong leadership) and 'backbone Conservatives' (patriotic, nostalgic, secure).[14]

The segments were rebooted and some renamed in 2025, taking account of further de-alignment from old left–right divisions. Their purpose was to demonstrate that Cox was right; there is more common ground than division. The British public are not all stacked up neatly on one side or the other of contentious issues. We shake out in a kaleidoscope of views and oppositions depending on the issue. The segments are a valuable tool, taking account of class de-alignment from traditional party affiliations. They're useful for campaigners too; climate folk have been using them to try to focus their efforts beyond their own bubbles.*[15]

More in Common has made specific studies of the ten percent or so of the population it calls 'progressive activist', reporting, usefully, on our tendency to overestimate by a factor of two or three the extent to which our views

---

*   See Chapter 7 for more on this.

are shared by the rest of the population.[16] Its 2021 report
on culture wars, *Dousing the Flames*, was addressed diplo-
matically to 'leaders' on both sides, calling on them not
to allow debates to be framed as binary cultural divisions,
and to assume greater complexity in what people believe.
The message for politicians was implicit: grow up and act
responsibly. But there was an explicit telling-off for activists:
'For those on the left, demands for change that rally activist
bases on Twitter can alienate the public at large,' More in
Common wrote. 'The wider public is acutely sensitive to
others looking down upon them, and judging them for
not using words with which they are not familiar… An
all-or-nothing approach to social progress will not secure
the base of public support required for progress.'[17]

It's not like social justice activists themselves weren't
talking about this too. The respected Detroit-based author
and activist adrienne maree brown (she is deliberate in not
capitalising her name) published *We Will Not Cancel Us* in
2020, drawing attention to the experiences of trauma and
harm that can lie behind our attacks on each other, encouraging us to notice how 'call outs elicit both a consistent
negative and dismissive energy, and a pleasurable take-down
activation, regardless of what the call out is addressing.'[18]
However, the 'depolarisation'-related critiques of activist
excess like More in Common's were placing themselves in
a middle space, somewhere between, on the one hand, the
gentle from-within critique by adrienne maree brown or
the civil rights activist Loretta J. Ross,[19] and on the other,
the shrill moral panic of the culture warriors blaming the
downfall of liberal democracy on 'woke-ism'. (Centrists do
this too. I know that the culture wars are a strategy of the
right but I do wonder: if you had never contemplated capitalism's effects and consequences and weren't willing to do

so, maybe 'woke' is where you'd start in trying to understand what's going wrong?)

Newspaper mentions of 'culture war' in the UK went from 178 in 2019 to 534 in 2020, and of 'cancel culture' from zero before 2018 to 3,670 a year in 2021 (23% of those in the *Daily Mail*).[20] More in Common's was not the only contribution to that middle space of critique from 2021. Others came from academic departments, think tanks and public intellectuals. Researchers at King's College London noted in 2023 that the proportion of people (of all persuasions) who think politicians are fuelling culture wars is growing.[21] In the same year, Sunder Katwala, head of the think tank British Future, encouraged the Labour Party and progressive left to find a route between panic and complacency, warning that while the UK was at the stage of 'culture clash' rather than full-blown culture war, it was 'misguided' to see it as 'nothing but a Conservative ploy.'[22]

To my eyes, the Fabian Society's contribution stood out in its recognition of what was – and still is – going on.[23] Firstly, they acknowledged that some activists on the left *respond* to culture war provocations with relish, that righteous progressive rage at inequality can tip into self-righteousness and zero-sum thinking, and that to onlookers the fights appear to originate with the progressive activists because they are about issues those activists are pushing. Culture warring is, nonetheless, being driven by actors on the radical right who are using it for distraction and division to their advantage. Secondly, they noted that the greatest division in the UK remains that of wealth inequality. So it's a trap and a distraction, the Fabian authors warned: don't go there. Instead, name the traps and distractions; concentrate on articulating a vision of the future that everyone can see themselves in; build inclusive movements. Another way of putting this is that the 'culture war' framing sets up a false equivalence between two 'sides', disguising systematic attempts by those in power to stigmatise the work of fighting economic inequality, racism and sexism and make it look abnormal.[24]

This advice remains solid, though I'd go further. The 'depolarisation' conversations risk missing the point that the insurgent right – in various incarnations – has been prosecuting a war on all of us for decades. The first phase occurred through successive neoliberal restructurings from the 1980s onwards that have impoverished the collective sphere and concentrated the wealth of the very few.[25] The second phase began with the catastrophe of Brexit. Both phases have been driven by the ideology of deregulation – and another way of saying 'deregulation' is to say, the evisceration of our capacity to protect people, society and the natural world from the quest for profit. Right-populism provides cover and a powerful vehicle for this agenda. While some of its followers have real grievances, its leaders and spokespeople are useful idiots for the very wealthy capitalholders funding it, and anyone paying attention knows that those holding the purse strings are not done yet. There's little value to 'depolarising' by meeting in the centre, in other words, when the centre is swinging so fast to the right.

And so there's little tolerance over on the left for the argument that it's progressives and leftists who are worsening polarisation with their purity politics. They notice, in 'depolarisation' discourse, a discomfort with the necessary confrontations of politics. In this view, you're more likely to be squeamish about agonism – the idea that conflict is an inevitable aspect of politics – or to think that your respectability requirements are a good political instinct, if you haven't had to fight for your existence. Nor is there much tolerance for how easily the 'activists are making polarisation worse' criticism elides into the suggestion, not hard to find in centrist commentary, that perhaps 'activists are pushing people *into the arms of* the far right'. This would hardly be necessary, when the mainstream is so full of anti-immigrant messages and a Labour prime minister boosts the far right by talking about an 'island of strangers'. In fact, left-wing and progressive people are sometimes at risk of a right turn themselves; the hard right's tracks are easy to fall into when you're disgruntled, suspicious and unwary. The *Guardian* columnist George Monbiot dubbed it the 'hippy-to-fascist pipeline', and the BBC's disinformation correspondent Marianna Spring documented several of its pathways in the UK in 2023.[26]

There is understandable defensiveness, then, about looking at the responsibility of campaigners for what is going on. Yet at the same time, there are things that we could do differently, so that our purity instincts can't be used so effectively against us. I looked at communication in the last chapter; that's certainly part of it. But it's also about how we turn towards or away from each other when we find what others are saying difficult.

BREAKING AND BRIDGING: IN THEORY

At least three inflammatory things have been happening around the issues that progressives speak out about. Firstly, the populist right fosters backlash against any campaigning action – whether on gender diversity or improving teaching of imperial history – to provoke a strategic culture war. Meanwhile, the extreme right appropriates the same issues for its own nativist purposes. 'In western Europe the far-right narrative is "We have to protect our women and gays against Muslim migrants, so we must close borders". In eastern Europe they'll say, "We have to protect our culture from gender ideology… and migrants."'

This is Sara Grossman, who runs the Democracy & Belonging Forum in Berlin, a project of the Othering & Belonging Institute at the University of California, Berkeley. Grossman tells me about the third tactic: the furtive weaponisation of differences among progressives by those seeking to undermine democracy. The malign power of this approach was demonstrated by the collapse of the coalition that organised the 2017 Women's March in Washington, DC. According to a *New York Times* investigation, the movement was derailed by trolls, some with the backing of the Russian government. They sowed acrimony along existing lines of friction within movements that were trying to work together against sexism, racism and homophobia, posing as Black feminists accusing white feminists of not getting it, or conservative women feeling pushed away.[27]

Grossman and her colleagues – including the Othering & Belonging Institute's founder, the legal and civil rights scholar john a. powell (he is deliberate in not capitalising his name) – are concerned about the 'breaking' that occurs when social justice groups, feeling under fire from such frightening developments, turn inwards and bond with each other rather than reaching out.[28] These new threats are of a different magnitude, Grossman says, to classic progressive infighting. They are threats to democracy, in this view, because if existing activists turn inwards towards their own groups, and everyone else turns away altogether because it all looks so fraught, then there is nobody to fight for democracy and the shared space for deliberation, citizen-ship and common action as even bigger threats arrive. For this reason, powell and Grossman prefer to use the term 'fragmentation' over 'polarisation'. While their analysis originates from the more polarised and more fragmented US situation, they see it increasingly occurring in Europe too.

And I would add that while they are on a different scale to change-makers' existing purity habits, these threats to democracy nonetheless exploit the purity habits. This is why it is important to examine them. In lieu of 'breaking' into smaller, more fragmented groups, the Othering & Belonging Institute points to the need for 'bridging': the difficult work of forming bonds even in the face of dif-ferences in background, political focus and strategy; even when it feels safer to turn inwards. It's not about moving to the middle, that soggy compromise.[29] Nor do we have to agree with each other. 'But can we hold the relationship and the difference?' asks Grossman. 'Mostly what people are really afraid of is being outcast by their own group.'

'Part of our call at OBI is a world of belonging without othering, and the not othering is the hard part,' she says. 'There's a lot of belonging in the world that's rooted in othering: I am *this* but not *that*.' Her current task is devel-oping a network of people willing to bridge: 'People who are developing capacity to counter the far right, but are still willing to grapple with questions around social justice and who hold power and resources.' She and powell observe – and as I was describing above – that while the people working on democracy and depolarisation tend to be scep-tical of the tactics of social justice even if they agree with the aims, the people working on social justice are wary of 'depolarisation' discourse.[30] Not just because they know that polarising is often part of the strategy to win,[31] but because 'a lot of protecting-democracy discourse comes from elite institutions: let's all get along to counter the far right,' says Grossman. 'Social justice people hear that and think, why should I defend democracy when democracy has harmed my group: am I just defending a flawed system? It's not that they're defending authoritarianism, but it's not at the centre of their work. They don't want to bridge with powerful institutions that don't care about their issue.' And so not everyone wants to do it, she acknowledges.[32] A consistent finding in the social-movement literature is that coalitions that bridge across different backgrounds and issues are hard to build and maintain.[33] It's easier, Grossman says, to bridge across smaller ideological differences. Short bridges, as structural engineers will tell you, are more straightforward to build.

After several years of conversations about this with change-makers, I agree with her that whenever we feel we can 'bridge', we must do it. Whether the purity is over lifestyle, methods or goals, whether it derives from personal perfectionism or trying to navigate through complexity, from turning-inwards responses to long-standing harms or to newer weaponisation of our issues – or, indeed, from any combination of these – the consistent outcome of purity politics is the loss of potential power. Plural, massive movements of people are needed in response to climate breakdown and anti-democratic forces. 'Movement ecology' doesn't just mean leaving space for other people to do it differently without giving them a hard time over their tactics; it also requires getting together, combining our assets and skills, to become something bigger than the sum of our parts. When we retreat into smaller groups, we can't grow our power. We're doing exactly what authoritarians, the far right and anti-democratic libertarians want: fragmenting.

BREAKING AND BRIDGING: IN PRACTICE

'People outside might say "The left is a circular firing squad", or "We know that people have a pop at each other." But I don't think they quite realise the visceral emotionality of the arguments that go on around justice,' says Clare Farrell, a designer and one of the co-founders of Extinction Rebellion, as she rolls a cigarette. 'My justice is bigger than your justice, you don't fucking get it, this is the justice, this is the right justice, oh but you're not… justice enough!

'I want to talk to people in a way they understand. About how unfair it is. It's about inequality, it's about loads of stuff that you would put underneath the justice word – but I'm interested in what's underneath. The word itself is not helpful, especially if you're going to use it to bash each other. Thousands of Zoom hours, God knows what the carbon footprint is, of people wanging on at each other who basically agree on almost everything – and they've found the one, minor, narcissism-of-small-differences point where they can go, do you know what, I think you're shit because of this. Open letters being written, "If the strategy team releases this, you're going to have blood on your hands because you're not talking about justice enough. This is about destroying indigenous people's lives. You're all part of the problem and you're all going to turn into eco-fascists." I mean literally, going from zero to you're-a-fascist.'[34]

Farrell sounds like she's letting off steam, though she's not describing a current situation.[35] She's recalling what was going on a few years ago and has a lively way of describing it – one of many reasons why she was a powerful media presence when Extinction Rebellion kicked off. In 2022, trying to bring some fresh air into these internal fights, she was introduced to a methodology for global-citizenship education that helps people have conversations that reveal where their own perspectives sit in a wider picture.[36] She developed a version for Extinction Rebellion's fractious teams to use to hear each other, test their own views, and try out modifying them.

'We'd do a group enquiry into a statement like "climate justice is racial justice." And then you critically look at that; look behind it. You ask, who would say that and why? Why would they think that? Do you agree with it? What else could you add? You just go round the group, three times, listening. You're not responding to something someone *did* say, but what they *might* say, so there's nobody to shoot down. You might get someone saying, "I don't like that, because I think xyz from my own experience, and that's why I think that's wrong." And the next person might say, "I thought that's the kind of thing I'd say myself, but now I've heard you say that, I'm not so sure, because I understand where you're coming from." So you foster a space where you can actually listen to each other, and there's no agenda, it's not like you're trying to decide anything or have an outcome — you're just going to learn some shit about each other.'

Groups trying to make change can grind to a halt in their outward work if they can't find a way to work through this stuff, and to take the ego defence out of discussions of ideas. 'I can't remember who said it, but the prison you build for others is the prison you build for yourself,' says Vanessa Faloye.[37] We've worked together in her daytime capacity as an educator and trainer of change-makers — rather than her night-owl incarnation as a DJ — and have been talking about perfectionism on and off for a few years. 'If I am building a cage of perfection for other people where they are not allowed to make mistakes, they're not allowed to change their mind, they're not allowed to be a certain way — and a certain way that is different to me – that is a prison that I'm also building for myself. I also remember it when I'm on the receiving end of someone's contempt or disappointment. I can think, "I see that you're treating me like that because that's the standard that you're holding yourself to." I remember that I didn't sign up for that standard, so I can be with their disappointment when I fall short,' she says. Faloye runs training programmes for Democracy & Belonging Forum participants who are learning how to 'bridge', and what she's describing here is one of the capacities that it requires.

The aggro is not over a confected issue. The people banging a drum within Extinction Rebellion were trying to say something that regularly arises in criticisms of middle-class white environmentalism: that it can fail to centre justice for the poorest, whether in the UK or in countries already more affected by climate breakdown, and fail to acknowledge the fact that those are the poorest countries because of colonial histories of extraction. That's what that phrase 'climate justice' encompasses. It's true that some of those who go hard with these criticisms can end up brandishing other people's experiences to prove their own credentials as 'good'. But they're also pointing out something that does actually happen: that white and middle-class environmental activists don't always make a bridge to everyone else who cares.

There's an old view – that it's 'distracting' or 'divisive' to address class or racial injustice as part of the urgent fight for a liveable climate – that sticks around in white, middle-class and, dare I say it, middle-aged environmental activism.[38] Extinction Rebellion (XR) was often all three of those things. I heard it articulated a few times – not from everyone, and not from people in leadership positions, but it was present among the rank and file: someone was talking to me about it as lines of police approached to arrest us while blocking Waterloo Bridge in April 2019.

This view extends beyond XR, however. 'Let's not be divisive' – I've also heard this cover for a certain kind of issue-purity in local politics, from centrists and progressives, and just generally around the place in majority-middle-class and majority-white settings. Emma River-Roberts had seen something similar. 'There was this utopian, we-all-need-to-be-united and so we can't talk about the uncomfortable things,' she told me, of her uneasy experiences in middle-class environmentalist settings. 'I think because a lot of middle-class groups have their underlying degree of relatability with themselves, this idea of having to unpack difficult conversations isn't normalised,' she added. The ironic result of this earnest desire for unity, then, is the opposite, because wide movements cannot be built from groups that are fragile when reminded that there may be other perspectives.

The climate-only view activates the old trope that speaking up about exclusion and oppression 'gets in the way' of the smooth running of things: businesses, organisations, politics… and responding to climate breakdown. In that old story, when feminists and people of colour protest about discrimination, *they* become the problem.[39] Without claims for social justice, the story suggests, we'd just come together and 'get on with' pursuing technical policies that reduce carbon. Yet it's politically unrealistic to think that any division can be avoided: the kickback against ultra-low emission zones from tradespeople faced with buying unaffordable new vans (let alone from wealthy male motorists or conspiracy theorists)[40] was a reminder that there will always be political contest, and that climate politics are not separate from the politics of inequality. With the radical right taking an anti–net–zero stance, it's important to show, explicitly, how efforts to protect against climate breakdown could potentially make life better for everyone.[41]

Also, like all single stories that claim they're the only story in town, climate-only is a kind of purity fantasy, a wishing away of other problems in which we might be implicated. Suggesting that climate work should not include racial justice, in particular, involves – once again – white people drawing lines around who's in and who's out. Climate-first also draws on another old story, that 'material' (in this case climate) and 'identity' issues are separate: as if class, race and gender do not, under the world's current arrangements, also have material consequences for our lives. Another version of this 'material' vs 'identity' story gets used to devastating effect to split united working-class resistance to inequality and excessive wealth into the 'white working class' on one side, who in this confected narrative are concerned with the material economic problem of getting food on the table, and 'immigrants' and the 'woke' on the other, as if they are not actually concerned about the same thing. Versions of these old stories have been weaponised by those in power for centuries; turning working-class men against working-class women;[42] turning white people against people of colour.[43] Fragmentation, again.

My friend Nick Anim, an activist and scholar researching why climate movements are so white, has seen the 'tackle climate first' story within the Transition Town movement, a community-based energy-downshift and local resilience project, whose Brixton group in South London he ran for several years. If you drew a Venn diagram of people involved in Transition and Extinction Rebellion, there would be more than a sliver of overlap. In 2023, he told me, someone in the Transition movement in Sweden published an article suggesting that they shouldn't be talking about racism in their environmental work, because it emphasises difference, which is the opposite of what we need to pull together. Nick worried that such arguments offered 'an open window for eco-fascists'. He means people on or susceptible to the far right, who will connect fear of climate breakdown to fear of immigration in order to pursue their white nationalism. He was concerned they would hear a coded dog-whistle in anything explicitly suggesting that environmental work shouldn't have racial justice at its heart.

Nick's fear of eco-fascism is well-founded. The far right are *already* at the table of climate politics, warn the Swedish academic and climate writer Andreas Malm and his colleagues in the Zetkin Collective,[44] a group of scholars thinking about climate and the far right together. I was initially surprised when I saw them saying this; many far-right political parties are steeped in climate denial. But environmental purity and population purity have an old relationship,[45] and there are far-right groups using growing climate concern to rehash their supremacist bile. In an unpleasant hour on the website of Patriotic Alternative, one of the UK's largest fascist groups,[46] I saw multiple blogs on environmental issues. Except for the white nationalist inflection, the topics sounded like a typical agenda for the lefty-greenies I hang out with: connection to land, hiking, camping, going plastic-free, allotments, overuse of pesticides, rewilding, opposing housing development, and the construction of hedgehog accommodation. There were even relatively sympathetic opinions of Just Stop Oil protesters.[47]

To read conversations suffused with hate that touched on my green 'home turf' was jarring. Hilary A. Moore, an American activist and researcher of the far right, warns of the need for great care when speaking about the environment or climate, which are value-neutral in themselves, so as not to leave the way open for far-right interpretations. If you speak about nature being 'threatened,' they may add, louder than you, their own view of what that threat entails: immigration.[48] Living in Kentucky, where the Appalachian landscape has been devastated by mountaintop-removal coal mining (this is, sadly, exactly what it sounds like), Moore has seen it happen first-hand, she told me. Local environmental groups' concerns about destructive mining were taken up, using very similar imagery and language but with added racism, by far-right groups seeking recruits.

So we must be explicit about the futures we want when we talk about climate and ecological breakdown. There's been good work in the UK in recent years creating and testing narratives for campaigners to talk about climate while being clear about justice for the hardest-up; and to talk about the hardest-up while being clear that it's about the working class in all their diversity. The UK 'Race Class Narrative', for example, was a messaging tool developed by the sadly now-closed Centre for Labour and Social Studies with the support of the communications expert Anat Shenker-Osorio (see Chapter 2). Silence about race does not work, this narrative advised; you need to name explicitly the united diversity from which you speak − 'whether we're black, white or brown, we all want...' − right from the start of the message.[49]

Trying to be pure about the *issues*, then, is a bad idea because it leaves openings for the far right to exploit, or for our opponents to divide us. But the opposing response to such a view − like those campaigners Clare Farrell was describing, condemning each other as 'eco-fascist' if they don't mention every aspect of justice − can involve purity reactions too.

Let's look at a conversation I had with an experienced campaign professional who's worked for decades on both environmental and social justice issues – let's call him David. He was telling me that in planning meetings he has heard, to his frustration, climate-justice folks saying that they couldn't bring themselves to invite the National Trust into their coalitions, because its properties were built on the proceeds of slavery. 'Five million Middle England members who would *terrify* the government – of course they've got to be involved!' he said. 'But they can't be involved because [in the view he was describing] they can't part be part of a conversation about climate justice until we've had reparations for slavery. Actually, it would be really good if an organisation of five million members, who are situated politically right in the middle of where you need them, is talking to the government about climate and encouraging them to be more ambitious on energy efficiency and land management – that's a good thing. It doesn't mean that you don't need to deal with colonialism – of course you do! But they're not the same thing,' he said.

They are related. Imperial extraction from colonised nations and enslaved Africans fuelled the Industrial Revolution which put Britain and other early-to-industrialise countries ahead in both wealth and cumulative contribution to carbon emissions. The first to suffer from increasingly destructive weather events are those who contributed least to atmospheric carbon dioxide and – for example in Caribbean nations – the descendants of those who were enslaved.[50] Countries that are desperately short on financial resources for adaptation and resilience preparation experience ongoing trade, tax and debt policies that *still* keep wealth flowing towards the richest countries. Actual climate justice would require massive financial support from the nations most responsible for climate breakdown.

The thing is, *I know* that David knows all this. But I realised later that if I didn't know him and I heard him say 'they're not the same thing' out of context, I might have reacted to an older white man *sounding* like he's saying that what's important is to have a big climate coalition, and that the National Trust's tangled history with colonisation and slavery is secondary to that. I might have assumed he didn't know they were entangled; I might not have taken his other points seriously. I might have dismissed him because he didn't 'get it'. And yes, I might also have been trying to keep myself pure, good, and on what I thought was the right side. I'd have been 'breaking', which is so much easier to do than 'bridging' when we respond from our unexamined reactions. And if, by chance, he *didn't* know about these connections,[51] I wouldn't have been any more justified in my decision to 'break' rather than 'bridge' – especially as a white person who is not repeatedly weathered by experiencing racism. I don't need to turn away from such 'debates' for self-protection. Rejecting a potential bridge in a flounce of my own moral righteousness would achieve nothing.

Of course, both things are true at the same time. The National Trust's history *is* entangled with slavery, and the campaigners David was telling me about were right that the institution should be part of conversations about reparative justice. *And* it might be a really good idea, strategically, for climate campaigners to involve the National Trust's mainstream membership in climate action (indeed, they are beginning to do so[52]), even if the national conversation about reparations has a long way to go.

The problem is that we can't hold that '*and*' if we're in strong reaction to one of the statements on either side of it. Our reaction keeps us in the '*but*'. It elicits a lightning-fast response from our sympathetic nervous system, priming us for the zero-sum scenario of conflict or flight, survive or die, right or wrong, rather than the holding of plurality that we're more capable of when we're feeling settled. Experiences of repeated harm – including from structural oppression – might have put us in the activated mode where we jump to the *'but'*. Yet even if we haven't experienced such harm, so, in a different way, might our inability to tolerate ourselves in all of our complexity. That intolerance comes out in our reactions to others. We talk about the polarisation of politics and culture out in the world, but there's a potential polarisation within each of us, leaving us disconnected from the aspects of ourselves we don't feel good about. Somehow we have to make a bridge to the part of ourselves that might hold views or feelings we fear, that's vulnerable, that's never going to be good enough, that *doesn't actually know*. If we can't do that within ourselves, how are we going to find the *'and'* so we can bridge across to others when there are differences of opinion or situation?

To loosen that judgement within ourselves, we must learn to recognise it. There was a clue scattered through the conversations I was having. People often referred to 'hard' activism. They'd be talking not about issue-purity but tactics-purity and its hierarchy of 'what counts', where the 'hardest' activists are those doing risky, frontline action. The point here is that word, *hard*. It can be useful to be tough and unbending in the face of pressure and opposition. But the word is also a clue to a somatic state, a body state, that comes with perfectionist judgement. By tuning in, I notice that my compulsion to make things right locks up my neck and jaw; lends an angry edge to my voice. For years, a familiar critic would deliver commentary on myself or others in what sounded like my own voice; I'd wind myself tight before I realised what was happening.

Now I know that voice is not my better self. To soften requires compassion for that judgemental part and its survival strategies that are no longer required. I can practise disarming in my personal relationships and when I'm doing politics in groups. Both are ongoing work. The body softening is a sign of judgement relaxing, but it works the other way too; consciously changing our body state, letting go of the clenched jaw, helps to shift our minds.

So much for handling our own judgemental voice. But when we face a choice between making a break or a bridge, we also need to recognise our habit of seeking the rewarding dopamine hit of a 'win' because we're right and someone else is wrong. Again, we cannot simply will ourselves to change this: the reactions are happening too quickly. They are below the level of conscious thinking.

So there's work to do. We can practise noticing the reaction, which means stopping and observing the feeling in our bodies when something has 'hooked' us. Each time it happens, we can pause, notice, observe the thoughts that come with it, remind ourselves that we are not our thoughts. This begins to open the space to respond differently. At first we won't catch ourselves quickly enough; we'll be reviewing in hindsight. In time, we may sometimes get there before we speak.[53] But it does need practice, and it's good to do it with somebody we trust, so that we can hold each other gently to account and offer reflections. 'When we give our brains information about a thing without being deep in practice with it,' warns Susan Raffo, who writes about embodied habits and their consequences for politics, 'it just gives us more tools and strategies to protect ourselves from change.'[54]

I've met people constructing bridges of all kinds in their climate campaigning. Some are bridges across issues; some are bridges to people who don't think of themselves as activists. I'll briefly outline three of them, that illustrate the potential of this practice – and how we can't always build all the bridges at once.

Green New Deal Rising is a movement of young people tackling climate breakdown and inequality together. 'We come from towns devastated by cuts and we grew up in cities choked by air pollution,' reads their website. The first 'Green New Deal' proposal came in the wake of the 2007–8 financial crisis from a group of economists, campaigners, the Green MP Caroline Lucas and the Labour MP Clive Lewis. Take the concept of Roosevelt's New Deal investment into employment, they said, and put it into the necessary low-carbon transition: public transport, energy generation, retrofitting homes. You can work for both economy and planet together. The idea grew in prominence as Democratic politicians tried to push it into US legislation in 2019.[55]

'The mistake they felt they made the first time was that it was a policy-led intervention, but actually what they needed was a movement-led intervention,' said Fatima Ibrahim, co-director of Green New Deal Rising in the UK. Young people who sign up are encouraged to challenge their MP publicly and film it; the resulting videos go viral and are used for recruitment. The aim is to get the need for a Green New Deal into the headlines and into people's minds as a defining political issue. The connection they make between climate politics and economic and racial justice is instinctive – as it often is for younger campaigners who were raised in or radicalised by financial crises and austerity.

'It feels so simple to us,' Ibrahim told me. 'We were already in an emergency when I was born – so of course this is what we're trying to deal with. There's not a mental separation. The more I understood the climate crisis, the more it became obvious that we have got things wrong and that we're trying to fix a symptom – and we're never going to fix a symptom in this way. You cannot separate the climate crisis from the material conditions of people, the rights of people, how we decide who and what is important in our society, right?'

While she bridges comfortably between justice and climate, Ibrahim is happy, however, to be pursuing confrontational (albeit legal) tactics that spook some funders. 'I'm not inherently allergic to polarisation, it's one of the things that happens on the road to change. Anything important, you need people to pick a side.' She thinks there's a fear about respectability among these funders, one that affects her less. As a young Muslim woman growing up in the UK and Canada in the early 2000s, she became accustomed to her identity being politicised. 'Some of the people running these organisations and foundations are nervous about being involved in something that results in them being on a side, where they might face marginalisation or polarisation. It's not an experience they, in their bones, are used to – "We just want everyone to believe the thing that we're working on, and this is the safe space, and let's not force the issue,"' she mimics, waving her hands melodramatically. 'But that's how change happens.'

The Climate Majority Project, meanwhile, is keen – in a very different way – not to wish away people who disagree. With the challenge of climate breakdown calling for mass action, participation from the usual left or green suspects won't be enough, they say. They want to bridge to the 'concerned majority': those who'll never see themselves as 'activists'. 'A genuinely inclusive movement has space for those whose first priority is intersectional social justice as well as those whose principal motivation is love of nature, for example, or a sense of heritage and posterity,' write two of its founders, Rupert Read and Rosie Bell.[56] 'There can be no insistence on a single ideology or set of values, and no group should present itself as a gatekeeper for the movement at large.'

I hear an implicit criticism of purity politics, and in those words 'heritage' and 'posterity' I hear them deliberately invoking the more conservative-facing 'moral tastes' identified by the psychologist Jonathan Haidt in his 'moral foundations' theory. This suggests that moral views are not singular, but based on several principles or, in his metaphor, 'taste receptors'.[57] They are focusing on the UK's need to adapt to extreme weather, working with businesses, trying to get companies to call for clear climate-related regulation from government and, in a 'climate courage' project, with educators and psychologists to share resources for young people experiencing climate anxiety.

I asked one of their coordinators: who shows up for their meetings and talks? Some, though not all, she told me, are left-leaning. Most are not self-defined 'activists'; these are people who aren't attracted to more radical spaces. So the bridge to the 'not-activists' from the organisers (some of whom have been 'activists') is working, although – perhaps inevitably – it may not be attracting what we might call the 'really-activist' into the same space. That's probably inevitable.

And as I was coming towards the end of writing this book, Clare Farrell, having mostly moved on from Extinction Rebellion, had a new project. She was working with Lee Jasper, a well-known anti-racist activist of many decades' standing, and Nick Gardham, an organiser and former teacher, who runs the Cost of Living Alliance, a national network of community groups supporting people in poverty to organise for change. Their coalition is called the Humanity Project, and brings together people working on poverty, on racial injustice, and on climate. 'We could all furrow away in our individual siloes – if I got race equality for individual Black people by some miracle tomorrow, would that impact the climate crisis? It wouldn't,' Jasper told me. 'If they [Farrell and her crew of climate-focused folks] got the UK government to end all licensing of oil and gas tomorrow, would that end white supremacy? No it wouldn't. Our view was – and coming heavily from the Black experience – that you had to build a critical alliance.'

'People in our network may sympathise with environmental concerns but it's not their primary concern because most can't afford to pay their bills,' said Nick Gardham. 'They're not thinking about what's happening in the next fifteen years, they're thinking about what's going to happen on Friday. It became clear to us there needed to be an extraordinary alliance of people from different backgrounds coming together to think about how we could do something. The core ambition of the Humanity Project is to connect the person in Hartlepool or Haringey who's got a housing issue with an environmental movement down in Cornwall because their sea walls are collapsing. All this does link up.'

The initial connection came when Lee Jasper was working with a group called Blaksox – which is 'not like an organisation,' he said, 'it's just a name, a convening platform for Black people who are willing to put their hand in their pocket to fund initiatives they think are needed, or contribute their time and expertise'. They were challenging white-led organisations on their anti-racism. Blaksox came to an agreement with Just Stop Oil and Extinction Rebellion to offer anti-racist training and mentorship in exchange for commitments to anti-racism being at the centre of their work. This led to thinking together about what systemic change would look like.

The Humanity Project is a 'build parallel institutions' project, rather than a 'resistance' one. They organise local grassroots assemblies which they intend to lead to national ones. It's an experiment in deliberative democracy. 'The politics of Westminster is fundamentally corrupt in that it's subject to corporate capture,' said Jasper. 'That's the poison in the well of British democracy. To meet the challenges of the twenty-first century you're going to have to have a more representative, more transparent, more decentralised democracy, and that calls for a democratic reset. That requires us to think about a new way of doing things. You almost have to create a new politics to go with it. We say we're not quite sure what it looks like, but what we do know is that we've been artificially divided when we have common interests that should be shared. The way we can try and facilitate that – and that's a big ask – is to facilitate conversations between people who wouldn't normally come together. To make that a virtue.' In the pilot phase they held forty-six assemblies around the country and trained 200 people to run them; in 2025 they were directly funding twenty local organisations to build further assemblies in their communities.

It's a strong start, though there will be much work when people are coming from such a variety of life situations. The next two chapters are all about some habits that can get in the way of coming together: knowing-better and being a saviour.

4

'I KNOW BETTER THAN YOU'

The truly hard problem is that the fragmented knowledge system in use today is unable to deal with the real issues confronting humanity because it neglects the experienced side of reality.

Minna Salami, *Sensuous Knowledge*[1]

The truth is that, to many people calling themselves Socialists, revolution does not mean a movement of the masses with which they hope to associate themselves; it means a set of reforms which 'we', the clever ones, are going to impose upon 'them', the Lower Orders.

George Orwell, *The Road to Wigan Pier*[2]

LIVED EXPERIENCE

Roger Harding was hiding who he really was at the homelessness charity where he worked, until an awkward conversation with one of the charity's trustees. 'They told me why I was wrong in our approach, because they didn't think the campaign would speak to or work for not very well-off single-parent families. It was a weird dynamic, getting an evidence-free lecture from someone who was quite posh about what my childhood was like.' Later, in a new job, Harding and his colleagues at Reclaim, a young people's charity in Manchester, surveyed working-class charity employees. 'The number one thing that pissed people off the most,' he told me, 'was the use of language about people on low incomes that they never use about themselves, language that is patronising or distancing. It's very much "they" and "them": "What you need to understand about people in poverty…"-type stuff that you just wouldn't say if you were talking about mates, or aunts and uncles.'

That trustee was performing a classic rendition of 'I know better than you.' We saw shades of this line in the save-the-world script in Chapter 2, during those moments where we condemn people for not knowing everything we do, refusing them space to learn. But then there's the version this trustee was doing: assuming that you know better off the bat.

I wanted to meet Harding after reading Reclaim's research, *Missing Experts*, published in 2022. It was a damning account of UK charities' failure to understand the life experiences of the people they are trying to help, ignoring the expertise of their own working-class staff, who often keep quiet about where they're from to fit in with middle-class norms.[3] Harding appreciated finding so many people who 'found it really cathartic to see that their experiences were shared. They were worrying: am I just an angry person, have I got a chip on my shoulder? Or maybe I'm not good enough, maybe I'm coming up with excuses as to why I'm not getting on? We got endless comments saying, "Thank you, because even if this changes nothing else, I know this is structural and not something that individually I'm going through."'

'The backstory,' he explained, 'is that I was really pissed off. Initially I didn't talk about my background while working in those organisations.' It wasn't a conscious decision. 'I just didn't see anyone else doing it. You are playing mimicry when you're in professional settings for the first time, so I copied what was around me. You wouldn't necessarily know it now, not in how I speak, but I grew up in a low-income family, in the South East, in a lower-income bit of an otherwise well-off town. And because of that experience – my mum raising me and my sister in a council house, and she was a dinner lady, and times were tough – because of all of that, I wanted to do social justice work.' But because Harding kept quiet about his background, charity colleagues, who were nearly all middle class, assumed he was too. That's when the conversation with that trustee happened.[4]

On another occasion a junior colleague told him it was a shame no one in senior management understood what it's like to grow up on a low income. 'It was like the crowning achievement of my passing,' he realised. 'My acting ability reached a crescendo, but I also felt a moment of shame, because it hadn't fully dawned on me how much at a sub-conscious level I'd made a decision to change how I speak, to not talk about aspects of my upbringing. I didn't really talk about it until I was a senior manager. Finally, something in my brain switched, to say: I'm probably safe enough now to mention this.' His research, done with Kirsten Graver, a colleague at Reclaim, looked at the consequences of not employing working-class staff or failing to listen to those who were there: lack of connection with communi-ties, clumsy mistakes, erroneous assumptions and missed opportunities.[5]

It's not that charities don't know they should root their work in the experience of those they want to help. The discussion has been going on for generations.[6] But for the past decade or so there's been a storm over this relationship between those with experience of the difficulties the organisation works to alleviate, and those without.[7]

The ruckus has been happening both in UK-focused organisations, and in the international aid and humanitarian industries, which have for so long been structured around a power differential between those who help and those who receive. 'Lived experience' has become a widely recognised term and a funder requirement. Consequently, charities' campaigning materials, their tone, their public faces, look a bit different to how they did twenty years ago. Yet there's still an underlying ranking of knowledge. The very framing of life experience as something requiring attention still implicitly centres the learned knowledge of the staff, who are more likely to have degrees and be middle class. The Sutton Trust found in 2025 that a third of charity CEOs were privately educated, and a fifth had been to Oxford or Cambridge.[8]

In the Reclaim research, Harding said, people spoke of 'a strong sense that, if you've got direct experience of one of these issues, that you're good for a "lived-experience group" or a case study. Here we have senior management. Over there's our lived-experience group. Here is our "board" board. And over there is our "lived experience" advisory board. And it's constantly clear that when it comes to the power, one is valued more than the other.'

Part of the problem is the mental structures that can underpin the very idea of 'charity'. In some contexts – for instance, the UK's class system and long legacy of empire – charity can take on a subject–object, doer and done-to dynamic.[9] But the problems in the charity sector are part of a wider difficulty across social movements and other forms of change-making, even when they are not explicitly oriented around a charitable relationship. When people from more privileged backgrounds assume that they (I could say 'we' here, as I have done this) know best, it gets in the way. Or they (we) take over. The relationship remains hierarchical.

This matters because – bigger collective 'we' coming up here – together we face challenges that require solidarity and cooperation: fighting grotesque inequality, overturning the influence of corporations and oligarchs on democracy, coping with climate breakdown, resisting the rise of far-right ideologies and political parties. Power dynamics are inevitable: our positionality within the world's current systems of domination affords some of us more power than others. We can't help who we are and where we're from. But we can help what we do with it, and knowing-better, that tool of status-quo hierarchies and obstacle to genuine solidarity, is something we have control over.

However, the instruction to 'step back' and 'pass the mic' to avoid I-know-better behaviour, currently felt strongly within the charity sector and wider activism, can seem like a directive to stay away, to not try to act. There are already high barriers to getting involved in social change: the practical problem of having enough time after working long hours to pay the bills as the cost of living rises, and the sense in modern Britain's increasingly individualist culture that we don't have a stake in the lives of anyone beyond ourselves, or any responsibilities beyond our own immediate spheres. That 'step back' directive adds to this problem. It's what many people outside of change-making circles already feel they must do, because like other instructions on the save-the-world script, I-know-better also works in its inverse: to keep people from trying to do anything. Thinking that we must know what to do, or must have first-hand experience of the problem to act, can prevent us from standing up *at all*. Even if we'd like to contribute, we may not be sure what we can bring. Specifically, we're worried about getting it wrong because we don't have experience of the problem ourselves and we intuit, even if we haven't been following all the talk about 'lived experience', that this might be an issue.

I attended a wedding while writing this chapter and was seated next to a chap in his thirties who, after responding to my polite enquiries about his work in finance, asked what I did. 'I've been a campaigner and at the moment I'm writing a book about how not to save the world,' I said, trying to keep my tone light. 'Oh, God,' he sighed, slightly dramatically, although not without genuine feeling. 'I know I should do something, but I don't feel I can. What have I got to offer?'

I have heard this for years: that if we don't know what we're talking about because we haven't lived it, better to steer clear. People hold back from volunteering, from speaking up, from getting involved in politics. But underneath the wanting to get things right – and that terribly British desire not to embarrass oneself by being inauthentic – I hear something else: the guilt and fear of being in relation across difference. It's one of the (unarticulated) reasons that some middle-class people wanting to change the world tend to congregate in NGOs and charities – where we can spend most of our time with people like ourselves.

It's quite a situation. Change-makers are feverishly debating who has credibility to speak, all while the very basis of truth and credibility are being so rapidly undermined across the globe that many people no longer believe anything they read or hear. We desperately need to come together. Is stepping away from change-making – so that those who are more authentic or credible can do it – the best way to avoid the traps of knowing-better? Or are there ways to be involved in making change, but without falling into those traps?

WHO KNOWS BETTER?

The authority to say what's true and what's not; what's worth attending to and what isn't: this is why knowledge is tied up with power. It's why 'I know better than you' is a power move, and why the denial of others' credibility as knowledge-holders — scholars call it epistemic violence or epistemic injustice[10] — could become a tool of class, empire and patriarchy. The charity staff and trustees' knowledge, in Roger Harding's example, is seen as 'objective' knowledge: objective because the knower is detached from what they are observing, and the knowledge is observable and confirmable by others. It's propositional knowledge: *that* something is so. It's learnt: from education, books, research reports, peer-reviewed papers, and professionally accumulated strategic know-how. It's in contrast to the 'subjective' and experiential knowledge held by the person who knows something about their own life, community and situation, about how to do things and how to be, about what it takes to survive, and what would actually make a difference. It's on the basis of objective knowledge, proven through degrees and CVs that list knowledge-handling jobs, that people obtain employment in the public sector and in charities helping other people who may — because of the workings of class and the education system — have less of that kind of knowledge.

'You're a twenty-two-year-old from a council estate outside Manchester and you left school at sixteen because the teachers were dickheads. Because of your life experiences or something you've seen on the internet you go, "I hate the police, I want them to be abolished, so I'm going to go along to a meeting about that in town." And it's far more likely that you'll have friends or family in prison than anyone else in that meeting. Everyone's explaining, "this is wrong and that's wrong", and at the same time you're feeling the judgement of that space because you can't talk like they do, because you can't walk like they do. Imagine that repeated ad nauseam for so many of these folks. So they're just like, "Fuck it, I'll have nothing to do with them".'

This is Dom Hunter, a community organiser and sociology researcher in Sheffield. Now in his forties, he spent years involved in leftist politics before returning to university. He has written two powerful books about his childhood experience of surviving abuse and being in and out of the care and prison systems, blending memoir and theory to analyse the relentless intrusions of the state and capitalism upon the chances of those already most harmed by them.[11] He receives regular invitations to speak about fighting for change, often with lower-working-class communities like the ones he grew up in, who are 'trying to do something, or start something'. And he's critical of the limitations of many do-gooding efforts, whether through social work, or leftist or social-movement politics. Most of the communities he spends time with, he says, just don't want to know.

His experiences and knowledge make him at home in more than one context. 'I can go into some spaces now, and can claim that space a lot easier, just by referring to the fact that I work in a university. Ironically, I can go into some spaces and say I've been in prison,' he says. 'But if I do that it's to the detriment of other people who can't claim that space, or can't articulate in a way that is as comforting to the person hearing it. "I was in prison" sounds a lot better coming from me than it does coming from any of the young people I work with, because I can sound like I sound and I can dress how I do. I code switch constantly,' though, he adds wryly, 'it's not necessarily good for my own psychological well-being.'

In his view, knowing-better arises in many kinds of change efforts, not just in the charity sector. Hunter observes how people 'don't view their political work as a space in which they need to behave differently to their work life. I hate to pick on teachers but they are pretty bad at this. When I was participating more in lefty spaces – and I'm talking socialist-y, union-adjacent, and union spaces – and it's partly because teaching has got a much higher [union] membership than many other occupations, you go in there and it's teachers holding forth, exactly as you'd expect them to in schools.' The many people who haven't had a good experience with school feel alienated. 'It's not just teachers,' he says, 'it's a whole – let's call it the intermediary classes, everyone gets a bit fragile if I say middle class – everyone thinks they have the information, and everyone wants to explain it.'

Hunter thinks people in all kinds of situations do this. He described a training session he'd sat in on. A third of participants were from the area local to the community centre where it was held. Another third were students or recent students 'who'd just discovered anti-capitalism.' The rest were more seasoned, some from old-school direct action, some now on the fringes of professional campaign groups. What happened, he says, was that 'in that community centre, the local activists were just as bad, as far as "We know what's right".' Everyone was at it, but 'they had a little bit more confidence because it was their space. Working-class activists from the community, doing decent stuff – but they had entrenched views: we have lived experience, therefore we are right. Everyone thinks they know they're right. If they thought they were wrong, they'd change their minds!'

So there's an inevitability to people thinking they're right – especially in change efforts when views on what's necessary to make things better are so contested. You could argue that it's part of the territory; everyone has strong views and the whole point of politics, in its broadest sense, is to agree on some shared goals to work towards. But perhaps the bigger problem is when knowing-better combines with power and its capital resources. This doesn't just push people away. It keeps change-making on limited tracks. Professional campaign-group types who haven't known poverty may not be best placed to determine the extent of the political demands that are necessary to end poverty.[12] Well-paid philanthropic-foundation employees deciding which organisations receive funding are more likely to choose familiar reformist than radical approaches to change.[13]

Attachment to knowing-better also gets in the way of relinquishing space and leadership to those who have lived it. For those in professional campaigning roles, there may be an unspoken reluctance to undermine paid employment prospects. But where change efforts are happening outside of work, there can still be the same unwillingness to be alongside and not above or out in front. It gets in the way of coalition, so it's worth looking under the surface of that reluctance to relinquish the position of being the one who knows.

NEEDING TO KNOW

For any of us, needing-to-know can be an adaptive habit. Certainty can bolster us against feelings of vulnerability, conscious or otherwise. We might be drawn to the certainties of people offering simple answers: this is one of the ways authoritarianism makes its appeal.[14] But even if we're fighting authoritarianism, we can get self-righteous, attached to our own certainties. We may try to fix people by offering information when all they want is to be heard. We may refuse to admit we might be wrong or that we don't know. We reach for a certainty that we think will make us feel secure.

Being the one who knows also offers security to anyone raised to value knowledge and education highly. (Perfectionism offers a similar reassurance, as we saw in the previous chapter.) I'd like to venture a suggestion: I am less sure how this operates in people from class backgrounds different to my own, but what I do know is that this is part of a certain striving middle-class way of being. The upper classes pass on privilege in the form of land and property, and to a lesser extent the middle classes may be able to do this; but one of the key ways they have passed on their privilege is through the possibility of professional success.

It makes sense, then, in a fiercely competitive culture, for parents to focus on achievement. Being taught to value our achievements and knowledge, however, can come at the cost of being able to value who we are intrinsically. This is not great for our own existential comfort. Nor is it good for our perception of the fundamental equality of others. Our status as someone-who-knows can bolster our own inadequate internal sense of equilibrium. But it can also create an unconscious assumption: that if others don't have the same knowledge, perhaps they are lesser; perhaps our position is justified. This isn't operating consciously: it's a conditioning. And it interacts with power and social status to create a barrier. Knowing-better becomes a shield we hold up in front of us, in place of the instinct for human connection that was partially trained out of us while we were learning to wield our knowledge in competition for advancement.[15]

Let me go gently here. I am *not* suggesting that everyone who passes exams has lost their capacity for connection! I am suggesting, though, that the conditioned habitual use of our knowing as a psychological defence can hinder our perception of fundamental equality with others, even if in our professed politics we are avowedly working to end inequality. If we want to develop our capacity to be alongside, we have to practise putting that shield down, however exposing it feels to do so.

And look, it's one thing for me to say that, as a statement I've processed intellectually. It's another to allow myself to let this understanding reverberate in my body, and to experience for a moment the fear that may hide behind my status-as-knower. Receiving criticism can activate that fear. Controlling the narrative, I could tell you that – naturally! – I have blind spots. But it's easier to write retrospectively, as I do throughout this book, about the blind spots I've already brought into awareness over many years, than it is to be reminded anew that there are still more. In the moments when someone does remind me – whether softly or bluntly – the effect of being exposed as not-knowing feels existentially awful, like a chasm opening up.

I could now start to make defensive noises about how you might think that sounds rather melodramatic or fragile. But naming that awful feeling is a step on the way to anti-fragility. If I can name it, I don't need to project it onto someone else and make them feel bad. If we've been using knowledge as self-defence, then the task is to develop enough resilience to tolerate our own discomfort without having to wield our knowledge over others in order to feel better. I should add that just saying something analytic like that shifts my inner state so that I'm no longer touching the awful feeling so directly. Instead I am thinking *about* it. Phew, back to easier ground. Such analysis is a good example of knowing-as-comfort in action. Knowing, in lieu of having to feel. The shield is back up. Self-critical talk that I am being melodramatic is also part of my arsenal against vulnerability because it puts in charge a more commanding part of me. (My self-critic is often in command.)

To be clear: there is no equivalence between the pain and difficulty experienced by those who are oppressed and exploited, and the emotional vulnerability of those who are more comfortable. So much work and care is needed to attend to the former, and to stop the systemic violence that causes it. And yet, unless we bring the latter dynamic into the open, the drive to quash vulnerable feelings by hiding behind the status of knowing-better will continue.[16] It's not only a driver of helping-from-above or its inverse, the avoidance of getting involved at all, which are our topics here. More widely, it helps to crush empathy, and thus helps to drive the creation of policies that cause harm. Needing to keep feeling certain even when you're not is behind the bullshit of those in power who cannot admit when they've gone wrong, even as they continue to make terrible and compounding decisions that affect the lives of millions.

OUR INFORMATION IS NOT ENOUGH ANYWAY

Zrinka Bralo was a young journalist in Sarajevo during the Bosnian war in the early 1990s as the former Yugoslavia disintegrated. For eighteen months she reported as the city was shelled by Serb forces. She fled for her life at the end of 1993 and came to the UK, where she was initially refused asylum. She helped support some of the thousands of Bosnian refugees who followed, some after torture in Serb concentration camps, and has been working on migrant rights ever since. As the internet and then social media developed in the 1990s and into the new century, she became '100 percent convinced that if we'd had the internet then, there would have been no genocide in Bosnia, and the war would have ended like *this!*' She clicks her fingers rapidly. 'I truly deeply believed that if only people knew…'

She no longer believes it. That view – that information would have been enough to make the killing and torture stop – really shifted in her when the Syrian civil war began in 2011, as Bashar al Assad turned on his own people. 'That's when people started sending images, and for me that was very personal because when I saw pictures of Aleppo, they looked exactly the same as Sarajevo. In the same way that Gaza looks like Sarajevo. And look at us now.'

All those images flooding social media were not – are not – enough. Attachment to our knowledge has consequences for our strategies. Valuing it so highly, we place too much trust in information-deficit theories of change: if we only provide the relevant information, people will do the right thing.

Of course, information *is* needed. This isn't about moving away from facts and reason; they are essential, increasingly so in a world of conspiracy and disinformation. And as Corinne Fowler's story about imperial history in Chapter 2 showed, sometimes offering the facts is specifically what's required. It's easy to forget, however, that facts are a means and not an end, and only part of the means at that.

For Bralo, being a journalist early in her career helped to inculcate an information-provision view. 'As a journalist you have a different approach to change. It's hit and run. We're going to do this story and then, boom! Stuff will happen, like *All the President's Men*.'* As a migrant rights campaigner – she took on the leadership of a group called Migrants Organise in 2001, when it was still called the Migrant and Refugee Communities Forum – Bralo pursued an equivalent approach. 'We write reports, we write submissions to select committees, we work with local authorities. We reason with people. And the theory of change was, if people know and understand the injustice, we can work together to fix it.'

This has a lot in common with the kind of information-provision, policy-advocacy model of change I was pursuing as a human rights campaigner at Global Witness. We dug up facts about corporate complicity in human rights violations and environmental destruction, stood the stories up and took them to the *Financial Times*, the *Economist* or the BBC's *Newsight* programme. We'd go to court to protect sources or keep information in the public domain. Several of us were former newspaper or wire-service reporters. There was indeed a copy of *All The President's Men* knocking around the office to show newcomers how you could build a big story one piece of evidence at a time. We were working on an information-provision model (look at these facts we found!) and an insider-access model (look at *who* we know!), developing contacts within the structures of power who could be persuaded or already wanted to act as we did. Policy campaigners spend time framing what they want so

---

* Bob Woodward and Carl Bernstein's classic account of their reporting that brought down Nixon in the Watergate scandal.

the targeted policymaker might recognise common interest. We must be presentable, and articulate our demands so they are legible to someone operating within the existing system. I was quite good at this, my path smoothed because I looked like, sounded like, was educated like lots of people in power.

Many campaign groups were following this model during the New Labour years, ever since the increase in NGO campaigning activity in the last decades of the twentieth century, when human rights and environmental campaigners put on suits, incorporated or registered as charities, and professionalised themselves.[17] Sometimes the insider–access approach worked, depending on the issue. It was during David Cameron's coalition government that – somewhat to our surprise – we persuaded Number 10 to pick up, and propose as law, one of our 'asks' from the campaign I'd helped launch for transparency over the real ownership of companies.

This is fine if your interests coincide with governments' interests. But there are limitations. One is that you are assuming a policymaker who will do the thing you want upon receiving the facts you present. This fictional policy-maker is a cousin of the fictional *Homo economicus* beloved of classical economists, that purely rational person who will – with no other emotional considerations – weigh up the financial pros and cons of any course of action and respond based on nothing else. But humans aren't like that. We have emotional investments and tripwires; prejudices and biases; tactics to seek comfort, stability and acceptance from our peers, and to avoid what might bring discomfort. Strategic communications can put the right headlines in front of them and give the impression of growing support, but policymakers receiving facts have no incentive to act upon them without wider pressure.

Access to people in power to place your evidence in front of them is not the same as actual power. It became clear to Bralo earlier than it did to me that reports, meetings and providing information was insufficient. If those in power are doing the opposite of what you want, you have to build some power of your own. And if you're outside of state systems of power because you don't share the state's interests or are negatively affected by its pursuit of its interests, the only available power is people power.

People struggling against the sharp edge of the power of the state and capitalism have always known this.[18] Others have to learn it. Climate campaigners have learned it over years of failed climate summits. Like other advocacy-focused campaigners of my generation who'd come of age at the 'end of history' in that triumphant unipolar world of the early 1990s, and who saw our friends and colleagues go and work for the New Labour government where we had easy access to their bosses, I began to understand it only once the Conservative coalition took office in 2010, and then for sure at the 2016 votes for Brexit and Trump. As Trump's second term began in early 2025 with the shocking closure of USAID and mass firings across federal agencies, it became inescapable.

Bralo and her colleagues were learning it as the UK's 'hostile environment' for migrants was turning its screws. Officially announced in 2012 by Theresa May, then home secretary, in effect it was ratcheting up much earlier under New Labour, from the Immigration and Asylum Act of 1999 onwards (and indeed, Bralo thinks, much earlier.) The 9/11 attacks in 2001 and the 7/7 attacks in 2005 caused a surge in Islamophobia and racist attacks in the UK, and her workload of protection and advocacy for migrants increased. During the financial crisis in 2008, she says, 'we were the first to be cut out of money from the public sector. Nice people who I had relationships with in local authorities and NHS trusts, who were trying to provide services properly, were saying "Oh Zrinka, equality is nice but there's no money!'" The government now tried to discourage arrivals by making it harder to exist here.

'So okay, people are not allowed to work, study, volunteer, they're given supermarket vouchers. We organised a local action where we were exchanging vouchers, one for one, for cash. I think I "laundered" ten thousand Sainsbury's vouchers in one year... the auditor had some questions.' She has the journalist's gallows humour, but her rage is biting. 'Then they created a special charge card for asylum seekers: more money was going into these punitive measures. They started dispersing people, often to condemned properties. At first local authorities were getting money from the Home Office to do this, then they started hiring private companies like G4S. We had a case where a single mum who'd been trafficked had a security officer in a stab vest going into her bedroom at 6 a.m. in the morning in order – he said – to check if she had a TV, which wasn't allowed. That was the minutiae of the hostility. And I thought, this isn't working. What are we doing here?'

BRINGING IN THE NUMBERS

From about 2005, Bralo began to shift to an organising approach, which generally consists of building a movement of people, one one-to-one meeting at a time. It's not the opposite of providing information to people in power; you might still do that. But it would just be a tactic, not the whole strategy. The key to organising is developing relationships with people affected by the same problems, and maybe with others who want to see change. You listen and start from where people are at. Finding and focusing on the issues you all care about can help to get around some of the purity challenges that we saw in the last chapter. Together, you strategise, build your collective power and take action to apply pressure, choosing tactics according to the situation.

People who've not had to campaign for the conditions of their own lives may hear that word 'organising' and think of trade unions or campaign organising, the door-knocking that political parties do to fight elections. But organising can be done outside the workplace and outside of elections – in communities, or around particular issues or identities. Sometimes it's presented as an American thing: that organising was central to the US civil rights movement is fairly well known in the UK. Stories from closer to home are sometimes less known.[19] The Suffragettes used organising. So did the Bristol bus boycott in 1963: the local bus company refused to employ Black and Asian drivers and conductors, and Bristolians boycotted its routes for four months until they overturned the policy.[20] (The Race Relations Acts, outlawing racial discrimination, followed a few years later.) Years of organising were behind the beautiful moment in 2021 when residents of a Glasgow street filled the road for hours, gathering a crowd of hundreds as the day went on, to prevent Home Office vans taking away their neighbours for deportation.[21]

It was organising in 2022 by young people desperate to attend university but unable to access student loans that achieved a reduction in the number of years young migrants have to wait for settled status in the UK.[22] Meanwhile, organising by tenant unions like Acorn and the London

Renters Union has brought together private tenants to keep pushing for secure tenancies, and controls on rents and bad landlords.

'Let's scramble the grannies!' my boss in the press office at Christian Aid's head office would declare, when I worked there briefly. If a campaign group or charity whose mailing list you're on asks you to email your MP or turn up for a march, you're being *mobilised*. But even if you take action, you might turn away afterwards; it risks being transactional. The grannies might go and do something else. Organising takes longer, its outcomes are harder to predict, but it's potentially deeper, wider and longer-lasting. It builds movements of people who may continue to act long after the original intervention or after the original instigators drop out. The US political scientist Hahrie Han has found that organising is more likely than mobilising to engage people who were previously uninvolved.[23] It's also more likely to bring the most marginalised into action, whereas mobilising tends to target – and work best with – people who already have more agency to take action; people who expect to be listened to.

At first Bralo and her colleagues worked with Citizens UK, which pursues a particular style of community organising imported from the US. Its noted success has been winning the argument for a living wage, which was adopted into legislation by the Conservatives in 2016.[24] Citizens UK works through institutions like churches and schools, drawing on their existing networks to identify and train 'leaders' who will then organise their communities on issues that trouble them.[25] With thousands of participants across the country who wanted to campaign on migrant rights, they were in a position to bring the kind of numbers that Bralo needed. As migrants, she said, 'we have a democratic deficit issue. There's never going to be enough of us to make the point, we're always going to be the minority. We need to hop on other people's power.'

Together and with other migrant rights groups, they made a few breaches, over the following decade, in the wall of institutionalised hostility. In 2010, they got Cameron's coalition government to commit to ending the detention of children; the law was changed in 2014.[26] In 2015, with outrage over pictures of a drowned two-year-old Syrian boy, Alan Kurdi, whose family were trying to reach Europe, Cameron agreed to twenty thousand Syrians resettling in the UK. In 2017, Migrants Organise worked with Citizens to set up a Community Sponsorship scheme.

Bralo is circumspect about calling these achievements 'wins'. In practice, she points out, the Home Office was and is still locking up children, with little accountability or oversight.[27] The agreement for twenty thousand Syrians was 'immediately diluted to five thousand people per year over four years and then further complicated into a bureaucratic process, which made it hard for communities to organise and support people.'

Bralo parted ways from Citizens in the mid-2010s, wanting to take a longer view on building power that wasn't so focused on tactical wins – even if those wins have a positive effect, however temporary or limited, that prevents or ends harm to a few people. 'The system is called the hostile environment, and it's doing exactly what it's meant to do,' she says. 'So there is no fixing it. In order to change it completely and replace it with a vision of a better system based on principles of dignity and justice, we need to build power through a long-term deep-roots organising of people affected by the issue.' At the moment, she thinks, 'we are still in the resilience-building stage, reframing the charity into solidarity. With large majority governments hostile to immigration, just surviving is a victory.' In late 2025 the

Labour government proposed extensive new barriers to migrants' routes to settlement and refugees' rights.

As of 2021–2, only 0.3% of giving by the UK's largest grant-making foundations went towards community organising;[28] it dropped to 0.2% the following year.[29] Recently established initiatives are trying to change that, like the Civic Power Fund, which channels money from big funders to grassroots organising across the UK. Charities and campaign groups are turning their attention to organising now that they've realised the limitations of their previous campaigning models in a situation where the centre has shifted rightwards, and as the early enthusiasm for online mobilising has curdled into concern about the limits of 'clicktivism'.

It's still too early to tell how this will go. Some fear that established charities and campaign groups' ultimate desire to preserve themselves (whatever they say to the contrary) will lead them to pursue routes acceptable to those in power rather than really getting behind the issues that communities want to fight for.[30] And I know from experience how charities and funders can jump on bandwagons, turn things to their own use, make groups seeking grants jump through hoops to prove paper adherence to strategies or concepts that were actually always theirs to begin with.[31] There is a risk they will do this with organising too.[32]

Others I spoke to object to organisers going into communities that are not their own. Dom Hunter, in Sheffield, said that organising has long been handed down through the generations in some working-class communities: ways of getting together to resist and get what they need, 'rather than big white saviour man writes a book and everyone copies it.' He's worried about the proliferation of imported organising models that risk flattening what's there already. Instead of middle-class activists bussing in from leafy suburbs to organise in poorer communities, Hunter said, 'I'd be much happier seeing them move into those places – as a bus driver or shop assistant or whatever, and go to their community centre: where can I help? What needs doing? Is it just cleaning after the youth club? How can I learn from this community? How can I embed myself in this place and understand its ebbs and flows and its struggles, and then, with those with lived experience, they can bring in any analytical thoughts they might have, and develop strategies from within. Rather than come in from outside with a strategy and be, "I'm being paid to implement this strategy."' If they're keen to organise, he wants middle-class activists to 'move back to the towns, villages, suburbia, where they're from and organise their own classes *there*, and push them as far to the left as we can take them. We're simply not going to win without those places being sympathetic.'

'WHY DO YOU CARE?'

Organising is no panacea. I met many organisers who are willing to be in service and not make it all about themselves, but ego and power trips can and do occur. People throw their weight around. Initiating groups try to remain in control of the topics that communities organise on, or push 'cookie-cutter' models that don't respect the complexity of what's going on in a neighbourhood. It can be 'differently elitist', as one organiser put it. In short, there's still lots of knowing-better. Nor is there a hard binary between organising and elite-access advocacy approaches; many effective campaigns blend them. Lots can still be done by approaching and working with people in power. There's also still much to do to integrate social media with traditional organising techniques.

And yet, so many of the organisers I spoke to also enthused about the *principles* underwriting the process that, when it's working, make it effective. By 'principles' I don't mean the different models for how-to-do-it, but their underlying guidance for relationship, which help dissolve the hierarchies that can come with charity. The reason I'm writing about organising is that I think these principles offer guidance for anyone seeking to act in solidarity where they don't have lived experience of an issue – whether or not it's organising that they are actually doing.

Enthusiasts note that organising can stop us seeing ourselves as so different. At the heart are relationships, and at the heart of any relationship is listening. The organiser listens to what people are saying about their needs and difficulties. They don't have their own agenda. But this goes both ways. The organiser also gives something of themselves.

'I hear people saying, we're here to listen to people with lived experience talk about this, or that. And I say yeah, you're talking to people who are living their lives in this struggle. But *you* also need to talk about how you are impacted. Why do you care? It's not a chat where you just take all this information out of this person and then say, "Well, we're going to design an action around that",' one organiser told me.[33] Another said, 'My self-interest in all this is, I don't want to live in a country where we treat immigrants appallingly, where our NHS is falling apart, where the cost of living is blighting the landscape we love.' Organising relationships allow the possibility that while the ways in which we are each not-okay are not the same, we are nonetheless all of us not-okay when some people are struggling.

*

'As a community organiser I'm not here to help you – at all. I will support you to help yourself.' This is Jack Spooner, a local organiser in Plymouth for Shelter, the housing and homelessness charity. It was in conversation with him that I saw, by contrast, how self-focused many of my own and my former NGO colleagues' efforts have sometimes been, often all about what 'we can do'. Good organisers do bring their own expertise: in how to gather people and then front up to those in power to apply collective pressure. But they are explicit that the goal is not their business. In Plymouth (as in many places), house prices and rents have risen much faster than incomes, there's wildly insufficient social housing, and nearly half of private tenants need housing benefit to meet the rent.[34] More than twenty percent of properties in the city's private rented sector don't meet the Decent Homes Standard, the benchmark used for social housing.[35] 'If it were up to me to say what we're going to campaign on, I'd say we're probably going to try to get derelict properties turned into social rented housing,' says Spooner. 'But it's not my position to.'

Spooner is one of a team of eleven organisers employed by Shelter in different cities, working to support people in insecure or inadequate housing to push for what they need. The people he's working with wanted to push for a landlord register, collating information on bad landlords so they can be banned when they next overstep.* 'My colleague in Birmingham has managed to get the council to declare a housing emergency and put extra resources into it. My colleague in Bristol is pushing for rent controls. And

---

* The Renters' Rights Act which became law in October 2025, after we spoke, includes a mandatory landlord database.

that's because it's come from the individuals we've been speaking with.'

I was struck by how differently he spoke about his work, compared to many of the campaigners with whom I have worked. There was little ego in it; he had little desire for control. 'I'm not going to dictate what the change should be,' he says. 'But I'll help you to connect with others who might feel the same way, help you understand the power systems that might be preventing you getting your way, and encourage you to get together to solve it. I think that's a lot of our job: helping people to understand power, and not fear it. Maybe the councillor's not listening to you because the chief whip is having a go at them. Maybe you've written to your local MP but the MP doesn't have any authority. So don't get angry because you're complaining to the wrong person, break down that issue, find the people who do have the power to do it.'

Liam Barrington-Bush, a Canadian organiser now settled in the UK, believes it is possible to offer support in solidarity with a community that you're not part of. In 2014 and 2015 he turned up to help council tenants in two London estates who were resisting eviction, trying to prevent the replacement of their current housing with unaffordable developments. In Newham, to the east of the city, a group of mothers calling themselves Focus E15 were occupying houses, and, inspired, other tenant groups under similar threat of being scattered to unsuitable housing across the capital were getting in touch to request support. One of them was from Sweets Way over in Barnet in North London, where Barrington-Bush ended up spending months helping out. Sometimes he was using his skills to write press releases or attend meetings with council officials; sometimes he was making tea or on the residents' rota to hold down the occupations of already-evicted properties. They didn't ultimately prevent final evictions and demolition, but, he says, the dogged resistance they put up secured better housing options for many of those being moved.

Barrington-Bush knows that what he was doing wouldn't have been possible at a different time of his life. He had set up his living arrangements – shared houses with low rent, travelling by bike, procuring food from supermarket skips – so he needed only a couple of days' work a week to get by. He's now a father, with a mortgage, and such a lifestyle is not possible – as he knows it's not for most people. But there are underlying principles, he suggests, that are important for avoiding knowing-better. Having fought gentrification in his home neighbourhood back in Toronto, he sees the same principles for offering support to a community as those for avoiding being an 'asshole gentrifier'.[36]

'You're showing up somewhere where something already exists, and don't forget that!' he says. 'And it exists in so many more complex and fucked-up and beautiful ways than you could possibly imagine when you arrive.' The story does not begin when you get there, in other words. Also, he says, be aware that the skills you may bring with your middle-class training – like writing press releases, conducting official meetings – are typically those that make it easier to get on that trajectory from grassroots politics and resistance into paid employment with organising outfits, NGOs or political groups and parties.

'Most people who have organised in their own communities for a long time don't easily have a CV that comes out of it that can get them hired into something,' he says. The people with professional skills can end up holding more power than communities, and part of the work, he thinks, is making visible the kind of labour that professionals might contribute, and supporting people to take more active roles in it, 'so it wasn't just this unknown form of magic that I could sometimes get journalists to come to housing occupations, or housing-office execs to change their line on what housing was actually available.'

Dom Hunter had said the same thing more explicitly: don't leap straight towards these kinds of political roles that give you power over people who are doing it as part of their life. Do a 'normal' job for a few more years; show up to volunteer; keep learning.

KNOWLEDGE AS RELATIONSHIP

The injunction to put lived experience at the front and centre is not a rule saying 'stay away' to people who haven't lived it. Organisers I spoke to had seen people with useful professional skills hang back from getting involved; they would focus on the listening aspect of organising, but then not step in to act.

'I sit on a funding committee and we're always talking about how organisations need to make sure there's lived experience at the centre of what they do, and I sit there like…' This is Dami Makinde, and she is miming tearing her hair out. On leaving school in 2013 and realising that she wasn't eligible for a student loan, she organised dozens of prospective students to intervene in a legal case which overturned the restrictions on loans for young people who didn't have settled immigration status.[37] She then set up and ran a group called 'We Belong' with Chrisann Jarrett, another young woman in a similar position. They organised young migrants to use their stories to pressure the government – successfully – to halve the route to settled status for young people from ten years to five. It was a brilliant piece of organising success, by anyone's definition. 'What's making you cringe?' I asked.

'It's like "lived experience" is almost the gold standard, and for me – I'm still developing my thinking, but as much as it's important, I think it's not the gold standard,' she said. 'Change can still be made even if the majority of people don't have lived experience. And the reason my view has changed is that when I talk to people with experience of the migration sector, a lot of them just want to sit back! They don't want that position. A lot of them are burned out, and it's an added burden. Not only are you doing the work, but your whole life is constantly on display so something can be changed in society.' (We Belong worked hard to provide care and psychological support to the young people it supported to speak about their situation.) 'It can be very draining,' she said, 'and that's not even to talk about the backlash you may get. So, much as I believe in the lived-experience model, those without it have a place within activism and community organising and they can actually do more good than harm.'

It's true that the most oppressed can often see most clearly the problems of the dominant culture.[38] It's also true that resistance movements create a collective alchemical container in which experience can be transmuted into voice and then power. Yet there are risks in constructing hard rules about who speaks and acts. As Makinde points out, if those who are more comfortable don't step up, that leaves the work of changing an unjust system to those suffering most under its burdens. Another problem is the difficulty of 'who speaks'. There is the risk of 'oppression Olympics', as it sometimes gets called, where the person or group with more marginalised identities is seen as having more credibility.

Of course, understanding the particular and specific experiences of people dealing with combinations of different forms of marginalisation *is* necessary – that's where the word 'intersectional' came from.[39] But trying to rank degrees of marginalisation serves nobody. Also, it's not always evident if someone has lived experience anyway. I've met so many activists who appear not to share the experiences of those they are supporting or working with – but then when we talk about their lives, there is often a close personal connection to the work they do.

The American philosopher Olúfẹ́mi O. Táíwò coined the term 'deference epistemology' to describe the phenomenon of passing-the-mic to someone who appears less privileged, in order to do the right thing and be a 'good' social justice activist (or academic), rather than because it's appropriate. The dangers he noted include homogenising entire groups of people, power accumulating with elites within marginalised groups, flippant assumptions about what it takes to speak from experiences of trauma, and failure to attend to the needs of those who aren't even in the conversation because those 'in the room' are focused on squabbles for relative prestige.[40] Nor does it foster resilience. The kind of people produced by these deference messages are not trained to stand up to power, he said in an interview.[41]

Táíwò began his essay on the topic by discussing an occasion when a white colleague suggested that she pass a writing commission to him because she wasn't the 'right person' to do it, and he concluded the essay with an alternative suggestion: that they should, perhaps, take on the writing of that piece together. I was happy to read this – not, as cynics might suggest, because I'm a white woman who writes – but because I had reached a similar conclusion. What I'd been hearing from organisers over three years of conversations was the foundational principle of connection and relationship, and that change-making *can* (albeit not always) work by combining the different knowledges of both parties: those with and without personal experience.

It is well-established that the 'subjective' knowledge held by individuals becomes politically powerful when it is joined with others' similar knowledge so that a class of people can recognise and articulate a common cause. This is what happened, for example, in the women's consciousness-raising groups of second-wave feminism in the 1970s. But in a different way, so can the knowledge of people with diverse life experiences when they come together. If a certain kind of policy advocacy is saying, *my* research is enough to make change, then the relationships at the heart of organising are saying (and I don't want to play down the challenges of this in practice) *all of our experience and information together* may build the power to create change. It's co-creation of knowledge, albeit with the opportunity for leadership, should they wish, of the person who has lived it. But it's the relationship that's central.

So there are things we can do to reduce the knowing-better. Nonetheless, you might not be wanted in some change efforts, *and* you can learn to handle that. If you are a middle-class person, some working-class people may not want to organise with you. If you are a white person, some people of colour may not want to organise with you. Just as, while I very much do want cisgender men to *do their work* – so they can understand patriarchy and its violence and teach the next generation of boys to do things differently – I don't always want to be around while they're doing it. Sometimes I find the things they say and write, while they are working patriarchy out, tiresome. And

I appreciate some readers might find parts of this book tiresome, for the same reason.

But there are also many people with 'lived experience' who think that those who haven't lived it can and should come and work alongside them in the struggle, and will welcome your skills, even if some do not want to deal with what you bring and may tell you so. And even if you are welcome, people may tell you if you fuck up, and you'll just have to take it. I've been there a few times, and I'm risking it again with this book. But the ground of solidarity is to keep showing up without assumption of leadership or superior knowledge to build relationships and work to transform this unhealthy culture and support those who are harmed by it, even when we inevitably do fuck up and people tell us so. The ground is learning, through practice, to be resilient enough to take the criticism and stay in the conversation, even if it would be more comfortable to remain in familiar spheres. We're going to need that resilience. And we're going to need the relationships that it will open up. The task is practising the use of some phrases that may be unfamiliar, like these: *I didn't know that. I'm not sure. What do you think?*

It will be near impossible, however, if some part of us believes that it's our job to save people because we are 'okay' and they are not, which is why the next chapter turns to the saviour in us.

5

'I SAVE PEOPLE'

Denounce the white saviour!
      Emma Dabiri, *What White People Should Do Next*[1]

The coalition emerges out of your recognition that it's fucked up
for you, in the same way that we've already recognized that it's
fucked up for us. I don't need your help. I just need you to recog-
nise that this shit is killing you, too, however much more softly…
      Fred Moten, *The Undercommons*[2]

WHITE SAVIOUR

'I met a guy, and he asked, "Are you intending on working
in the east?" "Maybe," I said. He told me there were a couple
of places left on a UN trip up there: "Ask for Des. Jump on
the helicopter and go and have a look." The next day I'm in
one of those big white UN helicopters. I'm flying over the
diamond mines. I'm flying over this war-torn country, and
we land, and a battalion of Pakistani peace-keeping soldiers
were there, with their little jeeps. We got four in the jeep,
then there were two guys, one at the front with a machine
gun and one at the back with an AK-47 or something, and
off we went into the bush.'

Matt is describing his first few months working for a charity in Sierra Leone in 2001. He went after spending the second half of the 1990s – his twenties – working in London for an internet start-up. I worked in Sierra Leone too, in 2004 and 2005 after Matt left, and he and I subsequently met back in the UK and became friends. 'Was part of you enjoying dashing around heroically in helicopters and jeeps with guns in a very recently ex-war zone?' I asked.

'Hell yeah,' he said.

These days he's a wiry fell runner with teenage kids, who gets a bit antsy if he hasn't fitted in his daily run. But back in 2001, the dot-com bubble had burst, his dad had just been diagnosed with Alzheimer's, and he'd realised he wasn't going to be a millionaire. 'I was doing a lot of recreational drugs, living in a flat in Chiswick, earning a hundred grand a year, had an Audi TT. Everything a young bachelor might want, but I was realising that my relationships were quite dysfunctional and that something wasn't quite working in my life.' One night he saw a *Newsnight* bulletin from the decade-long civil war in Sierra Leone: about child soldiers and the diamond trade that was fuelling the rebel groups. He found himself in tears. 'There was something in me that said, *Fucking hell, go and do something about it, go.* It wasn't so much a saviour thing at that point, it was *Shit, I've got to do something, I've got to go and* do *something, different from what I'm doing now.* The next day, I googled volunteering in Africa. I paid ten quid to get a report, I put in my skills, and I got a list of NGOs who might match my skills, which were computer and business skills.'

Matt took a sabbatical from his job and arranged to volunteer for six months with a small British charity that was supporting children who'd been separated from their families, including boys who had been forced to carry guns and kill, and girls who'd been abducted, raped and forced to work for rebel fighters. He would end up being offered a job, and stayed nearly four years, setting up projects, getting them funded and employing nearly sixty staff, turning into the kind of 'development' professional who ran organised programmes supporting thousands of people. He would go on to a postgrad degree in development management, and these days he has a senior role at a charity that works across several countries in Africa.

But when he started, he knew nothing. The big aid agencies and humanitarian organisations have their own problems with saviourism, but would never have sent someone so inexperienced, he later understood. Between one and two million people, up to a quarter of the total population, had been displaced during the conflict, and Sierra Leone was now the poorest country in the world. The war wasn't officially over, though the worst violence had ended. There was still insecurity, and thousands of people were stuck in displaced-persons camps. The day he arrived, his plane sat on the tarmac for hours due to a security curfew. Everywhere he looked were ruined buildings, checkpoints and blue-helmeted peacekeeping soldiers.

He was supposed to be teaching computer skills to teenage girls in a displaced-person camp in Freetown. Many such rehabilitation projects for young people focused on training that might support their reintegration into society. 'But when I turned up they barely knew I was coming, none of the computers worked and there was no electricity. So I started to teach them English. Mostly, we just sat and talked for three or four hours each day. I knew not to ask questions about what happened to them, I wasn't qualified for that. I think we all just enjoyed talking and learning together.

'One day in those early weeks a girl came to me with her baby who was in and out of consciousness in her arms. She was crying that the baby was going to die, and I thought, *Right, I'm going to help.* We spent the next three or four hours going round various hospitals and nobody would see her. Then we went to a private hospital, and the doctor would only see her because I was British. He admitted her, and the baby lived. And it cost me about four quid. In my head I scaled that up across the whole camp, across the whole country. How many other babies were there who didn't have someone to help them? That's when it hit me. The scale of poverty and desperation, just the imbalance, the inequality. I cried my heart out that night.' He ended up supporting many families out of his own pocket; in the evenings there would sometimes be queues of people outside his house.

'I never went there with a big altruistic "I'm here to save." I wanted to do something different. I felt called, when I saw that *Newsnight* report, to go to an extreme of where I was. It was almost instinct – to respond, to help. And at that point, I had no awareness of the power dynamics in aid, and me being a white guy in that situation. I guess those first few months, I let ego get involved. *I saved that baby's life! I'm making these fifty girls feel better about what happened! I'm saving the world!'* Later, he realised, 'It's like I was a little boy, I was so far out of my depth. Was I making any difference at all, or was I part of the problem? I could point to people that I had helped, but in the wider context, it was nothing and the system was stacked against them.'

The scale and severity of the challenges people faced; the complexity of what it might take to change the underlying global structures that generated poverty and conflict, rather than just hand out money to people he met; the depth of people's trauma that he was encountering in his interpersonal dealings: there was so much he didn't know. He became friends with a young man who'd been a child soldier, supporting him through his degree and transition into a new life, only realising years later that he had 'dined out' on his benevolence towards someone with such a disturbing story, when asking friends at home to chip in for tuition fees. In fact, he himself was equally looked after: this friend opened doors in Freetown and occasionally helped extricate Matt from the pickles into which his naivety led him.

To those who have experienced it or can see it – or are enraged by it – this is classic 'white saviour' stuff. White saviourism is the hero, plus a power imbalance. It's benevolence and altruism mixed with blindness to the racial hierarchies and colonial histories that created the poverty you're trying to alleviate. It's one of the assumptions of whiteness: thinking that the 'developed' outsider can solve problems created in part by their own culture.[3] You could argue that the white saviour derives from several instructions on the save-the-world script – being good, knowing-better, being a hero – when they are infused with white supremacy, which sees bodies racialised as white as the standard for humanity and everyone else as a deviation from that.

Matt didn't know about white saviourism then, but he does now. The internet has made this conversation – an old one among those who don't want to be saviourism's target – more mainstream. I'm telling an illustrative white saviour story from more than twenty years ago because these days it's less likely that a young person who has volunteered abroad or worked in international development will confess to anything that smacks of saviour heroics. Matt is willing to talk about it because to some extent and through two decades of subsequent work, his attitudes and assumptions have changed. There is a bit of distance.

I realised, as we conversed, that I wasn't thinking about saviourism twenty years ago either.[4] During my months with a charity in Sierra Leone I hoped I was avoiding the typical symptoms of what I thought of as aid-worker nonsense. I didn't drive a white SUV or live in a big air-con house with staff, but used public transport and shared a flat above the office with a local colleague. While I was doubtless much wealthier than many people I met, I couldn't afford to hang out at the fancy places by the beach where salaried 'expats' spent weekends. 'But where have you *been*?' asked a young British official from the High Commission when we were introduced shortly before I left.

I also thought I was one of the good ones because I understood the colonial histories that had led us all to this point. Being there showed me how Sierra Leone's impoverishment was still being generated in the City of London where the mining companies were headquartered, and later I worked to tackle it there. But while I knew a fair amount about imperial and capitalist theft of people and resources, I knew less about the historical creation of racist ideologies and of Western fantasies of 'Africa'.[5] I sought adventure, and I'd grown up on Graham Greene and Somerset Maugham stories from a different age. So while I was motivated by compassion, I was also there, in my late twenties, to be the number one character in my own escapades and to revel in the storytelling props.

Then there are people who are well versed in no-more-saviour discourse because they work in development or humanitarian assistance where the topic is live, and try to do it humbly, in organisations that are aware of and try to mitigate the risk of saviourism. But their priority remains the immediate problems they are trying to alleviate, especially so for those working in emergencies. They point out the humanitarian crises that get little enough attention from the world, like the killing and hunger as a result of the conflict in Sudan. They know they run the risk of being targeted themselves. And they know that if the projects they work on weren't there, children would go hungry. The starkness of this reality was revealed as Trump closed USAID in 2025; *The Lancet* has predicted that by 2030 these aid cuts could result in fourteen million deaths, a third of them children under five.[6] Or they have worked for years to improve rich countries' policies, pushing Gordon Brown twenty years ago to lead an effort to write off £30 billion in impoverished countries' debts,[7] or pressing for the UK to meet its commitment to giving 0.7% of GDP in aid, fighting rearguard actions as it was pushed down to 0.5% during Covid and, under Starmer's cuts, to 0.3%.[8] I want to honour everyone who is moved to help those who are struggling, hungry, dispossessed: 'those to whom the miseries of the world / Are misery,' as Keats put it.[9]

I want to recognise the compassion and commitment that drives so many people to give service, sometimes at great cost to themselves. When we are so motivated and involved in a humanitarian life, it can be hard to hear any questioning of how it is done. 'But if you just saw how it is,' people say, 'I cannot not help.' The saviour discussion, put bluntly, can sound like it's saying, 'Stay away'. I'm not sure that works for people who so want to help. This is not about *whether* we show up to do good, but *how* we do so in the context in which we find ourselves: as heirs, one way or another, to half a millennium of European empires and millennia of class domination.

There are also plenty of folk who don't really get it. 'I don't see what's wrong here,' said a friend with whom I discussed this chapter, whose work is unrelated to aid or campaigning. 'What Matt's doing might not be perfect or consistently impactful, but he's trying to do the right thing, having an impact in the immediate situation and learning things that will help him become more sophisticated. It strikes me he gave up his capitalist life to try and make a difference, and his naivety in that first phase is part of the experience that has made him more aware now.'

I agree that it's no bad thing to ditch a producing-and-consuming-focused life to orient towards service. Whenever I hear that someone is considering doing so, I encourage them to go for it. It's also true that altruism is good for the well-being and mental health of the person doing it. The problem, however, is that the white saviour is not just an individual person making decisions about what to do with their life. It's the combination of that person and the wider context.

SAVING AS A POWER RELATION

What we might like to tell ourselves is just our neutral 'compassion' may actually be shaped by unexamined ideas about the world – like the idea, with white supremacy at its heart, that Europeans and North Americans have the answers to problems elsewhere. Extreme consequences of this attitude can be seen in the lethal actions of Renee Bach, a young white American missionary with no medical qualifications who in 2009 set up a charity to care for severely malnourished children in Uganda, running a facility in which 105 children died while under her care. In 2023 Bach settled a legal case brought by the mothers of two of the babies who died, paying them about $9,500 each in compensation while admitting no liability.[10]

In 1968 Ivan Illich, the Austrian Catholic priest and social critic, addressed young Americans travelling to volunteer in Mexico in the coruscating speech known as 'To Hell with Good Intentions': motivated by their own 'bad consciences', he said, they would be better off working among the poor in their own country, who can, at least, 'tell you to go to hell' in a language you understand.[11] The critical academic literature on white saviourism has multiplied over the decades. It was social media that turned up the volume in the 2010s, together with the backlash to a viral campaign video called *Kony 2012*, released that year by a white American man and his charity, about the warlord behind a long-standing conflict in Uganda.

It was true, as Amnesty and Human Rights Watch had reported for years, that Joseph Kony and the Lord's Resistance Army were responsible for terrible human rights violations in Northern Uganda (he is still at large pending possible trial at the International Criminal Court in The Hague). But the film ludicrously simplified the situation and made no mention of the years of efforts by Ugandans to resolve the conflict. Instead, Westerners could donate, sign the petition, get the bracelet, share the video. Teju Cole, a Nigerian-American novelist and photographer, composed some punchy tweets and an article in *The Atlantic* in response: 'The White Savior Industrial Complex is not about justice. It is about having a big emotional experience that validates privilege.'[12]

Critics of 'international development' from the Global South had long observed that the very concept of 'development' emerged from the colonial 'civilising' mission and that the structures of empire were recreated in the white European charities that set up shop after independence, employing former colonial officers and assuming that they knew best.[13] In the years since Cole's intervention, and especially after George Floyd was murdered in 2020, the humanitarian and development industries have come under pressure, often from their own staff, to 'decolonise' how they operate.[14] There have been moves to diversify their staff and leadership, change their language, and wrestle with what they call 'localisation' and 'shifting power', which often means moving decision-making and budgetary authority to the locations where the funds are being used.[15]

Philanthropic foundations and grant-makers also talk about 'shifting power.' The problem here is that many of them run endowments earned through oppressive histories, that they are still required to grow by investing in companies and funds… many of which profit by extracting resources and wealth from the poorest countries.[16] The foundation Lankelly Chase announced in 2023 that it would 'spend down' its endowment over five years and close itself down, rather than continue to profit on the stock market and hand out the interest on funds it controls.[17] Other foundations are aligning their investments with their values, or setting up 'participatory grant-making', where previous recipients decide who gets funded next. There are growing alternatives, too, like Baobab Foundation and Kwanda, which are Black-led funders established to provide money independently of old charity relationships.[18]

The BBC's annual Comic Relief fundraiser has ditched its poverty-tourism 'celebrity hugs African kids' slot in favour of hiring local film-makers.[19] Potential volunteers can now find plentiful guidance online. The strongest point echoes Illich's from two generations ago: could you do it in your own country, where you might find less picturesque forms of poverty? If you must go, can you avoid 'orphanages' created by 'voluntourism' and filled with children who actually have families, or where the shifting rosters of transient helpers who then disappear are harmful? Can you ensure the money you fork out goes to the community and not to commercial fixer-type companies? Would you still go if you couldn't post any images on social media? Will you educate yourself about the colonial and enslavement histories, about the structural-adjustment programmes of the 1980s and '90s that used debt as a lever to force deregulation and cuts to social spending on poor countries, and about ongoing global trade, and debt, and offshore tax havens – and your own country's role in them – that have created and that perpetuate that country's impoverishment?

That last question is not just for potential volunteers but for everyone. Since the end of empire, citizens in the Global North have been directed to view the relationship between rich and poor countries as a one-directional flow: of aid and charity. Give humanitarian support in crisis, and offer 'development' aid to help them become more like us.

Jason Hickel, an academic, calls this the 'development story'.[20] But by far the greater flows of money are heading *the other way*. Globally, 1.3 billion people were lifted out of extreme poverty between 1990 and 2019, many of them in rapidly industrialising Asian nations, especially China and India. But three-quarters of those living in extreme poverty are now concentrated in sub-Saharan Africa and in fragile and conflict-afflicted nations.[21] The standard narrative is that poor countries remain poor because there isn't enough economic growth, and because of bad governance and corruption problems. The last two are very real, especially when it comes to the 'resource curse', in which revenues for oil and other commodities are captured by elites and moved into private bank accounts offshore, and the disproportionate weight of oil or mining within a country's economy stunts other potential industries.

What gets talked about less is what Global South scholars have been showing for decades: that the poorest countries continue to bleed wealth – far more than the aid that comes in – in the direction of the richest, according to a set of global rules that look pretty rigged.[22]

These rules include that the head of the World Bank is by tradition an American, the head of the International Monetary Fund a European; voting power within these institutions, as in the World Trade Organization which sets international trade rules, is skewed towards the richest nations. Since the 1980s debt crisis on the back of the soaring oil prices at the end of the previous decade, the World Bank and IMF have been able to impose policy – in the direction of cutting public spending, pushing privatisation and deregulation, and forcing opening of markets to foreign companies – on poorer nations' governments in return for access to necessary finance. I was working on campaigns against this influence nearly twenty years ago, and it is still going on: the IMF's conditions for loans during the Covid-19 pandemic included cuts in government spending that took nearly $10 billion off public sector wages across fifteen countries studied by Action Aid.[23]

So wealth flows from poor countries to rich via the interest paid on external debt: that's about $300 billion per year heading into the rich world's banks.[24] By contrast, total global aid flows the other way were estimated to be about $180 billion in 2025.[25] Wealth also flows north because of how trade rules are structured. WTO rules permit wealthy countries to subsidise their own farmers while preventing poor countries from doing the same and forcing their markets to be open to imports, devastating the livelihoods of small farmers. Quotas and tariffs restrict poorer nations to the export of raw commodities, preventing them from developing the valued-added processes that turn raw materials into more profitable consumer products. WTO trade deals allow companies to sue sovereign governments outside of the judicial system if they enact unwelcome regulations.[26]

Another reason for the flow from poor to rich nations relates to economic power and stability: rich nations have reserve currencies in which the rest of the world is keen to safely invest. So they can issue low-yield bonds, pulling in savings from other countries – which means they pay low rates of interest to borrow, and can then invest the money profitably elsewhere. Economists at the World Inequality Database, an international collaboration of scholars, calculate that the bottom 80% of countries that don't have this privilege lose 2–3% of GDP each year, along with influence over what kind of activity receives investment.[27]

Another way of looking at South-to-North flows derives from what some political economists call 'unequal exchange'. Because global power imbalances and border controls keep the costs of resources and labour much lower in the Global South, low-income countries in the South have to sell far more labour or natural resources in order to maintain a balance of trade in money terms. Scholars try to estimate the impact of this price discrepancy, measured either in the worth of what they call 'appropriated' commodities or labour at Northern prices. By one estimate, high-income countries 'appropriated', in effect, commodities worth $2.2 trillion in Northern prices from Global South countries in 2017, enough to end extreme poverty fifteen times over.[28] By another estimate, the Global North appropriated 826 billion hours of embodied labour from the countries of the Global South in 2021, equivalent to

$16.9 trillion. This, say the authors, 'drains the South of pro-
ductive capacity that could be used instead for local human
needs and development.'[29]

Then there are all of the methods by which tax revenue is
denied to poorer countries (these harm the public sphere in
rich countries too). Some are not illegal, like multinational
companies using tax havens to shift profits away from the
countries where they were earned. Other outflows from
low-income countries are illicit: trade mis-invoicing by
companies, outright tax evasion and corruption by elites in
those countries – all of which deny tax revenue that could
be spent on public services. [30] What these methods have in
common is the use of tax havens – secrecy jurisdictions, as
campaigners against them prefer to call them – which can
hide the ownership of companies, assets and flows. Many
of them are British Crown Dependencies – like Jersey and
Guernsey – or Overseas Territories, like the British Virgin
Islands or the Cayman Islands. Lower-income countries
lose at least $46 billion a year in tax revenue to multina-
tional corporations shifting their profits to tax havens, a
process with spillover economic effects that multiply this
loss by a factor of up to three.[31]

The 'development story' legitimises the international
political, economic and financial order that maintains
these neo-colonial flows of wealth, and it is persistent. So
when a 2022 parliamentary investigation into racism in
UK aid made recommendations for anti-racist actions that
critics have been demanding for years – UK aid should
be targeted at locally led organisations, applications and
meetings shouldn't always have to be in English, language
should be more inclusive, and patronising images should be
avoided – the cross-party MPs still found it hard to query
the underlying logics of the development story, or to hear

what one witness was really saying when she suggested that 'what we need to talk about is what other countries want.'[32]

This remains a radical suggestion. Governments that give foreign aid do so to pursue their own interests and diplomatic imperatives, hence the fluctuations in aid budgets. The aid cuts of 2025 were not changes to the underlying logic of saviourism or to the development story. They did not propose, in aid's place, tackling sources of poverty and dependence like trade agreements or multinational companies' profit-shifting activities. They did not propose, in aid's place, cancelling crippling debts or curbing flows of guns and ammunition. Forty percent of countries in eastern and southern Africa spent more on debt servicing in 2024 than on their education and health budgets combined.[33]

If this is beginning to sound a little circular, that's because it is. More awareness of the white saviour has altered the discourse, offering new opportunities to prove how 'good' we are. 'Look at those saviours over there! Glad *I'm* not like that!' But there are limits to declarations of independence from a story that runs so deep. The development story and the saviour story persist together and reinforce each other. If fewer of us were caught up in the unconscious superiority ideas behind our 'saving' instincts, more of us might be willing to look clearly at the truth behind the development story and to push for fairer economic systems rather than more aid. And if we weren't so caught up in the development story's promotion of Western modernity's idea of progress[34] – *everyone should be like us!* – we might be more willing to admit our own saviour tendencies.

Recognising saviourism might also be useful outside of the politics of international aid. Because it's a hierarchical relationship, saviourism is about keeping control of power. When philanthropic funders, for example, provide project funds but not core funds, restrict grants to two or three years' support at most, and insist on indicators of impact within short time frames, they are not just keeping the power and hierarchy in place, but limiting the kinds of interventions that campaigners and culture-makers can attempt. When democracy and freedom are up against such a generously funded, widely dispersed and free-ranging radical-right and far-right information and influence ecosystem, this is a terrible failure on the part of progressive-minded foundations to use their resources well. At a time of mounting crises, the saviour mentality has opportunity-cost effects that go far beyond literal attempts to save.

So after years of campaigning to undermine the development story by showing how financial institutions and multinationals continue to extract money from the poorest,[35] I'm now also interested in exploring the saviour story. Where does it come from, and what does it look like to help without being a saviour? When do compassion and wanting to act tip into 'saving?' How can we know when we're getting saviour-y? Like the commandment to respect lived experience in the previous chapter, is the no-more-saviour discourse telling us to stay away? The British saviour complex has been centuries in the making and these questions could fill a book of their own; what follows are some contributions to the conversation.

SERVICE, NOT SAVING

Not unlike Matt, who we met at the beginning of the chapter, Abdirahim Hassan was in his early thirties and had spent his first decade of working life in the private sector before moving into community work. Born to Somali parents and raised in Tower Hamlets, just to the east of the City's shiny money-palaces, Hassan had done local voluntary work and activism since his teens, organising protests and taking part in local campaigns against immigration raids and police brutality. Now he wanted to spend the best of his time and energy supporting people in his own community.

'We have the poorest children in the country in Tower Hamlets, the highest crack and heroin use in London, all these inequalities, the highest housing waiting list,' he said. 'Within a month I'd put in a bid, without really knowing how to write a grant application, and I went onto an enterprise programme.' Having learned how to run a social enterprise, he opened a crisis café in Hackney to provide food and signposting towards services for people struggling with mental health, homelessness and drug problems. 'It was so hard,' he remembers. 'We had no funding. I was mopping the floor. We had a woman come in and threaten us: acid attacks were quite common in London at that point, and she wanted to…' He trails off. 'She was obviously in psychosis, and I had a moment and I thought, *What have you done with your life? How did you get here?*'

Hassan is speaking softly and rapidly while we walk in Victoria Park, near where he lives. Six years later, he has set up seven hubs, employs twenty-five staff, eighteen of them full time, and they turned over £1.4 million in 2024–5. They're running youth services, outreach for drug users, and women's support and campaigning cooperatives. They're picking up NHS mental health contracts and offering digital peer-to-peer mental health support for Somali women.

I'd been asking people for months: who's doing good work *and* managing to avoid saviour-ish relations? Several mentioned Hassan and the organisation he set up, Coffee Afrik. The saviour arises, he said, when there is a power differential. Theorists of the white saviour, as we saw earlier, describe it as benevolence or altruism combined with unawareness of how structural inequalities work.[36]

Something landed in me, listening to Hassan speak. The unawareness isn't just blindness to the power imbalances out in the world. It can be unawareness of your own power. So if you're doing saviour-relating, you are subconsciously exerting the power *that you're not acknowledging in yourself.*

Hassan is sometimes on the receiving end of this kind of saviour behaviour from foundations that fund justice and change work in the UK. They're run by people with good intentions, he thinks, who still, despite the talk about 'decolonising', end up causing problems in how they wield their influence. Their decision-making about who receives funding can be unaccountable to the communities they serve, or they make intense demands on tiny and under-resourced organisations who must jump through time-consuming hoops to apply for and then report back on grants. Funds and their purpose can be expressed in abstract terminology which excludes people and groups who can't relate to or see themselves in that kind of language.

But Hassan isn't just on the receiving end of it. The saviour behaviour could potentially arise in Coffee Afrik's work with its own clients. There's an inevitable power differential between someone in a vulnerable situation needing support, and someone with a job and funding at their disposal who can choose whether, where and how to set up and run projects offering that support. The critical thing, Hassan says, is how you handle the potential power disparity – which means, first of all, acknowledging it, and being really clear about your position. 'My name is

Abdirahim, which in translation from Arabic is "the servant of God",' he says. 'And I see the work as that – that in the team we are servants of the community. Do we steward the work, do we carry the work as custodians? Our job is to go into each of these spaces and deliver for communities as though we are servants of the people that come into that space.'

What does that look like? 'One of the many principles of Islam is recognising that your neighbours have rights over you,' Hassan said. 'That means you move differently in your neighbourhoods, in your community.' They can call on you for support, for mutual aid. 'We do that really well within the Muslim community, we do that when we're sick and we visit each other: it's a condition that we visit someone when they're sick.'

And regardless of who he is helping, he says, 'it's an act of love. When we're delivering projects it's not because the commissioner needs a data report or monitoring form, we're doing it genuinely because we see it as an act of love for the community. Actually, of course I care about the funding, and I care about the funder, but I care about the community more. That's what really matters to me, that I deliver it in a clean way, in a just way, that it's transparent.' Coffee Afrik had just won a £500,000 grant from the National Lottery, and their plan was to 'co-produce, from day one, how we allocate the budget with the community.' This means – and it is unusual – monthly budget discussions with the recipients of the services they're providing, providing information about what has been spent and what's left. 'It's about transparent charity. So many people are disillusioned because too many organisations have promised to deliver something, to transform a community, or to rebuild communities like this.'

Hassan also works hard to try to avoid a saviour-y feeling in his own staff. He's seen it happen in his own community. The hero feeling can arise in any of us, as we will see in the next chapter. 'And I saw lots of other people doing it – talking about, "Oh, I've done this," or "I've helped a community do that." What happens is that among marginalised folk or organisations, you have this thing where charity bosses and teams walk around like mini-celebrities, I've seen it so many times.'

'Or,' he continues, 'the founders become the face of it. I've no interest in being held as the blueprint of something.' He doesn't have full control over this. BBC Radio 1 Xtra anointed him one of its 2023 'Future Figures' who are 'Making Black History Now'. University researchers and NHS people want to understand how his colleagues co-design and co-produce their services with the people they're supporting.

I had been wondering for a while if the desire to show that they are not white saviours – that they are passing the mic and a bit of the power – influences the way that funders and big charities latch onto 'hero' figures from marginalised communities, who then receive funding which helps them to grow their influence. This heightens the risk of passing on the heroism virus. Here I am, voice recorder on, interviewing him for a book. 'I found this really uncomfortable at the beginning,' Hassan said. 'That's why it's taken a while to really do the work within our team. The work, for me, is divesting from the saviour complex. The language we use is very nuanced. We are constantly regulating our ego. We are aware that we hold lots of power now in our work. I say to the team, it's your own self-regulation and being aware of yourself when you're coming into each space.'

I was noticing, in conversations with Muslim campaigners, how baffling they found the saviour attitudes that
they encountered. 'Generally we work in the poorest areas,
but it doesn't come across as saviourism because in Islam
we're taught to see everyone as equal,' said Bushra Ahmed,
the Croydon community campaigner from Chapter 1 who
had battled for compensation after the 2011 riots. 'It's not
us doing to them, it's us empowering and involving them
as well. As I was brought up, charity is not only one of the
pillars of Islam, it's our reason for being. Volunteering is part
of our life. From six years old if you're at an event, you're
doing water duty. My dad had seven girls and one boy and
he treated us as equal, and he never told us that we weren't
equal. I didn't know that I wasn't. So when I went into a
room with all of these English white people who had the
saviour attitude, I suppose I presented as an equal and they
found that quite offensive, because they thought I should
be grateful to them.'

When Ahmed first started lobbying for government
support when her family's business was burnt down in
2011, she met people who wanted to help her. But when
she began to use her own voice, to stand up for the whole
community who had been affected, some of those mentors
turned on her, almost as if they 'had an obsession with me
being able to speak. They didn't want to recognise that
anyone else had anything to say.' It sounded, hearing her
stories, that Ahmed's refusal to behave as if she was in the
lower position in a hierarchy had got under these worthy
people's skin.

These conversations were also showing how a 'saving'
frame is not an inevitable way of relating to people when
we're trying to help, even when there is a gap in material
resources. For some people, it may not be news that saviour

approaches are avoidable. A former colleague from Amnesty International told me she never felt any sense of trying to 'save' anyone in the years that she worked there – even though she was surrounded by people who did[37] – and even though the work was about as close to an actual practice of 'saving' as it gets: trying to help political prisoners at immediate risk of torture or execution. This was because, she says, she was motivated by *ubuntu*: the southern African principle that 'I am, because we are.'[38]

Ubuntu is a philosophy that underpins a whole ontology – a way of understanding what and who we are, that is embodied, felt intrinsically, not just as an idea. It's about being inextricably part of a whole, and how we only exist in our relations with each other – as opposed to the individualistic view that says we are individuals who form relationships with other individuals. The relationality of *ubuntu*; the focus on community in Muslim charity and campaigning; the solidarity – regardless of ethnicity or faith – of working-class communities anywhere, that support each other and practise mutual aid because everyone is in the same boat: all illustrate the limitations of a view that any of us, individually, can be a saviour. Retiring the saviour means understanding ourselves as inherently part of a collective: something not always central to middle-class life in Britain, and that, more broadly, capitalist modernity and two generations of neoliberalism have been keenly undermining.

While it's important to see examples of non-saviour interventions, I don't want to get good-versus-bad about this. Comparing the work of observant Muslims with that of secular post-Christian white charity folk is hardly the point. As Abdirahim Hassan was noting, any of us doing charitable work or public service is at risk of status claims and grandiosity. Humans are prone to egotism; we must all work to keep ourselves in check. And I don't want to lift any one approach onto a pedestal, or shallowly to appropriate principles or practices from other cultures than my own: that's the imperial habit and there is enough of it going on already. I was interested to talk with Hassan to hear how someone from another faith tradition thinks through the risk of saviourism. Nor, on the other hand – given that I have raised the question of religious traditions – do I want to dismiss the motivating power of Christianity towards loving service. But it is true that I have questions about Christianity's effects, and these conversations – and many others – were making me wonder if and how it might be contributing to the very particular British version of the saviour complex.

There would appear to be some obvious reasons to head in this direction. My twenty-first-century communications training – and picking up from the last section of Chapter 2 – tells me that any tradition that has foregrounded the idea of 'saving' for two thousand years will be having a powerful deep-framing effect on the culture, even if only a minority of those who consider themselves 'culturally Christian' are actually observant. With Jesus the solitary moral hero[39] dying to save us, and with the image of that death as the symbol of the religion, aren't we being told, at every level, that there is something important about saving, and might that saviour message still have some ambient power despite a century and a half of diminishing observance?

Among the faithful, the message might be stronger. I spoke to a young woman working for a charity supporting people in the UK – she is Christian, though the charity is not – who took seriously the example set by Jesus, though she knew she couldn't meet it. 'Saviourism comes from the

idea of the ultimate saviour being Christ, where he sacri-
ficed his life on the cross to save humanity,' she told me.
'And while none of us can claim to be the second Messiah,
I think some of us have that desire within us, and maybe it's
also compounded with a sense of guilt that maybe we can't
save the world.'

Other Christians push back on that. 'The world is not
ours to save', wrote Tyler Wigg-Stevenson in his book of
the same name; he's a nuclear disarmament activist from
San Diego who became a born-again Christian and is
now an Anglican priest in Toronto. His point won't work
for everyone: he argues that only God can save the world.
But he reaches another conclusion not so far from mine:
that the task of the young Christian activists for whom he
writes is not to hurl themselves into messianic attempts to
wrangle the world into the shape they think it ought to be,
but to find their calling and offer service.[40]

Mark Vernon, the psychotherapist, writer and former
Anglican clergyman we met in Chapter 3, told me that
Christianity can get 'reduced to moral imperatives' like
loving thy neighbour and being the Good Samaritan.
'People will say things like, "We are the hands of Jesus on
earth", which in one moment is sort of admirable but the
next moment is inflated,' he said. 'I feel quite strongly that
people confuse heaven and earth, and they feel the message
is to make heaven a place on earth – to quote Belinda
Carlisle! But that's a huge mistake. This earth, if you like, is
a place where we ready ourselves for heaven.'

Part of me finds it hard not to respond in an argumentative activist-y way to this, but he is not being literal, nor
saying there's no point in doing activism. He's saying that
the message of Christianity is not to try to save people or
the world – although you may end up doing good work.

The message, in his view, is 'to try and bring a different perception of reality' – to become more like Christ, in other words, in transformed consciousness. For many Christians, Jesus came not to end human misery, punish the bad or reward the good, but just to love.

Another reason to hold Christianity responsible for saviour habits is its entanglement with colonial history. The connections between Christianity, conquest and the white saviour were explicit in the colonial era. Missionary desire to save souls, imperial desire for resources, and myths about the white man's civilising burden were codependent. In one direction, the church actively helped to drive colonial expansion. In 1493, Pope Alexander VI issued a decree dividing what we now call Latin America between Spain and Portugal, for conquest and conversion.[41] Genocides followed.

And, in the other direction, it was colonial power that enabled missionary activity. 'If you were not our rulers, we would soon silence your preaching, not with argument, but with the sword,' an Anglican missionary in India in the 1840s was told by a recipient of his sermon.[42] Given the lines of descent from imperial-era missionary work saving souls to modern development-industry saviourism, it looks straightforward, in a broad sense, to hold Christianity responsible for our long saviour habits.

Could Christian thinking still be having an impact on a secular society now? In general, yes, says Jeremy Kidwell, an associate professor in theological ethics at the University of Birmingham. I asked him if he might help me think through my questions about the Christian connections with saviourism. 'The landscape of Europe was once relatively dominated by Christian ideologies. That is obviously no longer the case. We can see the attenuation of Christian forms of thought across the last century. But does that mean that Christianity disappears? The structures are preserved, but God is taken out of them.' He sees plenty of vestiges of Christian thought in the culture: in capitalism, in ideas about technological progress, and in the environmental activist groups he spends time in: 'try and find me a non–theological space in contemporary British environmental politics where we're not using metaphors of progress, or linearity, or activism which is focused around saving some-thing, or theories of change or transformation which sound a lot like conversion.'[43]

Christianity is thus having an influence on how we think about the possibility of us 'saving the world' at all, especially with respect to the climate crisis. But Kidwell is not sure that white saviourism is a specifically Christian vestige: in his view, the supremacy feelings that underpin the *white* saviour come more from ideologies of race than they do from Christian theology. On this basis, any of us potential saviours may have more work to do on how we show up with white supremacy baked into our embodied habits.

Kidwell also reminded me that from the very beginning – and indeed, as with any religion – Christianity's braided histories have included states and elites who co-opted the religion in their power plays and oppression of those they ruled... and they have also included the marginalised and those working for or with them, who have found spiritual nourishment, moral guidance and social resources for care and resistance in Jesus's teaching of service, radical action, solidarity and love. Both the power-over and the power-with, you might say.

Rowan Williams, the former Archbishop of Canterbury, embodies the latter when he writes that baptism does not bring Christians into 'a convocation of those who are privileged, elite and separate', but of those 'who have accepted what it means to be in the heart of a needy, contaminated, messy world. To put it another way, you don't go down into the waters of the Jordan without stirring up a great deal of mud!'[44] Even amid colonial conquest and murder there were priests and missionaries who persecuted, and those who, despite being there as part of the imperial cavalcade, stood up for indigenous rights, like the former colonial administrator turned Dominican friar Bartolomé de las Casas in the Yucatán in sixteenth-century Mexico.

Even within myself, I sense conflicting reactions to these two strands. On the one hand I deplore Christian institutions and what they have done over the centuries to indigenous people and their traditions, to women and children and the sacred feminine. On the other – well, how to describe this? I was raised as a Christian, though haven't attended church or felt that I'm Christian since my mid-teens. I optimistically thought that I'd formed, by my early thirties, a coherent sense of the sacredness of the universe, inclusive of its scientific principles, that was independent of Christianity or any other organised tradition. In the last decade I have begun to realise, however, the quite staggering extent to which there's nothing new under the sun: that our culture's and thus my own mental frameworks have been profoundly shaped by Christianity; and, even more surprisingly, that there is something about Jesus that still, somewhat against my intellect and will, feels like the familiarity of home. So I'm not just throwing stones here.

But to return to Kidwell's point: even as Christianity has been tied up with oppressive power, millions of Christians from different traditions around the world draw and have drawn on their faith to resist imperial logics and give service to those in need. Within the UK, powerful strands of Christian social thought and action, both Catholic and Protestant, were woven into the founding of the Labour Party and the origins of social work. Giving service and working for justice have been central to Methodism and Quakerism since their founding: my years working in the peace and anti-arms-trade movements were spent alongside Quakers. Catholic social teaching is centred on solidarity and the common good. Anglicans regularly reflect on how they are giving service. Pentecostal churches, whose congregations are growing in this country, focus on compassionate service, especially within the community. People who do voluntary work through their church or donate to Christian Aid Week feel motivated by service. People working for British charities with Christian roots will say that they are empowering and involving the people they're working with. Members of Christian Climate Action are at the front of many arrest-risking direct actions.

CLASS SAVIOURS AND EXCEPTIONALISM

Yet the saviour stuff continues – including within the UK. While the discourse is about the *white* saviour, saviourism isn't just a development-industry, colonial-hangover, perceptions-of-African-poverty problem. It is also a class problem. I was told several stories during the research for this book, where well-meaning people working with, supporting or mentoring people with less formal status or power had ended up exerting various kinds of control over them, or were in the end simply unable to contemplate seeing them as equal. Those on the receiving end of this consistently saw it as saviourism. People involved in UK food-bank charities told me that they had seen saviour-relating – helping that comes with a palpable sense of hierarchy – alongside, of course, the many expressions of we're-in-this-together solidarity. More fundamentally, implicit saviour attitudes can underpin acceptance of food-bank-style charity that obscures the need for different policies, like taxing wealth.[45] Social workers told me about the potential for saviourism in their field.[46] Funders continue to keep grantees on a desperately short leash. The saviour in us can manifest in any situation where we are trying to help across a power differential.

While the threads linking Christianity to the contemporary white saviour may not form a direct causal line, there is in my view a specific Christian connection to British saviour attitudes. It is rooted in a peculiarly Protestant view of salvation: the idea of the elect,[47] which arrived with the Reformation.

Christianity is hugely plural. Only the Western formations are so focused on Jesus saving us, and what we must do to ensure our salvation; the Orthodox church emphasises how we might become more Christ-like.[48] What are we being saved from, in the Western doctrines? The consequences of our 'original sin', which we inherit from Adam and Eve. How do we obtain salvation? For Catholics it's by repentance, faith, and the sacraments, like baptism and the Mass. Through prayer and other intercessions we can try to improve our prospects after death. Protestants have faith alone. Martin Luther built his rebel Protestant theology on the pessimistic views of Paul and the fourth-to-fifth-century North African bishop Augustine of Hippo, both of whom were preoccupied with our inherently dark, fallen human nature and its contrast with the light of Christ. Luther took a strong line: that God has already decided who receives his grace of salvation.[49] This is the doctrine of predestination. God's chosen are 'the elect'. If we have faith in God and Jesus, then we are among the elect and are saved. The theology of the two-decades-younger Calvin, which influenced the English and Scottish Puritans and was taken to America, diverged from Luther on some issues but largely agreed with him on predestination.

Sola fide, 'faith alone,' is not the source of the saviour behaviour. There was no literal message that engaging in charity – or indeed, for the missionary-minded, conversion – to save other people was going to save our own eternal souls. Quite the opposite: good works cannot lead you to salvation because it's not up to you. It's up to God. We should do good works anyway, as an inevitable result of faith. But the idea of being 'elect' puts you above those who are not.

This isn't about what it is to be Christian now, and it's not a mainstream Christian view anyway. Jeremy Kidwell considers the idea of the elect to be a rogue ideology that cut loose from a broader system of thinking. But, shorn of its theology, he says, 'a partial underlying structure remains, and the partiality of that structure renders it dangerous.' It's about the hangover in the culture. A sense of the elect was built into class attitudes and I see it doing something that works against solidarity.

I've homed in specifically on a Protestant doctrine here and in Chapter 3 because of how it has shaped the dominant culture in Britain since the Reformation. Tracing the effects of Protestantism on cultural values and, consequently, behaviour, is hardly a new pastime. It's been going on since the German sociologist Max Weber published *The Protestant Ethic and the Spirit of Capitalism* in 1905, initiating decades-long debates among historians and sociologists about the extent to which Protestant doctrine encouraged accumulation and investment, against the other, material factors that contributed to the rise of capitalism.

In my view, the Protestant emphasis on being the elect isn't the only factor in the British saviour attitudes that I'm trying to understand. But it's part of it. I turned to Christopher Hill, the prolific historian of the seventeenth century, who blended material and class analysis with a deep interest in the power of ideas, values and the commitments in people's hearts. It was in one of his last books, about the influence on seventeenth-century thought of the Bible being newly and widely available in English, that I found him tracing the long consequences of the idea of the elect for class and nation in England, in a way that has saviour implications. Yeomen and parish elites – the middling sort – wielded their Bibles and found the congruence between their Puritan ideology and their economic interests useful when it came to controlling their families and the landless poor. As the revolutionary and regicidal decades of the seventeenth century passed and a new king was crowned, the religious texts began to count for less. But, said Hill, even when stripped of its overt religion, and, eventually, without reference to the Biblical texts at all, an 'authentic English ideology of pragmatic empiricism' remained.

'The English pride themselves on "muddling through", "conquering an Empire in a fit of absence of mind", "the English genius for compromise". These apparent failings of which we boast with mock humility are perhaps vestigial remains of the Calvinist conviction that God will help his elect, regardless of their merits… The English were no longer the people of the Book but they seemed to have been selected.'

Hill died in 2003 and didn't live to see Boris Johnson in Number 10, but that is who I pictured when I read this, possibly because it is saying something about unmerited overconfidence. This attitude survived for centuries, Hill thought, because England became the world's biggest imperial power, succeeded by the US (also founded on a Puritan sense of being the elect). 'The gift for holy humbug among Anglo-Saxons,' he wrote, 'allows them still to believe that their use of power is different from, and nicer than, that of lesser breeds. It is so much second nature that it is difficult to know in any given instance whether the hypocrisy is conscious or unconscious.'[50]

Believing that your use of power is better and nicer than others! I have heard exactly such sentiments in the comments of British diplomats in various capitals across Africa when discussing their aid strategy vis-à-vis China's, or from middle-class NGO types justifying their interventions at home or abroad. This is the kind of process that Jeremy Kidwell described: the theology has gone, but the pattern remains as a self-image and a way of relating.

Protestantism's focus on each soul's direct relationship with God already encourages an individualistic way of seeing the world. But the idea of the elect, detached from religion, becomes a form of exceptionalism; an assumption of superiority. It's a strange kind of exceptionalism, though, one so insecure it needs constant reinforcement. Being the elect brought simultaneous superiority (I am chosen!) and a crisis of proof (but how do I *really* know I'm saved?) that imparted an existential and fundamental sense of scarcity. Both the superiority and the underlying scarcity are all too easily transmitted across generations through embodied individual and relational habits.[51] The superiority is a perfect shield to defend against feeling the scarcity. In the language of psychotherapy, it's a great recipe for inflation. The exceptionalism functions in the same way as knowing-better in

Chapter 4: it's the shield of being 'okay', which hides the fact that we might not be.

'The British saviour complex: it really is in a category of its own, isn't it!' remarked an old mucker of mine from Global Witness. My speculation is that two potential insights follow from thinking about the cultural heritage of the 'elect' in this country. One concerns our national self-identity: certainly English identity, and perhaps British too, especially that version of it that is, in former Green MP Caroline Lucas's description, 'the state within the state – the England which hides behind "Britain", "GB" and "UK", but which is by far its most powerful component.'[52] What might it mean or look like for Englishness and Britishness not to be built on feeling better than everyone else?[53] My sense is that attention to this tributary of our post-imperial hangover might help in the long quest for a healthier and more grounded national self-image – one that is less amenable to manipulation by demagogues appealing to nationalistic feelings among those who have been made powerless.

The other insight involves the British middle-class psyche. We're a funny bunch. The middle classes both kiss up and look down, like Ronnie Barker standing in between John Cleese and Ronnie Corbett in that *The Frost Report* sketch about class from 1966. Our sometimes complacent occupying of our station holds many of us back from protest, even when our rights are being lost and living standards falling. But it also makes us less likely to think about our power when we're looking the other way, trying to help those more in need. In both directions, you might say, we know our place. There's a reason to do with the translation from Latin of a key New Testament text that Luther's original Protestant doctrine of salvation for the elect was named *justification* by faith alone.[54] But it's interesting that the sense of being deserving (whether of God's grace, for Protestants, or of wealth, for those who have it) helps to *justify* greater access to material resources.[55]

The American political philosopher Michael Sandel takes up the Reformation's 'tense dialectic of grace and merit' in his examination of meritocracy. It was hard, he writes, to resist the meritocratic implication of the Protestant work ethic. Good works as a *sign* of being the elect curdled into good works as a *source*. The 'ethic of mastery and self-making overwhelmed the ethic of gratitude and humility.'[56] Sandel is thinking not about saviour politics but the dark side of meritocracy – those it leaves behind – and its contemporary role in contributing to the resentment that is exploited by the radical right. But underneath, we're talking about the same dynamic – and, in any case, grappling with our saviour tendencies might improve our chances of facing up to the far right. It's exceptionalism that puts us in the position of thinking that perhaps we can *save* others – rather than asking what they want and need. Exceptionalism is tied up with economic inequality, whether within Britain or in relation to other nations. If we've grown up with inequality, it can be easy to think that this is just how things are, rather than that it is the result of political decisions. If we think we deserve to be where we are, then we can be more complacent about why inequalities exist; we can think that charity or philanthropy is enough and that we don't need to push for fairer political and economic systems. Greater humility about the position we are in, and how things might easily be otherwise, leads to a different kind of relationship with those who are struggling. And in this bumpy post-Brexit world, it might help to build a different kind of politics.

'"I've got to save something," as an impulse, is not just misguided but dangerous,' says Jeremy Kidwell. 'It takes us into these spaces of saviourism where we objectify and control others out of a desire to ease this inner pain we feel around our own privilege.' He notices that prayer or meditation among Christian environmental campaigners can balance out the compulsion to save something or someone. How might that work for those who aren't religious?

'I don't want to say, give up activism,' he suggests, 'but I might want to say, find a way to balance your activism and your impulses. And if your impulses are about saving, how do you wrangle that impulse in a way that makes it safe for others? It means keeping yourself in healthy ways, social ways, and it may be a matter of finding forms of active contemplation and meditative practice that complement that.' This is a call for us to make enough quiet space to recognise what our own personal saving impulses look like, to notice that they come from within, as well as from the culture. But it's also an acknowledgement that the desire to avoid being a saviour does not have to stop us acting. There are, potentially, ways to temper the saviour inside us.

SAVING OURSELVES: ARE *WE* OKAY?

Do some of us have a personal saving orientation? I have met people who seemed to. There was the climate campaigner who spent her twenties trying to save a boyfriend from his own worst self, followed by intense action trying to save the world. She had begun to realise these tasks were connected.

'Many of us have a desire to be needed, that validates who we are and our place in the world.' This is Jane Stavert, a psychotherapist. Her profession needs to be alert to the inner saviour, lest it deny clients the opportunity to develop the capacity for change by working things out for themselves. I met Stavert when we were both on the board of a rape crisis centre. A few years off retirement, she brought to meetings a stately presence that might, to the unobservant, belie the fire of rage at patriarchal violence that burned within.

'For me it comes back to that very simple triangle, that as long as I am aligned with the victim, as long as I am supporting them in their victimhood and indignation, then I am not an abuser,' she says. She's talking about the 'drama triangle', a simple concept that reflects a consistent pattern in human behaviour, one that's easy to fall into. The triangle's corners represent three interdependent roles we can adopt: 'victim', 'persecutor' and 'rescuer'. We might be drawn to one in particular, especially if we grew up playing that role in our family, or watched our parents adopt a role when they argued.[57] Maybe we're the person who always tries to fix things when others are fighting. Or we quickly submit and let people push us around. But we can switch between roles according to the situation; we are not fixed by personality or experience in any position.

The mistake, Stavert says, is thinking that we have to be the 'rescuer' in order to avoid feeling like a persecutor (which might feel intolerable since we would not be 'good'), or like a victim (which might simply feel intolerable). Actually, we can be neutral, and still be supportive. We don't have to step into the drama triangle. But it takes awareness and practice not to jump into the rescuer ('saving') role, especially when activist, charitable and service-provision dynamics can all point us towards it. Thinking back to Chapter 1 and being 'good': the drama triangle risk in my investigative work was that if we put the corporate bastards we exposed into the role of perpetrators, and held ourselves up as rescuers, we risked casting impoverished people in low-income countries into the role of 'victims'.

When we worked together – in a very different context from my investigations into corporate malfeasance – Stavert would notice when a dynamic within the organisation might be tipping towards someone putting themselves in a saviour or 'rescuer' position. Rape crisis volunteers on the helplines are trained – and professional staff know very well – to avoid this. Constant attention and vigilance are required, because when supporting survivors of rape and childhood sexual abuse, one of the positions on the drama triangle is obviously in place: that of the perpetrator. A position being taken can be enough to propel us, unless we're alert, into one of the other roles. A rape crisis support worker in training might instinctively move into a rescuer position, which positions the survivor in a 'victim' role they don't want. Actually, there is no separate 'them'. No drama triangle. Rape crisis service users *are us*, and we *are them*, and all language used reflects this. It struck me that this is true three times over. It is politically true, because in our violent patriarchal culture any of us could be in a service user's shoes, having experienced rape, sexual assault or childhood sexual abuse.[58] It is ontologically true – despite what Western modernity insists about our individuality – because we are all interconnected humans. And it is morally true, in that it voices a profound ethic of solidarity that is the opposite of saviourism.

'When we're doing the saviour thing because that's what we need to feel okay, we miss the "other". We're not able to see what they may or may not need from us. We need them to be "saved".' This was Satya Robyn, another therapist. She's a Buddhist and an author; does lots of climate campaigning. In her early fifties now, she never saw herself as a big protester – 'I've always been rebellious but I did it in a very tidy way': she became vegetarian at thirteen and pissed her dad off by getting her nose pierced. In 2019 she freaked out about climate breakdown and got involved in Extinction Rebellion, clocking up several arrests. Every day for the year up to the 2021 COP26 climate conference in Glasgow, she spent an hour on the pavement in silent meditation in the centre of Great Malvern in the West Midlands, where she lives. She hoped this daily vigil might prompt reflection in passers-by. Again, every day for a year from mid-2023, she said a public prayer for the earth, always in the same spot in the middle of town. She knows that profound changes to financial and political systems are necessary. Yet at the same time, she finds, such small actions can maintain hope and potentially influence others.[59]

I was already aware that we might have unconscious reasons to turn to 'saving' strategies. We might have experienced or witnessed harm in the past, and thereby acquired a habit of swinging into action to try to prevent it in the present. Or we might in childhood have had to make things okay for a caregiver who required us to meet their emotional needs. By being good we might 'save' them from their own bad feelings. If our caregivers were not able to take responsibility for their own feelings, perhaps we might also save ourselves from their reactions, like shaming us for not doing the right thing.

Robyn has an additional perspective, however. 'The urge is coming from the saviour part that needs us to do something in order for us to be okay,' she said. The saviour *part* of us. What does that mean? That word 'part' reflects how

Robyn's psychotherapy practice has been transformed by an approach called Internal Family Systems. Many therapeutic models recognise the multiple nature of our inner worlds and that we are not one sole congruent self. Internal Family Systems (IFS) is a version of this understanding. Its founder, Richard Schwartz, chose that name when he recognised that the inner voices in his eating-disorder patients sounded like argumentative family members.[60] 'IFS has revolutionised how I do psychotherapy... and life,' Robyn told me. I'm sharing her view of IFS here because I find it a valuable tool to identify and stand down the saviour impulses within me.

We have two main kinds of 'parts', in the IFS view. 'Exiles' carry burdens from early life that we couldn't process: shame, fury, sadness, despair. 'The feeling is so big at the time, our system shoves it into a cupboard, as it would overwhelm us,' says Robyn. Then there are 'protector' parts, of two kinds. 'Managers' deploy critical voices to keep us hard-working and praiseworthy. 'Firefighters', meanwhile, ensure that we don't feel pain from the exiles. Any risk of that and they leap into action. 'The firefighting part might say, "You need a drink. Or more chocolate. Or let's just lose our temper",' Robyn says. 'Managers and firefighters get into fights. The managers say "Go on a diet." The firefighters say, "You need to eat or you're going to feel that rage." The protectors work harder and harder, but in opposite directions. But all parts have good intentions even if they're causing chaos.'

Yet there's another element that IFS recognises, which it calls Self.[61] It refers to our wholeness, and it has a spaciousness to it, in that we feel calmer, softer, more peaceful. The signs that we are acting from Self, rather than just one of our parts, are that we feel — and yes, they alliterate — compassion, curiosity, calm, confidence, creativity, clarity, courage, and connectedness. These are signs that our protective managers are standing down. Self, Robyn says, doesn't get overwhelmed by emotion and, crucially, doesn't have an agenda, 'doesn't need the other person to change in order to be okay.' When a 'part' is in charge, it does have an agenda: to keep us safe.

This, then, is how we can identify a saviour 'part' of us. It will have an agenda, it won't be driven by any of those 'C' qualities. It's likely to be a 'manager', generating a behaviour that, in the past, might have kept us safe from unbearable feelings. We don't need to have experienced adverse child-hood experiences (violence, abuse, deprivation) to have developed such coping strategies. We may have needed them just to fit in with family life and parental expecta-tions. If we stick at it – with a therapist, a friend or even by ourselves using resources available online – IFS can help us approach each of our protectors and find out their agenda, ask their permission to temporarily stand down their guard, and then to 'go to the exiles and witness them,' Robyn said. 'All these young parts want is someone to get it and not be overwhelmed. That person wasn't available at the time and Self wasn't available at the time, and so they were just left alone with it and that's the most painful thing.'[62]

Robyn thinks we can also use IFS to investigate our saviour instincts. She tried it out on me, live in a workshop we ran together for activists. We warned everyone there would be limits, since I'd inevitably hold back in front of a crowd. Still, we gave an idea of how it works. You find out the agenda by asking the saviour part of you directly – but only from the Self position. 'I'm tired of it,' I snapped when Robyn asked me how I felt towards that part. Here was a lack of compassion, a clue that a manager with an agenda held the mic. Once we notice some compassion and curiosity – suggesting that Self is present – towards the part we think is doing something save-y, we can talk directly with it. My own impulses to save, I've been working out, include being driven to 'help' to keep me acceptable. *Be a good girl!* I've begun to see that I want to fix people so I don't have to feel terrible around their pain; other people's pain may not be safe. I need to try to make things better for everything to be okay. And at the same time, none of this is to suggest that I'm not also motivated by compassion for suffering and rage at injustice.

The gift of IFS is that being able to speak and act from Self is a more generative spirit to take out into the world. Less energy is used attending unconsciously to our internal balancing act; more is available for service. Suddenly I could see *how* saving keeps things centred on us: because the intention of a 'saving part' is to keep our *own* internal system regulated, according to an old pattern. So it's not that we all have a 'saviour part'. It's that in some of us, saving might be a strategy that one of our protector parts adopts. Even if our consciously chosen values are to work in solidarity with people experiencing difficulty, we will undermine that intention if we're acting unconsciously from a saving part. We may continue to enact feelings of hierarchy in our interactions, even if our declared intention is not to be a saviour.

It is discomforting to acknowledge the vulnerability of these needy parts of ourselves. Especially so if we're used to feeling competent and resourced. When I began protesting, then volunteering, then working in professional campaigning environments in my twenties, I was struck by how many damaged people I felt I was encountering, compared to my previous job as a reporter in a commercial media company. It wasn't everyone, but there were people who seemed – this was a hunch – perhaps to be acting out their mental stories or past traumas through their work to save the world. They were often hard to work with: both demanding and flaky. When the difficulties they brought got in the way of 'my' work – my ability to get through my workload – I would be indignant. My compassion would fail because I felt I was being pulled down. It felt unprofessional, woolly; I wanted to get away. My sense of myself depended on a demarcation I'd made between those who were not okay and those (like me, so I thought) who were. Sometimes I wished I were back in a more mainstream environment where everyone appeared to have themselves together enough just to *get on with it*.

But what was I not seeing? That it felt important to me, for a long time, not to see myself as vulnerable. That in the more 'professional' environments I worked in before, there were also wounded or vulnerable people, acting out status and power games within a frame that looked like 'competence', or socially acceptable male anger or dominant forms of leadership. That often it is precisely those who have experienced harm of some kind, whether interpersonal or from structural injustice or both, who can perceive the system's problems and end up working to change things.[63]

These days I see all this in more political terms, and this is where the necessity of looking at our own 'stuff' becomes part of the bigger picture of collective change. Those of us with various forms of privilege might think that we must, therefore, be 'okay'. There's been a fair amount of this kind of unhelpful and rigid identity-based thinking in activist spaces recently.[64] Or, more unconsciously – and this is also a widespread phenomenon beyond campaigning circles – we might feel that our being 'okay' makes sense of, even justifies, the unequal wealth distribution that affords us more power. We're back with that feeling of the elect again.

Both ways, our attachment to being 'okay' allows us to keep on with the unconscious projections whereby we see vulnerability only in those with less status or power than us, and either that's acceptable to us, or we put our heads in the sand about it, or, if it's not acceptable, we need to 'save' them. Our own vulnerabilities – even if they are not the same as those of somebody living in poverty and experiencing oppression – hide behind our societal status, or what people who talk about this regularly call 'positionality'.* Being 'okay' in this way is a version of the hero's shield. It stops us having to look at painful or difficult matters: our own vulnerabilities, our racial, class or gender assumptions, and the need for more substantial material redistribution to tackle inequality, both nationally and internationally. To get over the British colonial and class hangovers, we are going to have to put down that shield.

But what if we still think we have to be the hero?

---

* See note 16 to Chapter 4.

6

'I AM A HERO'

Unhappy the land that has no heroes!
No. Unhappy the land where heroes are needed.
Bertolt Brecht, *Life of Galileo*[1]

I NEED A HERO

Before motherhood deprived me of whatever tolerance I had for the anxiety of being on the leading end of the rope, I enjoyed rock climbing. I discovered it in my late twenties, around the time I realised that the local indoor climbing wall was rammed with attractive, sometimes shirtless men; this was a few years before dating apps. I was never going to climb the higher grades on real rock because I lacked the head for the exposure, however strong and nifty at the physical moves I became. In the purist outdoor form of the sport, known in the jargon as 'trad', you place temporary protective gear as you go. You must ascend beyond the last tiny lump of metal you jammed into a crack and clipped your rope into, knowing that if you fall, you will descend twice that distance, plus the rope stretch... and that the protection might not hold fast anyway.

One way of describing trad climbing is that you feel an absolute hero when you reach the top. Another is that it's rather like childbirth: amid the subsequent euphoria you quickly forget the agony until you find yourself doing it once again. It's interesting that 'hero' and 'childbirth' are two such different mental frames. Despite my reluctant head for leading a route, I managed a few long multi-pitch climbs during those years. Once the second climber has followed up the first pitch, un-wedging and collecting the gear placed by the leader, you both clip yourselves to an anchor that you construct on the rock face. If you're lucky there will be a nice solid ledge – at least a couple of inches wide – to stand on. You retrieve a flattened Snickers from your pocket and scarf a few bites, swap the lead position, and start off on the next pitch. After a few turns like this you're a couple of hundred metres vertically above where you began, in what the route books drily call an 'airy' situation.

So when in October 2022 I saw the photos of Morgan Trowland and Marcus Decker slung in hammocks with a Just Stop Oil banner near the top of the cables of the 137-metre-high suspension bridge over the Thames estuary at Dartford, I didn't just have an abstract response. I could feel in every queasy cell of my body what that exposure might be like. The bridge, which carries the southbound lanes of the M25 motorway, was closed for forty hours until Trowland and Decker agreed with police to be taken down. The media debates about whether Just Stop Oil's tactics were counterproductive were well under way before they packed their ropes and harnesses to climb those cables, and I knew all the arguments for and against inconveniencing the public. A witness at their trial would later testify that he missed the funeral of his best friend of thirty-five years, and refused Trowland's note of apology written from the dock.[2]

Nonetheless, 'Heroes!' was my first response when I saw those pictures, just as it was when I saw videos of Greenpeace climbers on power stations or oil rigs. I was slightly in awe of this kind of thing because I was never that kind of direct-action person. I haven't put myself in real, physical danger. I could say that I'm not a good enough climber, or didn't want to risk a custodial sentence, or that I've tended to see my skills as doing something with words rather than direct actions. I could say that my status-needs and conventionality kept me 'in-the-system' for a long time, working for credentialed campaign organisations… or even that I wouldn't want to take those kinds of risks given my growing uncertainty about the effectiveness of holding-up-the-public tactics.[3] Those statements have all been true at various times. But I wondered, looking again at the pictures of Trowland and Decker in their hammocks, and thinking about their respective prison sentences of three years and two years seven months,[4] if it's also to do with feeling like I'm not someone who can do such heroic things. And this is many people's reaction to any kind of standing up and speaking out – even if it doesn't involve physical danger, or pissing off the public. *That's something for heroes, not for ordinary folk like me.* And we can leave saving the world to the heroes, can't we? That's what heroes do, after all, as the stories and films tell us.

WHAT DO HEROES DO?

In August 1971, Philip Zimbardo, an American social psychology researcher in his late thirties, conducted what would become a notorious experiment – the Stanford Prison Experiment. Needless to say, it would never pass a research ethics board these days. Zimbardo set up a mock prison in the basement of Stanford University's psychology department with cells and a solitary-confinement room, assigning student participants to the role of prisoner or guard. It was supposed to last two weeks but Zimbardo ended it after just six days when his girlfriend – and later wife – Christina Maslach, a researcher in the same department, came to see how it was going and was horrified. The 'guards' were dishing out humiliation and abuse around the clock; after an early revolt that was quashed, the 'prisoners' had all become powerless. Even Zimbardo, as the experimenter, had lost his perspective and was egging them on. Five of the 'prisoners' had already had emotional breakdowns, the first within thirty-six hours.[5]

Zimbardo wanted to build on the research of Stanley Milgram,[6] whose disturbing experiments into obedience, conducted at Yale a few years earlier, had found that people taking part in a 'learning' experiment were willing to inflict what they thought were electric shocks on fellow participants if somebody in authority told them to do so. The 'learners' who received shocks if they failed their 'tests' were in fact collaborators, acting; there was no electricity. But almost two-thirds of participants were willing to inflict shocks to a potentially fatal level. Where Milgram was demonstrating that tyranny is inevitable because so many of us will obey people in authority, Zimbardo was illustrating 'situational power': how easily 'good' people will oppress others when placed in a position of authority and given power. For many, their work confirmed Hannah Arendt's observation of the 'banality of evil', made in her 1963 study of the trial of Adolf Eichmann, and how the Holocaust was made possible as much by willing followers as evil leaders.[7]

You may well have heard of Milgram and Zimbardo's experiments. Their underlying message about how easily we slip into evil has persisted, though their methodology and conclusions have since been criticised.[8] But I was intrigued to discover what Philip Zimbardo did three decades later. In the early years of the new century, he had undertaken research projects into shyness and perceptions of time and hosted a PBS documentary series on psychology that made him widely recognised in the US. He was now president of the American Psychological Association and emeritus professor at Stanford. Flicking through TV channels in a Washington, DC hotel room in April 2004, he saw disturbing pictures of Iraqi prisoners being tortured and humiliated by American soldiers in a detention centre at Abu Ghraib, outside Baghdad. These images caused global revulsion, seeming to confirm the hubris and hypocrisy of America's invasion of Iraq the previous year. But Zimbardo was startled by the similarities between Abu Ghraib and the conditions he had created in the basement of Stanford's psychology building. He agreed to appear as a defence witness at the military trial of one of the soldiers involved, Staff Sergeant Ivan Frederick II.

'I knew that in the Stanford experiment, I began with good apples and that it was the place that corrupted them, so my hypothesis was that maybe these soldiers were good apples and it was the barrel at Abu Ghraib that corrupted them,' he said.[9] His intervention made no difference: Frederick was convicted of five abuse charges and sentenced to eight years in prison.[10] Zimbardo felt it was time to tell the story of his original experiment properly, which he hadn't felt able to do in its immediate aftermath. His 2007 book, *The Lucifer Effect*, relived each of those six days in painful and compelling detail and drew out the parallels with Abu Ghraib. But his last chapter hinted at the new turn in his interest: just as the perpetrators in Iraq had been 'ordinary', the person who exposed their crimes, Joseph Darby, was an ordinary twenty-four-year-old soldier. Appalled, he had handed his colleagues' incriminating photos, which were circulating in the barracks, to the United States Army Criminal Investigation Division – an act that triggered years of threats so severe he and his family required protection.[11]

The Stanford Prison Experiment had focused – as has so much work in this field – on what makes us innately susceptible to evil. But at this late stage in his life, Zimbardo finally wanted to focus on our innate capacity for *good*.[12] The opposite of evil is the hero, he began to suggest. To be a hero is not to have extraordinary powers of physical strength or moral courage. It is simply to act when something bad happens. Any of us can be a hero by countering the 'bystander effect' and standing up when someone is experiencing or at risk of harm. Echoing Arendt, Zimbardo called this 'the banality of heroism'. Just as evil is committed by ordinary people in particular situations, so it is situations – where someone or something is at risk – that can bring out the hero in ordinary people. He wanted to make being this kind of hero very ordinary. He founded an organisation, the Heroic Imagination Project, encouraging young people to intervene, including when they see bullying. Lesson plans are offered to teachers; there are TED-like talks to fire up corporate and nonprofit leaders to get in 'training' ready to act when the moment arises; Zimbardo gave talks internationally.

Realising that psychology researchers had neglected heroism and bravery, he worked through his late seventies and eighties with colleagues to publish papers establishing a behavioural theory, testing society's implicit views on heroism. In their view it involves a 'willingness to enter a fraught situation' – whether to preserve life or an ideal – and must have some kind of anticipated or actual sacrifice or risk.[13] They delineated duty-bound heroism (military and front-line responders like firefighters) from civil heroism ('everyday' heroes who act in the moment to undertake a rescue or intervene bravely). They argued for a separate category of 'social heroism', in which people stand up, sometimes over the longer term, for values that are under threat or that they want to become norms, in actions that may have financial costs and threaten their social standing. They tested whether people were willing to expand their implicit understanding of heroism to include some of these social-heroism situations. Good Samaritans, whistle-blowers and individuals standing against bureaucracies made the cut. Religious figures, scientific or discovery figures, odds-beaters, martyrs, adventurers and political leaders did not.[14]

I had seen some of this research before I made the connection, through Zimbardo's name, to the Stanford Prison Experiment. Already deep in conversations with psychoanalysts and myth-tellers about the ancient hero archetype and its workings in our unconscious selves, I'd found some of these explorations a little simplistic. Setting out conceptual distinctions is part of scholarly work, and I did recognise that what they were calling 'social heroism' was a description of activism as I recognise it: standing up for a principle, even at the risk of being ostracised. But I was looking for leads as to how we might engage differently with the idea of the hero when we're trying to change the world, and the instinctive reaction to this categorisation effort from the demanding campaigner in me was 'So what?'

However, when I realised Zimbardo's connection to the Stanford Prison Experiment, I found myself moved by this activity that he inspired when the horrors of Abu Ghraib brought his research to life. I checked that critical voice. I was reminded once again of the power of old and dominant stories to shape our understanding of what humans are like, and what enormous work it takes to shift them. Psychology researchers' long-standing focus on how easily any of us can commit evil, shared by philosophers and social scientists, was understandable in the second half of the twentieth century. But it had helped to reinforce the ancient Christian focus on humans' innate sinfulness, at the expense of our understanding of our equally innate goodness. Now, I couldn't help but see something almost desperately heroic about Zimbardo's quest: a late-in-life struggle against the odds to shift one of the most powerful Western stories about what it is to be human, which his own most famous research – whose fame he had never outrun – had helped to strengthen.

Zimbardo died in 2024. In many ways, his inclusive view of heroism is exactly the view of changing the world I want to encourage. Being this hero is not about the kind of person we are or think we are; it's about how we choose to respond to what's going on. It suggests that we don't have to feel like we are 'an activist' – or, indeed, a typical hero – in order to try to change the world. We don't need to do something physically strenuous, or that requires being able-bodied. We just need to speak out or take the necessary action, even if it feels hard. I find this democratic view of heroism helpful because I have seen the deterrent effect of the action-hero image. Many people wonder how we can help in a world in trouble, yet think it's not for us because we don't see ourselves as anything like that archetypal activist-hero who is either loathed, like those annoying folk from Just Stop Oil, or worshipped – safely after their time, once we no longer have to live with the difficulties they cause – like the Suffragettes, Gandhi or Martin Luther King Jr.

The secret I want to let you in on, however, is that many of us who are already trying to change the world are rather turned off by the hero too.

THE PROBLEMATIC HERO

I'm not talking here about the revered foremothers and forefathers of our movements. Nor am I necessarily talking about the direct-action types. Trowland and Decker are reportedly modest folk, as are other protest-climbers and tunnellers of my acquaintance. I'm talking about the people who, however unconsciously, are trying a little too hard to be the centre of their own story while doing good. The ones who make coalitions difficult because they insist on pursuing their own project's tactics or positions, even though the point of a coalition is finding the shared ground where you can all advance together.[15] The ones who find it hard to countenance that not being seen might be bearable if you're in service to the bigger picture. The leaders – to be found in every change-making organisation I've been anywhere near – who think leading means controlling, and who struggle to share responsibility, creating bottlenecks that block others' work and creativity.

There are practical, strategic reasons why these behaviours are frustrating; they get in the way of the work and reduce our collective chances of success. Business schools may not share activists' worldviews, but their leadership experts – with greater research resources than those outfits that support campaigners – have been onto this for two decades or more. The 'heroic leadership' model of an infallible, unflappable individual making grand moves and producing big ideas while keeping tight control is old hat. Executives are now exhorted to adopt 'quiet leadership' where they 'pick their battles and fight them carefully rather than go down in a blaze of glory for a single, dramatic effort';[16] they are reminded that instead of thinking their personality makes them a leader (typical hero-thinking), they must be able to flex between leadership styles according to the circumstance;[17] they are encouraged to be more human, vulnerable, in touch with their emotions and to develop their people and devolve responsibility.[18] Jon Alexander, a former adman who now campaigns passionately for us all to see ourselves as 'citizens' rather than the 'consumers' he used to sell to, argues that it's now time for the 'anti-hero' who is free of the individualistic self-reliance of the 'Consumer Story'. When the anti-hero turns instead to the 'Citizen Story', he knows it's not his job to access the rooms of power in order to rescue or save others, and instead hands over the mic and opens the door to everyone else.[19]

But hero-style actions may also irritate us because that traditional lone hero contradicts our political commitments. We might react to the very idea of the hero because our political view is that conditions make people, more than inner greatness (or badness, as Zimbardo was trying to show). We might be in democratic reaction to the persistent view that history is driven by 'great men', as the nineteenth-century Scottish historian and essayist Thomas Carlyle suggested. He was sceptical of the developing democracies on both side of the Atlantic, and thought we should look up to strong leaders who could do a better job.[20]

We might be in liberal reaction to authoritarian uses of the hero. Nazi Germany's militarism was enabled by heroic ideals of fallen soldiers,[21] and Hitler's supremacy fantasies were built on *Übermensch* theories appropriated from Nietzsche.[22] In our own age, we might be horrified by the heroic posturing of Trump or Putin. Our decolonising instincts might be aggravated by the hero's association with empire: if the hero stars in and writes the histories, the stories of the colonised will not be heard.

We might be swayed by decades of feminist objection to the association of heroism with men and their nation-building deeds, especially those involving violent militarism. It was from feminist peace activists working against the arms trade that I first learned how macho and aggressive saviour heroics are just another dose of the world as it is, and will not deliver the peaceful regenerative cultures we want.[23]

Our qualms about dominance hierarchies and commitments to the promised equality of horizontal organisations can trigger reactions when yet another person with a great idea is in thrall to 'my-thing-ism', pushing their project to the exclusion of other initiatives and wider cooperation towards shared goals.[24] Yet my-thing-ism is the flip side of something necessary: the fire-starting energy to work on a new concept, found an organisation, lead others, fight Goliath.

These negative responses to the hero image and those who invoke or occupy it have legitimate rationalisations, grounded in our chosen values and political reasoning. Yet they are, nonetheless, *strong reactions*, just as some observers' negative reactions to environmental activists are strong. So too are the positive, idolising reactions many of us have to activist heroes whose annoyances are safely in the past. Zimbardo and his colleagues likewise noticed people's fickle responses to the hero, and the tension between 'the desire to elevate and the desire to castigate [their] actions.'[25]

I usually take strong and polarised reactions as an indicator of psychoactive content meriting deeper investigation. Just as people on the left and in progressive opposition to the status quo have a conflicted relationship with power (we need to build or take it if we're going to change anything, but we don't want to become what we hate) and with leadership (we think we want equality, yet figureheads and

coordination are often required), we also have very conflicted feelings about the hero.

'It's a very divisive topic, especially for progressive, liberal,
psychologically sensitive Western citizens,' says Andrew
Samuels, a psychoanalyst, professor of Jungian psychology
and author of several books about politics and psychology. 'I
think anyone who denies some involvement or other with
a hero is either lying or has spent too much time looking
into the mirror. It is something that affects everybody...
And this is especially true – and I'm speaking now as a therapist – of people who say that they have no time for heroes.
For people who say the idea of a hero is just super-macho,
it's a boys' game, women are left out, spiritual people are left
out, people of colour are left out. This is not going to work,
simply announcing that you have detached yourself from
something as colossal, as widespread as a serious involvement with the hero.'[26]

It is possible, as Samuels has pointed out to me, that I
object to jarring heroics in other change-makers in order to
divert attention from my own. I could say, as I did at the start
of this chapter, well, I don't do high-wire dangerous deeds
and therefore I'm no hero. But I know that I've acted like
a fighting hero when it would have been better to coop-
erate, competing for press coverage in a coalition because
a press officer from another organisation had thrown their
weight around and undermined me. I know that I got off
on the hero kicks of working on undercover investigations*
and living at a distance of only one more shitty letter from
Carter-Ruck from a kleptocrat or mining baron's libel
claim. I may as well just say it: I enjoy being a hero. I have

---

* Not, I must clarify, as the actual person undercover; I am too earnest
and poor an actor for that.

broad shoulders, I'm good with responsibility, I've run great teams whose members liked working in them. I like the accolades when something goes well, I like it when what I do is noticed, and while I've been freelancing, raising kids and writing books, I have sometimes missed the adrenaline hits of a full-time arse-kicking job. And here I am now, proposing perhaps to save progressive activism from itself with a book like this one. I mean, *come on*.

But it's not surprising that change-makers struggle to escape the hero when so much of our culture is built around the heroic leader. It happens in politics, and in the way that the press – and all of us – treat politicians. The fallibility of a party leadership built around one person and their small team at the top is why an increasing number of people think that distributed decision-making and citizens' assemblies must be the next democratic frontier.

The unambiguous leader-as-hero image remains sticky in business, too, despite the anti-heroic leadership drumbeat coming out of the business schools. Researchers found that leaders-in-training on an MBA management programme – some early in their management careers, some with significant leadership experience – continued to see themselves in a 'heroic' leader view based on personal control, despite being on a course that emphasised 'process' leadership, which is more facilitative and brings forward the views of others. Their course reflection notes showed they had absorbed what they'd been taught about the benefits of processual leadership. But they couldn't apply this cognitive, propositional knowledge (see Chapter 4) to their reflections on their own situations at work. Their analysis of these situations still emphasised what they as a leader could do to better 'control' the situation and influence the outcome. Even if they could see what they, personally, had contributed to the problems of a situation (which not all of them could), their conclusion was that they, personally, should have done it differently – rather than thinking about whether they could have *interacted* differently with others to contribute, collectively, to a different outcome. Reassessed twenty months later, they were fully back in individualised 'heroic' leadership mode in their work.[27]

This inability to abandon the lone hero pattern, the researchers proposed, was either because they were still striving for individual control, or – for those who were a little more self-aware – because they remained bound by the heroic image of leadership, even though they recognised they couldn't meet that high bar. Instead of seeing unpredictable and complex circumstances as inherently impossible to control, they thought they'd failed if they couldn't rustle up enough hero vibes to control those circumstances. As a result, one participant in the research actually quit their leadership role during the training process, and took a post with less responsibility.

None of this is to say that leadership isn't necessary. But the hero is an illusion of individual control. Like any archetype the hero image is malleable and persistent, so each age has taken him up and presented him in its own light. From the classical semi-divine hero who would conquer and offer catharsis when his flaws led to his downfall, to the medieval knight on his quests for glory and love. From the early modern colonial conqueror to the Enlightenment sage. From the Romantic hero, alone on his mountain, to the modern hero who can earn and consume all he desires. We might be the postmodern heroes trying to change the world that those previous heroes created, but they are still in us.

A heroic narrative is the same shape as an arrow or spear, wrote Ursula K. Le Guin, flying to hit its mark.[28] But straight-line thinking may not help us to face problems that don't have simple lines of cause and effect, or that call on us to act when we can see no obvious outcome. On some level we know this, which is one of the reasons why so many people don't even try to make change. They see the complexity, see that we can't logically, straight-line, cause-and-effect have a big influence on it, and withdraw. This is true of people who've never tried, as well as of people who've tried some lever-pulling campaigning and then come to see how much more complex everything is.

When our thinking is shaped by the hero narrative's straight lines we're less likely to see that enthusing our neighbours to work together to stand as independents for the local council,[29] getting together with other parents to create anti-racism projects at the primary school or to fight for access to a piece of land for a community vegetable-growing scheme that improves mental health and food resilience, might be the sparks that begin to change things in our locality, or that if people everywhere did that, we'd be on our way to a culture shift. We're like those managers at business school who, despite their ambition, found it easier to think they'd failed if they couldn't control the uncontrollable, than to consider abandoning the internalised hero-leadership story which told them that control was the task. Actually, they needed to adjust their idea of what was being asked of them. So do we all, because we can't *conquer* the problems we are facing. Even if fossil fuel companies changed tack tomorrow, there is much to do to adapt and build resilience to the climate chaos that is already coming.

The novelist Amitav Ghosh suggested that the 'great derangement' of modernity is to have allowed ourselves to be taken in by the bourgeois delusions that emerged with industrialisation: that the forces of nature are regular and can be controlled.[30] The traditional hero is called upon to battle outrageous forces, and yet these stories of over-coming, control and battle are little help in facing complex problems requiring as much adaptation as mitigation.[31]

THE INNER HERO

So why is the hero narrative so sticky? Back to the hills, where I learn so much about myself and the world, even – perhaps especially – if not in the way I intend. In May 2008 I spent a night on my own on Rhinog Fach, a mountain in the south of the Eryri national park in North Wales. It's a few miles of raven-flight north of Cadair Idris, where legends famously say that a night on the summit will render you either a poet or mad. I was on a neigh-bouring mountain but I scared myself enough to wonder about the latter possibility. My journal for that year does not record the sequence of thoughts that impelled me to check the forecast, borrow my brother's car, drive to North Wales then, a little south of Harlech, to navigate up nar-rowing lanes to the road's end. A few hours from dark, I set off on foot uphill. Perhaps the reason I cannot remember is because it wasn't really thoughts that pulled me there. It was a deeply felt call: a desperation for solitude, for land as wild as possible, for a break into the depths within myself that had felt long blocked-off and, like a drumbeat underneath, for a sense of what my own significance and story might be. What was I really going to contribute to the world?

These desires had been growing for months, as I spent more weekends in the hills. In the wild and the green I relished the natural world for its own sake, but I was also approaching something elusive within myself. I didn't know what it was, but I feared something in me might die if I couldn't access it.

As I walked, climbed and slept outside more frequently, I became seized with the notion of spending a night up high on my own. No mountaineers' backchat and banter. I had recently read Robert Macfarlane's second book *The Wild Places*, and was inspired by his wintry night alone on top of Ben Hope, the most northerly high peak in Scotland, standing stark above the peat bogs of the Flow Country. He became dangerously cold and was keen to descend when dawn arrived, but something about the romantic excess of his heroic quest for wildness grabbed me, even though later in that book he realised that the 'wild' could be found anywhere, including in the small cracks beneath his feet.

It did not work out as I hoped. As I lifted my pack and walked unsteadily away from the car at the road's end, I heard a distinctive hissing. I turned back to find that I had punctured the side wall of the front nearside tyre when bumping up the final stretch of track, and would now have to deal not only with my own thwarted expectations if I turned around and left without trying, but that soon-to-be-flat tyre.

Already full of misgivings, I saw little alternative but to continue. The heathery path began clearly enough, but faltered as the ground steepened and the light faded. I'd come this far in a fugue state that left little room for doubt, but negative thoughts now intruded. What if I injure myself? My dad was a mountain rescuer in his youth and taught me the safety precepts. I'd left a note on the dashboard, saying where I was going and what day I'd be back. But I was breaking his bigger rule: don't go into the hills on your own.

Solitude was the point, however, and I'd chosen this location precisely because of the unlikelihood of meeting anyone else, especially compared with the honeypot summits around Eryri to the north. 'Utterly uncompromising', 'hard going' and 'roughest terrain in Wales', warn recent online walking guides to the area. 'Off-path progress is tortuous.'

I was careful to take a route that was marked faintly on the map, but long before darkness fell and I pitched my little tent near the top, a litany of fearful thoughts was beating in my ears. I tried to counter with rationality: *The weather is clement. This is within my skills and experience. There have been no wolves in these islands for five hundred years.*[32]

The thought of accessing depth, stillness or insight amid such a stupid cacophony was a joke. I surfed the edges of a panic attack, slept briefly just before dawn, then woke to gaze emptily at the impassive rocky wall of Rhinog Fawr's heights across the chasm to the north. I came looking for something of or for myself and the mountain was having none of it. Perhaps it was resisting 'being claimed by the educated middle classes on spiritual quests', as the Scottish poet Kathleen Jamie put it in her punchy review of Macfarlane's *The Wild Places*.[33]

I was thirty-three, which, some point out, is your 'Jesus year'. This was indeed a thing before young and online American Christians turned it into a meme. Like the rounding of each decade, it's one of those bullshit self-flagellation opportunities at which self-focused denizens of industrial cultures are encouraged – or pressured – to tick off the accomplishment of key milestones. The probable age at which our Lord was executed by his oppressors is deployed less as a benchmark of relationship, housing or other material success – thirty and forty are more appropriate moments to beat oneself up over these – than as a point by which we should, like him, have made our mark or, at the very least, found the path of our contribution to the world. It's a moment to consider the likelihood of our heroic significance.[34] And I wasn't feeling great on that front.

On the one hand, using my journalist's training to investigate and name corporate responsibility for corruption and environmental damage felt like a satisfying way of saving the world. My younger self would have been delighted. But on the other, I was having to suppress my growing understanding that our work was only picking at the worst excesses of capitalism to make it play more nicely. Even if we achieved the reforms we wanted, capitalism's destruction of life would continue unabated. I was very distressed to realise this. But another part of me was also distressed that I might not, after all, have found a delivery mechanism for my desires for personal significance. My hero desires were thwarted.

It was a few weeks later, having returned home tail between my legs (and having asked a farmer for help with the flat tyre), that I first heard someone talking about a 'wilderness quest'. They were referring to a modern version of the ancient pan-cultural phenomenon of going into the wild to seek initiation and insight into your place in the web of life; traditionally, on the cusp of adulthood, but in modern Western cultures that lack community support for such initiations, it could be at any time of life. You spend three or four days and nights in wild-ish country* with water, rudimentary shelter and no food, returning to a base camp where others will hear your story and help you make sense of your experience, connecting it to the bigger

---

* I say 'ish' because in Britain there is no such thing as truly wild landscape; for millennia it has all been settled, worked, cleared, fought over.

human and non-human stories of which you are part. You might be in search of insight, guidance about your place in the world, or a way to mark a letting go. By surrendering to the land, 'sinking deep into your beingness in the world,' as I later heard someone describe it, you may go beyond yourself and your previous questions. I felt substantially less mad hearing about this. The call to wildness and descent I was experiencing was shared, and recognised by healthier cultures than our own.

It's true that I hadn't been trying to fast, and, comparing what I had done to how these rituals worked, I could see other key aspects I missed. I just dashed off; wilderness vigil participants are encouraged to get very clear in advance about their intention. I needed longer; a night – or more – of fear, dread and small deaths might be expected over a four-day vigil. I needed a community tending the fire to set out from and to return to, rather than heroically trying to do it all myself. And I was lacking the necessary reverence to the ceremony in which I was participating; a non-transactional approach to the mountain and its beings.

But in the absence of any obvious cultural support for the shift of consciousness I was entering, I tried to initiate myself – just as adolescents often try to initiate themselves with alcohol, drugs and other risky undertakings, in the absence of adult support for their need for challenge and spiritual adventure. Raised in an individualist culture, I did so the only way I knew: on my own. In these modern times where we lack the sense of visceral and ontological connection to the rest of being, maybe it is no wonder I became lonely and scared, however much I felt at home in the hills and had craved their solitude.

What I'd also been toying with, unprepared, was the ancient threefold pattern of *separation, threshold* and *return*.

In this situation, separation may involve identifying habits and beliefs that must now be left behind. Threshold, or initiation, is the time alone in the wild. The return involves learning how to bring back to your community the insights you have been gifted, a process which, like integrating psychedelic journeys, can last months or even years and cannot be taken lightly.[35]

You may recognise this three-part initiatory sequence as the heart of the 'hero's journey': the narrative sequence made famous by the mythologist Joseph Campbell. Comparing myths across cultures, Campbell found a common pattern of severance (the hero hears a 'call to adventure' and leaves home), initiation or threshold (the hero meets difficult challenges which he must overcome) and return (coming home transformed).[36] Further broken down into detailed stages delineating the hero's challenges and finding of support, this map made its way explicitly into popular culture from the 1970s when George Lucas famously used it to construct the plot for *Star Wars*. An industry of screenwriting guides and teachers flourished, sharing its pattern. Many novels and scripts remain remarkably consistent in their adherence to the underlying structure. Campbell noted that this monomyth resonates because it fits the pattern of human psychological and spiritual development. This is why the hero narrative is so persistent; it illustrates something integral.

The psychological pattern that the hero's journey describes is what Jung called individuation: the process of becoming ourselves. The hero is a symbol of ego-consciousness;[37] the monsters that the hero defeats symbolise the expansion of our consciousness to include our shadow sides that we had projected away.[38] We must separate from the parental and especially the maternal matrix, seek our own soul's truth, then find a way to integrate what we've learned into how we live our life and find our niche in the world. This work begins in adolescence and can be lifelong. Campbell was showing, in a different way to Jung, how stories reflect that. Myths and stories are more attractive and viral than 'psychology' as a way to communicate the same cultural instructions. In this light, the Grail stories of Arthurian legend, with their sacred object to be sought, are a quest for wholeness. And while psychology, in its Western, individualised way, takes us down further into ourselves, with all the potential constraints of that move, myth and story can lift us up out of our individual concerns and connect them to something wider, older and shared.[39]

One of the ways I think I found the necessary distance to begin the process of individuation was through developing a political identity and getting involved in trying to change the world. This can be the very old story of generational conflict. Developing different political views to those of my parents was certainly part of it, though that kind of opposition is neither the only route to individuation, nor is it sufficient on its own.* But more generally in my early twenties, I was developing my identity by rejecting some of the norms of our unhealthy and violent culture. This is something anyone can do, whether or not it involves disagreement with their family.

That call to get involved in changing the world feels very like Campbell's 'call to adventure', the first stage of the hero's journey. We turn our backs on what we know and set out into the unknown. We are energised. We have a task. So even if we disavow the politics of imperial heroes, or condemn the my-way-or-the-highway behaviour of the wannabe

---

* It's not sufficient for changing the world either, as we saw in Chapter 2.

heroes we have to work with, or understand that our marination in Hollywood hero-culture obscures that we are only one of eight billion instances of just one species,[40] the hero's journey may still be the underlying template that is being activated in us. The trick here is to recognise what might be going on. 'Being the hero is very different to having a relationship with the hero archetype. Those are different things altogether,' said Dwight Turner, a Brighton-based Jungian psychotherapist who writes about psychology and social justice.[41] Seeing the hero as a role or vibe we can temporarily adopt or step into helps mitigate the risk of trying to occupy the hero position more permanently.

Jung warned that when we assimilate to our ego any of the archetypal images that properly belong to the collective unconscious (which he saw as our shared and inherited stock of images) the result is that we inflate ourselves.[42] We're not meant to contain all of the universal; our only task is to become entirely ourselves, and everyone doing that is what creates the universal. When we inflate, the hero becomes the dictator, the messianic leader... or, more commonly, the nightmare boss. By this route, we may become what we are fighting. In a workshop we ran together on the hero, the novelist and eco-feminist writer Sophie Strand encouraged campaigners to decentre themselves as the human protagonists, and ask who they might be a side story to. She told a story about rescuing a woodchuck – a small North American mammal also known as a groundhog – from a highway: 'Maybe my entire life was about aiding that woodchuck. Maybe I'm not the main character, not even the side character. I'm a side *side* character,' she said. 'And the main character is the woodchuck.'

But is it reasonable to ask young people to hold the hero at bay? I wondered if it wasn't, at a time in life when the drive for adventure and distinction runs so hot; when the hero's black and white may be more appealing than the contemplative's nuance. 'Why not be inflated?' asks Andrew Samuels, the Jungian analyst, only half tongue in cheek. 'Has there ever been a successful revolutionary who was not necessarily, gloriously and insanely inflated?'[43]

John Ashton, the former UK climate diplomat from Chapter 2 who became an anti-fracking campaigner, told me that in his experience younger activists could sometimes be resistant to the idea that they should, in their actions, take care to keep open a 'path to redemption' for those on the opposite side of their struggle, however wicked they might seem. When we are young and inspired by a cause it is natural to see ourselves as warriors, Ashton said; to surrender to the red mist; to take on, in a sense, the mantle of the Irish mythic warrior hero Cú Chulainn or his Norse counterpart the berserker. We can't in that role afford to imagine the world through the eyes of our enemies; if we did we might hesitate and ourselves be cut down.

I wondered, then, if something else I've been suggesting throughout this book is reasonable. I've been saying that we should try to withdraw our projections: of badness or evil onto political opponents (Chapter 1), or of ignorance onto those who don't share our experiences or education (Chapter 2). But – and bearing in mind the risk of generalising about generations – is this a reasonable ask of younger activists?

I asked this because even by Jung's own argument, individuation doesn't only comprise the search for identity. It's about becoming complete by bringing the conflicting forces within ourselves into balance – our socialised acceptable self, and everything else that we have pushed into shadow. Jung thought this shadow-work stage of individuation was something that couldn't really be done before midlife, which for him meant at least the mid-thirties. It was in the second half of life, Jung thought, that we move into service. Until then – through childhood, adolescence and young adulthood – we are building a healthy functioning ego, so that we can become clear about who we are and, critically, who we are not. Should we even ask younger activists, then, to do the work of shadow recognition, to try to be less driven by ego?

The psychotherapists I spoke to weren't much troubled, however. 'You've got a generation of kids coming through now who are aware of their mental health earlier on,' Dwight Turner told me. 'I think the more reflective people are from an earlier stage, the less likely it is that their egotistical side will impact on their activism. So that things become less stereotypical around activism, and more realistic in some ways.' Turner also pointed out that Jung certainly didn't have everything right.* So perhaps we can use, as Turner and his colleagues do, what is helpful in Jung's thinking without having to take him as gospel.

In a way, however, perhaps I already had an answer to these questions. It came in the form of the many illuminating conversations I've had over the last few years with younger activists. Some of them embody an approach that is subtle, aware of shadow and projection, conscious of power and its misuse, able to try on the hero role when required – all things that I didn't think about until my forties. This is cultural evolution. The conversation changes; the leading edge of the culture shifts. I find this life-giving.

---

* The charges against Jung include racism, antisemitism and cultural appropriation; some people also object to the idea of archetypes as foundational structures of being human, since across cultures there are so many different ways of being human; in this view he looked at other cultures through his existing filters, and may have found what he wanted to see.

LEARNING FROM THE HEROINE

We have now met a few save-the-world heroes. There's the bridge-scaling activist hero who we can rely on or hate while remaining, ourselves, on the sofa. There's the speak-up-even-though-it's-uncomfortable hero who, Zimbardo reminded us, can be any one of us. There's the persistent old conquering-hero who tells us we must strike out, command and control, achieve everything ourselves. We've seen the need not to confuse necessary heroic moments of stepping up with the ancient archetype of the hero, which we assimilate to our ego at our peril. And now, in Joseph Campbell's monomyth, we can see why the hero-image is so magnetic, because it's a metaphor for and thus activates our own deep desires for wholeness.

But ironically, for an image that was supposed to be about wholeness, Campbell left a lot out. Half of us, in fact. The lyrical narrative of *The Hero with a Thousand Faces* occasionally acknowledged that the hero could be a 'man or woman', and at a couple of stations in the hero's journey, he offered female examples: Psyche's quest for her lost lover Cupid, and the ancient Sumerian goddess Inanna descending to her dark sister Ereshkigal in the underworld.[44] The dreams of twentieth-century folk that served as his parallels to illustrate the links between myth and the unconscious did include those of women. But Campbell would default, when it came to the crunch – the moment of initiation of the hero – to the woman's presence in the story serving as the object of a man's quest. Or she was his mother, whether the good variety, or the variety to be escaped from.[45]

I've been hopping about this for years. But long before I could articulate it, or had found some of the many writers who were already articulating it,[46] I was already responding by trying to model myself on male hero patterns. I would show myself and the world (and, certainly, my dad) that I could do it too. I spent my late teens immersed in accounts by travel writers and foreign correspondents – often men – which shaped my desire to travel alone and report like they did. Before I started meeting my heroism needs through activism, my younger 'calls to adventure' looked like repeatedly heading off on my own with a backpack, even though I sometimes found solo travel lonely and scary.

I'm not saying that it's not a female thing to do any of these things on your own, or that it's only a male thing: that would be ridiculous. And there is class and Global North privilege in travelling freely at all. It's more about the underlying vibe. In retrospect I can see how, for a long time, my approach to being an empowered woman meant simply substituting myself for the chap in all those stock images of male adventure that I had absorbed, without questioning the hero narratives behind them. I did it in my attempts to change the world, too, enjoying the swashbuckling feel of investigating and chasing bastards. And I did it in my personal life when I was in crisis about that hero role, feeling like it was no longer working. Climbing up the mountain to spend that night on my own, I was turning myself into *The Wanderer Above the Sea of Fog*, the lone male gazing out over the mountains in Caspar David Friedrich's famous Romantic painting.

There are things to learn about hero-alternatives, I later realised, from the women who have tried to find their way in the cramped spaces left over. That one-of-the-chaps version of the hero I experimented with maps onto a 'lean-in' kind of feminism. Another thing that women have done with the immense cultural weight of the male hero image is develop their own version of it. So instead of saving the world as hero, we try to save the world through enabling, self-sacrifice and martyrdom. We become saints. We make sure to be virtuous and extremely good at what we do. For obvious reasons, this is a more socially acceptable accommodation to patriarchy than substituting ourselves into the male hero image (the crimes for which Joan of Arc was burnt at the stake were heresy – and refusing to stop wearing men's clothing).[47]

A masochistic martyrish form of female virtue can infuse even militant action, as the historian Susan Pedersen noted, somewhat sadly, about the hunger-striking suffragettes who were force-fed in prison. Alone in their cells, she writes, 'they girded themselves for assault: like medieval martyrs, they tested their faith by their endurance… Militancy unabashedly drew on, indeed drew its strength from, some of the oldest tropes of female difference and abjection: tropes of women's superior purity, their unique capacity for fleshly mortification, their willingness to bear on their bodies the stigmata of their subjection.'[48]

I have met many women in campaign and service-provision organisations who work in martyrish ways, depleting themselves in the process. It's how so many of us – and so few men – have been implicitly socialised: to sacrifice our own needs and desires in order to attend to others, to be always available to help.[49] One former colleague told me she'd previously worked with an organisation supporting homeless people, where she noticed a manager was always available on her phone, day and night, to staff and service users. 'And that sets up a model for everybody else working in the organisation,' she said. 'Not the men, funnily enough: they didn't adapt to that model. But a lot of the women did, particularly when they were new: "Oh, she's just amazing isn't she, wonderful, I can ring her any time and ask her anything.'" These women, I think, had been socialised, as so many of us are, to see that kind of giving, that availability and self-sacrifice, as a positive. In this manager's line of work, however, such unboundaried behaviour was counter-productive. 'Most people who are homeless have been traumatised, many of them repeatedly,' my former colleague said. 'So to be available to the service users in this way is not helpful to them, because the task is to find a manageable way of living ordinary life.'

A third option, when faced with the legions of old-school heroes, is to create some new heroic myths. If the heroes of empire and capitalism destroy worlds or save them only by their own logics of violence, then by all means, let's have something else. The individual conquering hero appeared with empire at the end of the Bronze Age, points out Sophie Strand, the mythologist who saved that woodchuck. Before that, as far as we can see, cosmologies involved ecologies of animals, women and men.[50] So if the conquering hero hasn't been here forever, why not be ambitious, and assume that he doesn't have to persist endlessly into the future?

All right, so it's unrealistic, as the psychoanalyst Andrew Samuels suggested, to think that we can turn our backs entirely on our hero desires. And there are perennial insights from within the myths of conquering-and-killing heroes that go beyond gender politics: that humility is essential; that the key to the journey is transformation; that the hero must reflect something larger than themselves. But fine: let's *compost* the conquering hero and see what other heroic myths might grow.

Ursula K. Le Guin's work is full of new myths: take the gender-neutral society of *The Left Hand of Darkness*. N.K. Jemisin creates survival myths amid seemingly impossible atmospheric, geological and social conditions in her *Broken*

Earth Trilogy, as did Octavia Butler in the burning California of *Parable of the Sower*. Naomi Alderman experiments with new myths in her incendiary speculative fictions *The Power* and *The Future*, which imagine, respectively, a world in which patriarchy is overturned, and a world in which the tech billionaires are overcome by – and I did hoot with joy here – having their own technologies turned against them. Both stories raise dilemmas about the use of old-hero means versus new ones.

Manda Scott does new myths too: her novel *Any Human Power* depicts a revolution in British political culture whose wheels are set in motion by a teenage girl's furious tweet about porn and rape culture. Back in the real world, Jacinda Ardern embodied a new myth during her premiership of New Zealand between 2017 and 2023: a young female leader who could do empathy as well as possessing the strength and decisiveness to defy terrorism and Covid-19.

In 2011, in her mid-twenties, Sara Zaltash began singing the Islamic call to prayer as a piece of public art. The new heroic myth she was creating, she says, was 'this liberated female Islamic channel of divine song that somehow manages to change the idea of what Islam is.' Raised in Reading by Iranian parents of Muslim heritage, she had developed a theatre performance piece that contained the call to prayer, and saw the impact it was having on people. So she started singing it on its own; in some performances she did so repeatedly, for an hour or more.

'The audience will show you the truth that it might be scared to express by what it enjoys and what it appreciates,' Zaltash told me. 'And what people really wanted in this mess of stories in the Middle East, and colonisation, and the Taliban in Afghanistan, and because of the way that Islamic patriarchy treats women, it's like there was this longing for an empowered femme queer brown girl singing the call to prayer.' For a decade she sang it at festivals, conferences and arts events.

'I got quite openly excluded, shunned, from any liberal Islamic conferences I would go to,' she said. 'People would realise who I was and just not talk to me. In both Sunni and Shia [Islam] any innovation of practice is *haram* [forbidden] – and in Iran, any innovation of practice is punishable by death – so people were just scared to associate with me. Sometimes they – normally men – would contact me on the internet, or come after a performance and try to explain to me why I shouldn't be doing what I was doing, and I would point towards the positive effect it was having on people hearing it: look, God is bigger than all of us, and this feels true. And normally I would be able to win them round.'

When we spoke she was planning new projects to change the stories of rape culture and of the Christian church's persecution of witches. 'You don't mess around, do you?' I said, grinning. These are not small stories to be playing with. 'The myths we've got are not meeting our moment,' Zaltash said. 'There is this movement of going into the mythos of different cultures to try to find new ways of understanding things. And there's also the feminist rewritings of old myths which can to a certain extent be useful. But why, as a culture – or me, as an artist – why are we not just taking the reins and creating a new story which can be held up for people to be inspired by?'

Why indeed, I thought. This is about creating narratives that shift our understanding of what a changed world might look like. I might say such narratives serve as rocket fuel for the imagination, though that would reveal that I'm still working on my alternatives to fossil fuel-based metaphors.

Working with narratives like this is a profound form of change-making, even if it doesn't look like protest, policy-making or community-building.

'Why is that not something that we're taking on as artists?' Zaltash asked. 'I feel like artists have just become these sort of edge-twiddling commentators rather than stepping forward and saying, "Okay, Hercules isn't really working any more, what do we need? What story is going to galvanise the change?"'

People steeped in the old myths can usually discern the structures of much older stories in anything claimed as 'new', and will point out that myths are never 'ours' anyway – they have their own gravity. The myth-teller Martin Shaw's books and electrifying live storytelling events are always clear on this. As Zaltash had acknowledged, the old myths do have much to offer – though we may need to get past what looks like a gendered surface.

To this end, I find feminist understandings of old stories particularly fruitful. I unearthed my copy of Clarissa Pinkola Estés's 1992 classic, *Women Who Run with the Wolves*, in a second-hand bookshop in 2004 and re-read it every few years. A Jungian analyst, she examines the old stories of folklore, the 'fairy' stories that women must learn from in the absence of great myths that centre us. What can look like women being injured in horrific ways (*The Handless Maiden*, *The Red Shoes*) are actually heroines offering sub-versive, coded warnings about the risk of sacrificing our full powers – to false men, false gods and false stories. In the last decade the Jungian psychologist and author Sharon Blackie has gained a following for her work on the Celtic mythological heritage of these islands. She sets out a 'her-oine's journey' and a 'post-heroic' journey that can speak directly to women, especially once they realise the futility of struggling for position in a culture and economy that continue to destroy the basis of life.

'But Joseph Campbell saved my life,' men sometimes say, when confronted with feminist killjoy complaints about their hero. I see my young son's growing interest in the male heroes of Marvel stories and ancient mythology, who reflect back to him something that makes him feel good. Many men like the old heroes, especially in a world where feminism has made great strides for women while our understanding of what patriarchy *does to men* lags behind. The susceptibility of boys to misogynistic appeals from influencers in the online manosphere arises, in part, from our collective failure to articulate this damage and offer alternatives. As Trump returned to power in 2025, I noticed conservative commentators appreciating the return of what looked like an archetypally heroic masculinity pushing back against the controlling norms of political correctness and 'managerial' bureaucracy (or what others call 'care' and the protections of the state). Whatever you think of that, it's delusional for any of us to think that the old-style hero has no place in the male psyche.

But I'm not so sure that it's Campbell's male-centric narrative that his defenders are most attached to. The core of his message goes beyond that. What is actually life-saving, when we feel in crisis, is to discover the ancient idea, lost in secular modernity, that our ground of being is greater than ourselves. What is lifesaving is to hear that our existence has meaning, that our task is to find a way to express it, that we need challenge and support in order to do so, and that modern life is not good at offering either of these. Trying to change the world and offer service can provide the challenge. But we must watch for grandiosity. Striving for significance through changing the world can have the same inner resonance and power over our psyche as the call to war.

And so there is a fourth option, relevant for any of us when we are confronted with the omnipresence of that hero's call to war. It's to draw on the many stories that are already here – even the simple ones we thought we knew.

Storyteller and scholar Joanna Gilar, who lives in Sussex, has been working with a collective of storytellers from different backgrounds and traditions to 'rewild' the tale of *Cinderella*; she's found a story that helps us to see one of our roles in a time of ecological breakdown.[51]

'Everyone thinks that *Cinderella* is about a glass shoe and a dress. We can also understand it as a much older story which holds layers of meaning around ritual, particularly ancestral rites,' she told me. In most versions of the story the magical helper is more-than-human. That fairy godmother as we know her first appeared in Charles Perrault's seventeenth-century version. 'In most versions across the world, the dead mother returns as a plant or an animal, the animal is killed by the stepmother, and the cinder child has to gather back the bones and bury them. It is profoundly sad that the complexity of this story cycle has been lost.'

'It's her tending of the bones that creates this magical dress that she then puts on,' Gilar said. 'The work that we've done with rewilding the story has been really interesting. I think Cinderella, the ash child, is a hero, but she's not a hero who goes out and fights. She's a hero who tends the hearth. There are feminist dismissals of Cinderella: she's passive, she marries the prince. But she holds the home and sweeps the hearth in the context of holding this liminal space between life and death, and between home and "other", or the wild – which is fundamentally heroic, otherwise we wouldn't be here. You have stories where the hero is going into the woods and battling with dragons, and you have stories where that's a man or that's a woman. And you also have stories when the hero is finding different ways of holding home.'

And this is the task for all of us in a time of climate break-down, Gilar thinks, where 'home' ultimately means an earth that can support human flourishing. 'That's what we have to do now if we're going to survive on the planet, we have to find different ways of holding home, and negotiating with grief, and negotiating with what we've lost.'[52] This means finding ways to make our communities more resilient to changing weather and faltering supply chains, including by building connections between people. It's the heroic work of continuing to show up even when relations are difficult, so that we can build supportive communities. It's the heroic work of quelling the instinct towards 'othering' even when we are feeling threatened and insecure.

Actually, let's just put down the hero for a moment, and all these questions of whether we adopt him, or try to be him, or replace him with a different kind of hero. This is bigger even than that. What we are talking about here is the vision that I hold even when I know it may not be achieved in my lifetime, of a world in which these values of holding and care of life are not just a way of surviving or resisting the current mess, but are the basis for organising human society, more important than money, growth or accumulation. And perhaps there is room in that vision, to create it and defend it, for anyone who still wants to be a hero of some kind.

POST-HEROIC ACTION

Just before dawn on an early January morning in 2024, Ruth Ben-Tovim, a grandmother and artist in her fifties from Devon, was dropped off in an industrial estate next to the M4 and M5 junction on the northern edge of Bristol. She was muffled against the cold in thermals, warm coat, thick socks and boots, and she was carrying a heavy bag containing sturdy metal tubes about the width of a drainpipe. With her were a small group of people, three of whom, aged between fifty and seventy, were similarly provisioned.

At a quarter to seven at an arranged meeting spot, a couple of dozen further people materialised from the darkness, with banners, keffiyehs and Palestinian flags in their backpacks. This larger group were set for a picket, though they didn't all know there was going to be some non-violent direct action too. Walking quietly, they approached a building owned by Somerset County Council and rented by Elbit Systems, a weapons manufacturer that supplies drones and other lethal equipment to the Israeli military, who had been using them in their attacks on Palestinian civilians.[53]

In moves they had rehearsed the previous evening, Ben-Tovim and the three others with whom she had arrived took the tubes out of their bags and inserted their arms, each clipping a chain round their wrist to a karabiner that was hooked to a metal bar welded across the inside of each tube's diameter at its halfway point. Imagine holding hands with someone at arm's length, with a straight tube covering the length of both of your arms. Attached to each other in this way – 'locked-on', in the direct-action lingo – the four of them lay awkwardly in a row on mats and a big Palestinian flag draped across the freezing tarmac. They were wearing nappies as they didn't know how long they would be there.

As the sky lightened, someone from their crew put signs saying 'Shut Elbit Down' and 'Palestine Action' round their necks, and placed theatrical props on the ground next to them, symbolising white-shrouded dead children. The morning became noisy. Somebody was playing loud recorded music, and there was shouting from the wider protest crowd who were holding a long banner. But every half an hour or so one of the close-support team would ring a little bell and say, 'Let's have a moment of silence.'

'Just to connect, and look round at each other,' said Ben-Tovim. 'It was constantly bringing us back into why we are here. It's less about "How can I influence the big picture?" If for a few hours we can stop a drone being made or developed, that might down the line stop one child being killed or a family being bombed – for me, that's enough.'

I wanted to talk to somebody taking a bold action yet in a non-heroic way. Ben-Tovim is warm and funny, though I would be scared to piss her off. She has probably always had an activist temperament, she thinks. But after some direct action in her youth, her change-making for many years was through her work in community engagement through participatory arts. She designed, curated and facilitated public events encouraging people to imagine the futures they want and start working towards them. It was only once she turned fifty and got involved in Extinction Rebellion that she returned to direct action. After the Hamas terror attacks of 7 October 2023 and the Israeli government's subsequent assault on Gaza – described as genocide by a UN commission of inquiry and scholars of genocide – she had been raising money for humanitarian aid and joining marches and silent vigils.

Her non-violent direct action against Elbit Systems was planned with a few others she met on those protests. They formed an 'affinity group' that could operate independently. Those offering flasks of tea, snacks, emotional support and a lift from the police station afterwards held equal status with those lying on the ground. (Extinction Rebellion worked the same way.) These were just roles they were playing, rather than some people being in the 'hero' position. Once they had a plan, the ten of them approached Palestine Action, a grassroots network doing non-violent direct actions to target – with blockades, break-ins and hoses of red paint – the premises of businesses in the UK that they identified as supporting Israel's war machine.

It was Palestine Action who rustled up the wider crowd with banners and noise, and whose reels of Ben-Tovim lying in the road – closing Elbit's UK research, development and logistics facility until well into the afternoon, when a specialist police unit with power tools eventually cut them out and arrested them – would later be seen by more than a million people around the world.

Ben-Tovim wasn't part of Palestine Action. Her group wanted to try something a little different. Perhaps some of it was about their accumulated years, but it was also her interest in actions that 'call in the ceremony', creating space for people's grief and their rage. I could see that incorporating a ritual aspect chimes with her artist's instinctive sense of theatre and performance. That's part of it, though I think the ceremonial aspect is also doing something deeper to puncture any potential hero inflation.

'A ceremony would usually have an intention and a sense of gratitude. It would have a sense of honouring, and of stepping into the unknown space, in the moment but also in its potential impact,' she said. That's why they were calling for those moments of silence. From her position of physical discomfort on the ground, there were moments when she was just looking up at the sky. She could see a drone overhead, which she felt connected her to what was happening in Gaza at the same time. The winter sun had made an appearance, and there was a beautiful tree. 'It was a really heart-opening experience. It means I can find my anger or grief but somehow it's supported and connected with the wider intelligence.'

One impact of this ceremonial feeling was feeling more resourced to face something difficult: 'Three of us had been arrested before, but it's never nice. It's horrible being in a police cell.' But they also had an effect on other participants. 'A ritual has a sense of intention, a sense of setting off, a sense of being in the liminal space in the middle where you're open – to what's unfolding, to the wider intelligence of everything, every being around you in that moment. You're in an unknown space. And then there's a sense of journey: an arrival, integration, return. Whether it's direct action or running events, I always see it as a shape. I'm really conscious about how we begin it, about gathering people together at the beginning of something to tap into their hearts as well as their minds.'

By creating a ritual with this familiar transpersonal shape of the hero's journey and of ancient cross-cultural initiation rites, they were helping to connect everyone present to something bigger than themselves.

The impact rippled out; perhaps there was a little transformation. Later she heard younger activists talking about how inspiring that day had been. 'People can be a bit excluded from the hero thing. Somebody goes up on a roof and the message goes out and people come to stand at the bottom and cheer. But there's a distance – there's the actors, and there's the spectators. I'm interested in blurring that. How do you build community, how do you value people who are there, how do you negotiate, how do people meet each other, so it's not just the actors, it's the "spect-actors"?'[54]

At the next action they were planning – derailed by a frightening police raid on the house where they were staying – they had intended to read out names of the dead in Gaza, and had asked a sound artist to create a war soundtrack to be played every hour, followed by silence. It struck me that she was speaking about a potential antidote to the individualistic hero archetype: designing an intervention or action that, while still courageous, decentres the potential hero actor at the centre of it, and weaves connection while doing so. There was a humility to how she spoke about this role that she had temporarily stepped into for a day. To many it looked like – and indeed was – a heroic role. But within that scene, she was working consistently to create a different feeling in everyone who was there.

A few weeks later, the police dropped charges against them. At a Palestine-support-group meeting I attended shortly after I interviewed Ben-Tovim, a woman described being told by a Palestinian contact in Gaza that she watched videos of protests on social media on her phone to get through the nights of bombing. That was in mid-2024. A year later, as the population of Gaza faced starvation or being shot while queuing for food aid, the Labour government proscribed Palestine Action as a terrorist group under the terms of the Terrorism Act 2000. Any perceived support for the group or its actions might result in a prison sentence of up to fourteen years. More than 2,700 people were arrested in the second half of 2025 for holding placards expressing support for the organisation. As this book went to print, a High Court judgment in a judicial review brought by Palestine Action found the proscription to be unlawful and disproportionate.[55] The Home Office was reportedly planning to appeal.

My purpose in sharing Ben-Tovim's story is not to comment on or to express support for Palestine Action, who were also involved that day. Rather it is to identify an example of nonviolent courage that is deliberate about creating connection and avoiding the lone hero. That said, it is also true that we are many, those of us who struggle to see how non-violent protest against war-making facilities can be equated with terrorism.

7

'I MUST SAVE THE WORLD *NOW*'

Our house is on fire.

Greta Thunberg[1]

The times are urgent, let us slow down.

Bayo Akomolafe[2]

TICK TICK TICK

During 2009 Ben Margolis, a climate campaigner, was pro-curing alarm clocks: the old-fashioned kind, with big bells on top. Hundreds of them. Campaigners sometimes find themselves doing things like this. There are only so many ways of saying: you *must* do what we say. A former colleague of mine once obtained a suitcase full of wind-up chattering-teeth toys for distribution at a meeting of governments that had signed a not-bad-on-paper anti-corruption treaty. Would the representatives ensure that the treaty had 'teeth' and was actually enforced? You could hear those gnashers going off in the hallways all week. The delegates and probably their kids loved them, although plastic-wise it wasn't the best idea. Enforcement briefly moved up the conference agenda, though the bigger forces impeding cross-border corruption prosecutions ultimately held sway.[3]

Margolis's clocks were for photo opportunities to launch a campaign about time running out to tackle climate breakdown. He was coordinating a network of hundreds of NGOs, trade unions and faith groups trying to influence the outcome of the COP15 climate negotiations in Copenhagen at the end of 2009.[4] The meeting of 192 countries managed to agree in principle that temperatures could not be allowed to rise more than two degrees Celsius above pre-industrial levels, and some funding – not enough – to poorer countries. But the binding agreement to reduce emissions that many of us were hoping for was nowhere near. For those who had focused their energies on these negotiations, it was a moment of terrible failure.

By the time of the Paris climate summit in 2015, which saw agreement on a 1.5C target – although with countries still able to map out their own emissions-reduction route to meet it – Margolis had, for a while at least, had enough. He was hosting asylum seekers on his permaculture farm in Norfolk, working together on the land, helping them to integrate into the local community. 'I wanted to do something that was tangible, that was connected to real human beings, and offers something practical, rather than this big, ethereal, international-policy work,' he said. But he did notice the press releases from climate groups trying to influence the Paris talks.

'I thought, these look familiar, and I went back to the ones I drafted from Copenhagen. They were, word for word, the same. When you're in a communications department and you're trying to get something picked up by a newspaper, it's quite difficult to not go with the headline that this is our "last chance",' Margolis told me. 'But there's more and more discussion about this version of urgency. There's been a bit of a recognition that we can't say every year, "There's five years remaining – this is our last chance!" Where do you go from there? In twenty years' time you're still asking people to come out and campaign.'

My friend Andrew Simms, another doyen of climate-policy campaigning in the UK, did something similar: in 2008, when he was at the New Economics Foundation (NEF) think tank, he fronted a '100 months to save the world' campaign, accompanied by a monthly column in the *Guardian* for the year up to the early 2016 deadline. One of his colleagues from NEF paid tribute to Simms' masterly ability to come up with headline-catching campaign hooks. But, this colleague told me, he was the one who then had to field the enquiries from journalists after that clock ran out: 'Hello, I can't help but notice that 100 months have passed, and we're all still here. Any comment?'

Simms laughed when I told him this because as he remembered it, the enquiries were forwarded on to him. He said that while it was a deadline-focused campaign – 'We worked out how long, on trends at the time, it would be until CO_2 concentrations got to the point when it would no longer be "likely", based on IPCC probability measures of risk, that we'd stay below two degrees' – the headline had been the *Guardian*'s. Invariably the media will choose the pithy statement ('x months to save the world') rather than the technical detail, and so the save-the-world trope lives on.[5]

There was a dramatic increase in the use of urgency, crisis and emergency language between 2007 and 2019, when Greta Thunberg told world leaders that 'our house is on fire'.[6] And that is the point: it *is* urgent: we're in a fight with the fossil fuel industry and its shills for the survival of life. Global heating exceeded 1.5C above pre-industrial levels during 2024.[7] The last ten years have been the warmest on record; the earth is already heading for two degrees above pre-industrial temperatures, which will result in unprecedented natural disasters and threats to food supplies. Immense flooding in Pakistan in 2022 affected a third of the country and 33 million people, displacing nearly 8 million and destroying agriculture.[8] Harvests are already failing: more than 90 million people in eastern and southern Africa were suffering extreme hunger in 2025 due to drought. Around the Mediterranean, persistent droughts are reducing cereal yields from Morocco to Egypt, have already halved the Spanish olive crop, and are increasing the frequency of wildfires across southern Europe.[9] In the UK, October 2022 to March 2024 was the wettest eighteen-month period on record for England, putting swathes of farmland underwater; this followed major wildfires, and 3,000 heat-related deaths, during the heatwave of summer 2022.[10]

The problem with the ticking-clock metaphor, however, isn't only that the earth's regular passage around the sun will invariably take us past whichever deadline the current clock is highlighting. It's that – as Margolis puts it – 'all of the evidence shows that sort of messaging doesn't land.' Metaphors evoking time as a limited resource which is running out are much more likely to be discouraging and promote anxiety, too much of which becomes paralysing.[11]

Yet the countdown metaphor continues to be popular. Another, bigger climate-clock initiative was launched by some New Yorkers in Times Square in 2020 and has spread around the world. The UK installation was unveiled by King Charles in 2023, with a five-metre clock at the Guildhall in the City of London and a takeover of the big digital board that looms over Piccadilly Circus. And these clocks come on top of the existing Doomsday Clock run by the Bulletin of the Atomic Scientists, which in January 2023 was moved from 100 seconds to midnight to 90, and then another tick down, to 89, in early 2025. I can feel myself going into shutdown just looking at the Doomsday Clock website.

Like many others, I have had periods of paralysing fear about climate and ecological breakdown for two decades. At some point between 2007 and 2010 came a series of moments when I realised they were no longer just two lines on a list of issues I was worried about, but the ground of them all.[12] Twice since then I have fallen into a deep hole and taken months to climb out; these days I can cycle rapidly between full awareness of what is at risk, and the kind of low-level disavowal sometimes necessary to greet the kids, prepare a meal and be on hand for homework and social crises when they clatter in from school. But I do know what the rising panic of running-out-of-time-to-change-things fear feels like in my gut. I recognised that feeling again in late 2024 and early 2025 when Trump was elected for his second term and began his autocratic takeover of government powers and reversal of climate action in the US, and the increased risk for more of Europe and the UK to head in a similar direction became clearer. I saw it in the messages my campaigner friends were sending each other, in their faces in the pub once the podcast 'record' switches were off and the op-eds were filed. This chapter is about what happens when we act (or don't act at all) from that feeling of urgency-panic, and the steps we can take to counter it.

URGENT ACTION

In October 2019, a decade after Margolis was gathering his clocks, two men carrying Extinction Rebellion banners climbed onto the roof of a morning-rush-hour train at Canning Town station in east London, holding up further services. As pressure built on the platform, a furious crowd of commuters pulled the protesters down and set upon them. One kicked and lashed out as they reached for him, a terrible moment for a movement founded on non-violent principles. I saw the videos circulating and felt sick. Many of us, inside and outside, feared that this was the moment that Extinction Rebellion was done for. How bad does it look for an organisation founded and mostly run by white people to disrupt a diverse community in a poorer part of the city where people were trying to get to work? The criticism was: here are some white men with a limited sense of the lives of others. By not working with people from different back-grounds, you don't just leave people out, but risk tactical and strategic mistakes.[13] And why target public transport when it's more environmentally friendly than cars, and we're going to need more of it to get people out of cars?

Extinction Rebellion – like Just Stop Oil, after it – leaned heavily on urgency messaging. I hated the 'talk' they did around the country during 2018 to gather initial recruits. Not because the information was a shock but because I worried that it was irresponsible to use panic and fear that way. Furthermore, at the one I attended, there was some-thing enraging to me about a man talking about mass rape in the event of social breakdown as a way of inciting fear and getting us to sign up for a climate campaign, when most men do so little to tackle rape culture. The talk format tried to give us a few minutes for digestion – in principle this is good practice, though it was not enough – in which we could turn to our neighbour and discuss how we felt about what we'd just heard. The chap next to me ranted about conspiracies, which hardly helped.

It was only after I heard people talking about the first bridge-blocking action in London in October 2018, and then attended thoughtfully run local meetings, that I changed my mind. I later realised that most of those who initially joined Extinction Rebellion were already aware of the extent of climate breakdown and had been stuck in a typical pluralistic-ignorance problem: desperately wanting to go beyond the usual earnest diplomacy or stunts, and not realising quite how many others felt the same way. During the few days that I was involved in holding up Waterloo Bridge in April 2019, I bumped into a stream of friends and acquaintances from two decades of campaigning, all of us having previously run into the same walls and now considering it worth trying something new to communicate the urgency of the situation. There was a powerful sense in which it worked: we won acknowledgement – from the country, and from the government – that we are in a climate emergency. It moved us to the much more difficult next stage: sufficient action, and dealing with the backlash.

Mark Ovland was one of the Extinction Rebellion (XR) protesters pulled off that train roof at Canning Town six months later. He agreed that while a lot of people in XR had been 'acting out of fear and distress', he drew on a sense of grounding that he carried from a 'spiritual opening' – an experience of oneness with the divine – years earlier. He was influenced in his protests by his Dharma teacher, Rob Burbea, who died young of cancer in early 2020, not long after Ovland was released from remand.

Burbea encouraged Buddhists to take a more active role as part of their spiritual path; he was responsible, Ovland says, for getting many Buddhists off their meditation cushions and into practical action. Ovland dropped out of training at a Buddhist retreat centre to throw himself into

Extinction Rebellion in 2019, and thinks he was arrested ten or twelve times for protests that year.

'I was doing what I thought was a good thing to do, with as much compassion and wisdom as I could bring to do that. I've seen the science and what everyone's said, I understand the urgency, but it doesn't or hasn't impacted me in a way that causes overwhelm of distress or despair. My question always in life is, *How can I best be of service?*'

The night before the action, he told me, the twelve of them involved (trains were held up at other stations too) were informed that Extinction Rebellion participants, via a poll, did not think they should go ahead. They decided to sleep on it and reconvene in the morning. It was gut-wrenching, he said: 'One of the loneliest times of my life.' He thought that many of the opposing views were based on fear that people might be trapped in tunnels, and reasoned that they might not know the action was designed for an above-ground station specifically to prevent that. The protests out on the streets were faltering, more proactive police action making them less impactful than the two-week roadblocks with the iconic pink boat in the middle of Oxford Circus six months earlier. 'There was this genuine sense of, this is the big thing and it might just cut through. Even if I'm hated afterwards, in the country or by XR, if it cuts through then I'm willing to do it.'

But the criticism was intense: in the media, and within Extinction Rebellion. Recriminations and arguments about democratic control of its protest actions – including ones, like this, that involved some central planning – raged into the following year. Ovland didn't know much about all that for the first two months because he was on remand, having broken bail conditions from a previous protest holding up the Docklands Light Railway in April. A friend posted some articles to him in HMP Thameside.

'I didn't take it personally,' he said. 'For the large part I saw where they were coming from, and if I had been a Londoner watching TV and saw this, I'd have thought, *What dickheads, what the hell are they doing?* We weren't from London. We had no idea that Canning Town is a working-class area. We were told it was the gateway to the financial district and we would be stopping bankers getting into the city. Whether I would have gone ahead knowing that, I don't know.' In court he said that in hindsight he thought it was the wrong thing to do, although, he added to me, he didn't regret doing it. 'Not because I thought we were "right" – I'm not even sure "right" and "wrong" are that helpful here – but because I'd done the best I could with the information in front of me, and acted in line with my conscience and my values. That's not something I can regret, no matter the outcome.'

It is easy to denounce what happened at Canning Town, especially if we're seeking to make ourselves feel 'good' or 'pure' or 'knowing better'. I was grateful for Ovland's openness to discussing his thought process, so that others in a similar position might potentially benefit in the future. We've spoken a handful of times since 2019; he seems sincere, less ego-driven than many campaigners I've met, and is consistent across conversations. 'I'm not interested in coming out of this shining,' he said at one point.

Yet while Ovland may have been driven less by a state of embodied personal urgency than others involved in Extinction Rebellion, the wider context for the action was a movement running on urgency. (Just Stop Oil was too; it would be fair to suggest it's a key characteristic of both movements' co-founder Roger Hallam, who in 2024–5 served thirteen months of a four-year sentence, reduced on appeal from five, for taking part in a Zoom call to plan a direct action.) And I think that in its extremity, Canning Town is a useful illustration of one of urgency's problems: that it cuts off connection.

'Urgency can serve a collective purpose in bringing people together,' says Nick Anim, who we met in Chapter 3. Nick is not short on motivational urgency himself. Over just one weekend while I was writing this chapter our messaging-app chat contained his photos from three different protests: on Saturday, for a ceasefire in Gaza, on Sunday against antisemitism and, the previous weekend, protesting outside BAE Systems against weapons exports to Israel.

'If we're fighting [the] government's policies on the environment, or draconian policies on protest rights, it brings a lot of us together. It can make this bridge. But it can also cause breaking,' Anim said.[14] (See Chapter 3 on the purity aspects of breaking and bridging.) The potential for 'breaking', at Canning Town, was with the community on that platform who were trying to get to work – and, potentially, with anyone who identified with them.

Thinking about what Ovland had told me, it seemed that good intentions and a personal spiritual foundation may be insufficient to prevent urgency-related misjudgements. Let's think for a moment back to that definition of white saviourism from Chapter 5: benevolence or altruism without awareness of the roots of material inequality. Here, we're looking at how save-the-world motivation without enough political-material awareness can create disconnection problems. It leads to a deprioritising of connection with those affected – either by the problem, or by your protest (sometimes they are the same people).

Once Covid-19 struck, Ovland left Extinction Rebellion. 'I didn't feel the disruption was that helpful any more...

Now we really need to connect more. I really want to be involved in connecting.' He read books about politics, race and inequality. He tried to get a campaign off the ground using direct-action methods to tackle inequality, and approached groups already working on the issue, but they weren't keen to collaborate. He has since returned to Buddhism, teaching and running retreats and, like his old mentor, 'encouraging people to act according to their conditions and what they're able to do.'

*

'It was like Mordor, or *Blade Runner*. Every few minutes a cannon would fire, to stop birds landing and keep animals away. Toxic lakes. I remember this moment where I thought, I don't actually know who we are, to do this.' Suzanne Dhaliwal is describing walking through the Athabasca tar sands in Canada – one of the biggest carbon bombs on the planet.[15] An area of Alberta bigger than England is being raked over for shale oil, composed of thick bitumen that is mixed with sand and is impossible to extract without vast quantities of power and water; without completely destroying the land and everything that lives on it. It was tar-sands mining trucks that I was thinking of when I saw Denis Villeneuve's vision of the monstrous spice harvesters in the *Dune* films.[16] These ones were being financed not by an intergalactic empire but by British banks, among many other financial institutions.

Tar-sands oil had been known about for decades, but as more conventional oil sources diminished and prices rose in the 2000s, it became more 'economic' to extract at scale. (There is, obviously, much to unpack in this use of the word 'economic'.) Oil companies including Shell and BP got involved,[17] as did UK financial institutions including

Barclays and HSBC.[18] The consequences have been catastrophic. Boreal forest that is as critical as the Amazon to global climate tipping points has been felled;[19] huge tailings ponds leak poison into ground water;[20] by 2024 the air pollution was found to be up to sixty-three times worse than the industry had previously reported.[21] To say that indigenous communities have lost hunting and fishing land and are suffering increased rates of cancer and other illnesses – all of which is true – doesn't begin to take account of the psychological and spiritual impact of this desecration of their home.[22]

I wanted to meet Dhaliwal because she worked hard, from the mid-noughties, to raise awareness of this devastation in the UK. In her mid-twenties she left her secure-ish NGO job and created the UK Tar Sands Network, a coalition of campaign groups highlighting the destruction, supporting indigenous communities and exposing the European companies and banks involved. They brought indigenous protesters to the UK to front the campaigns, booked them media slots, targeted shareholder meetings, and staged protests in front of banks and conferences.

I was interested to hear how she handled urgency and the desire to make a difference. She was swept up in it, and there was an intensity to living in that feeling. 'I got rid of all my stuff. I thought by 2012, we'd all be underwater. I only just started saving recently,' she told me. 'I was this five-foot-two Brummie girl running round challenging these corporations. We were under surveillance, I was listed as a terrorist by the Canadian government.'

As Ovland had, she described a sense of spiritual surrender to necessary work. 'I can understand it scientifically, economically, legally, but there's a spiritual direction for me because how could I possibly know how to respond to something so big?' she said. 'It's bigger than me. I know I collaborate with other forces to do the things that I did, and there's a humility: that's what I was trained to do. For me that reaction was very humble – clean up your house, minimise your things, pray, get your body strong and be ready for service – and that's part of being Sikh. When you can see that people are already dying, when you visit the tar sands, the sense of time is very different. The climate crisis is not in the future. We're in it, and we've been living through apocalypse – it just depends where you're situated on the planet.'

Dhaliwal criticised Extinction Rebellion at the time because, she said, it didn't check in with existing climate campaigns or communities in London before proceeding.[23] This risk – of not connecting – can happen across change efforts, and Dhaliwal was aware of it. A core principle of the UK Tar Sands Network, she said, 'was that all of the actions had to happen with input, consent and consultation with the indigenous communities.' But often the sense of urgency 'would mean that there's not enough time for that. Just get the press release going, make a plan. So that delicate work of solidarity which involves extra diligence, that late-night Zoom call – that work is steamrollered, and the justification is always the urgency. It's *always* the time. It's used as an instrument of colonisation, a deprioritising. That was something I had to rally against, which meant working around the clock, or being seen as someone who's slowing things down.'

Dhaliwal is also an artist, and one of her pieces is a megaphone, reverse-engineered to be a listening device. 'Somebody asked me to describe what I do, and at the time I didn't have language for all of the care and consultation and work that was going into it. Then I put this megaphone to my ear and it's just that. You stop, and you listen. You put your ear to the ground, and to the communities, to the land, to the sea – then you take that in, and with your strategies and your gifts and your positionality, your proximity to power, you develop the strategies that are in service. That's it really. Yes, we need to examine our power and our privilege, but [when it's] "go" time: can you quiet yourself? Can you calm your ego and your desire? When you work with artists, they're like – "I'm going to come up with something amazing in response to the climate crisis." And sometimes, what is needed is skills, is resources, is care for the people, for the lineages that you're now joining, who have been working to undo settler colonialism, to respond to extractivism. You're coming into a lineage – and how relieving is that?"[24] Another way of putting this: it's not actually all on you.

URGENT TALK

Urgency messaging might work to recruit the already converted – as Extinction Rebellion did with me and many of my friends, those of us most likely to get involved with that kind of climate activism because we already see ourselves as 'activists'. But away from the direct-action frontlines, it doesn't work with everyone else.[25] It doesn't work if you're already in the ongoing emergency of poor or insecure housing, income that doesn't cover bills and food, and the nightmare of navigating the Universal Credit system. To be heard, any climate messaging has to be part of a story about making life fairer, not a race for the same-old-shit but solar-powered.

Even if you're materially more secure, urgency messaging doesn't work if it makes you freeze in anxiety, or because you can't see a role for yourself in it. Some environmental groups had already turned away from sensationalist emergency messaging by 2014 — like images of London underwater — because they realised it wasn't reaching beyond the activist base. A grouping of organisations calling themselves 'Stop Climate Chaos' rebranded as the 'Climate Coalition' and developed a strategy to reach new audiences. 'Show the Love' was about getting people involved to engage with the aspects of nature that they love.

'Many of the activist groups hated it,' Ben Margolis said. 'Because it wasn't about panic and fear, it was gentle and lovely.' While he was running the Climate Coalition for a couple of years from 2020, Friends of the Earth groups were the most actively engaged in Show the Love. 'It helped them to reach new people and expand beyond their base. Suddenly they've got all the Women's Institute people coming to them saying "Let's make green hearts for you." They thought it was brilliant. It was activist groups in head office who sometimes find it more difficult. But they've come on a journey since then, they've realised this stuff works and they need an ecosystem of actors — some of whom are doing the more sensationalist, a lot of whom are doing the more pragmatic.'

For some, not even 'urgent' and 'emergency' frames are enough. The Climate Majority Project (see Chapter 3), while moderate in its tactics, thinks that the rash of declarations of 'climate emergency' after the school strikes and Extinction Rebellion protests of 2019 have normalised the idea of crisis, and we are back into disavowal — knowing the seriousness, but simultaneously turning away from it. They've been trying out a 'five minutes past midnight' message: it's too late to 'save' or 'fix' a world of taken-for-granted stability because further climate breakdown caused by historic fossil fuel emissions is already baked in, so the work now is to cope with adapting to an unknown future.

Acknowledgement opens up a radical space in which we can better face the disturbing task of adaptation to life with flood, fire and uncertain food supplies.[26] And one of the advantages of 'adaptation' over 'prevention' discourse is that with adaptation, it can sometimes be easier to see – and crack on with – what needs to be done locally. At the same time I worry that in an anxious world the paradoxical and nuanced truth of this message – that it *is* too late and yet this is where the work of adaptation really begins – may not work at scale. I worry that what would cut through would only be that 'past midnight', because we're so used to thinking in the binary terms of – as the writer Maggie Nelson puts it – 'fucked or not-fucked'.[27]

We can't get through to people if we terrify them, so we must stay optimistic – but if we do that, we're not going to get through to people. What are we to do? The research is starting to shake out, said all the climate-communications people I spoke to. For most people, an 'emergency' message is likely to disengage them and fuel fatalism – unless they can see something specifically for them in that message, something more than just being told to write to their MP.

'Is it important for my neighbours who don't think about climate change every day to know that it's urgent?' asks Margolis, who is now back working as a campaign strategist. 'I'm not sure how that helps us. What we need is for them to feel empowered to take the small actions, and ideally to take some bigger actions. This is about building a social mandate for change, and we do not have a social mandate for the type of political action that we need. Next time that there's a proposal for onshore wind turbines nearby, what's going to stop my neighbours from trying to close it down? It's not going to be because they're scared about the urgency. It's going to be because they see themselves in this positive green utopian future. And I think that's the important story for them to hear.'

Certainly, it is important to get strategic about how to communicate in a time of urgency. 'Strategic climate communications' became a thing after the failure of the COP15 meeting in Copenhagen, after years in which the sole success metrics for an environmental group might be how many people saw their outputs. Another buzz-phrase is 'narrative change'. But a number of people I met suggested – from various perspectives – that we must move beyond this kind of thinking. Emma River-Roberts, founder of the Working Class Climate Network, who appeared in Chapter 3, said that it was often better to be less utopian and use less abstract terminology, and instead talk about the steps that will get us there. 'I'm not saying throw net zero out, but where we've got these abstract goals where we can see we're failing on graphs, people think, what am I supposed to do with that? Whereas if we campaigned for nationalisation and affordable public transport across the UK, more groups would be aware of how to do that,' she said.

'There is a limit to looking at all this through a lens of "Is this good communication?" That's not how twenty-year transformations work,' I was told by David Powell. When we spoke he was working at Climate Outreach, an organisation providing communications advice. 'Whether or not Just Stop Oil's strategy is right we will only know in hindsight. What else did it enable? What space did it create for more moderate people to say, "I agree with what they're saying, but not with their action"? This is the activist's curse. Someone has to be the radical edge, it's a hell of a thing to bear and there's burnout, but if you don't do it, the more moderate stuff, which reaches eighty percent of people, isn't as stretched as it is.' (Indeed, Just Stop Oil already claim that what they did worked, as the Labour government stopped new oil and gas licences, which was JSO's stated aim.)

Tom Crompton, meanwhile, who introduced many campaigners in the UK to the possibility of using communications to shift people's underlying values (see the final section of Chapter 3), wonders if people's demand for a better response to environmental challenges will come from more than just talking about the environment. Our underlying values shape our perception of multiple issues – and our experience of any one of these issues can affect the strength of our underlying values. 'My experience of seeing a doctor for free on the NHS may be more impactful than the exposure I might have to an NGO communication on climate change in the *Guardian*,' he suggested.

These conversations, taken together, were leading me to the ironic conclusion – which had been growing as this book grew – that sometimes the last people who should be trying to communicate about the climate or persuade people to do things differently are the ones who see themselves as 'climate activists'.

Two things are true at the same time: that those who bravely step up to do direct action are doing what is necessary to break a collective silence. And, that by doing increasingly dramatic or weird things in order to get noticed above the media cacophony, the clearest thing communicated is that their message is not, in fact, about or for everyone.

But even in more moderate approaches, and even if we are desperately trying to figure out how to communicate with people who are not like us, the very fact that we're talking about how to reach 'ordinary people' can be part of the problem. We are still doing it from the awareness that we're something 'else'. And if the medium is the message, the message needs to be delivered not just by us, the niche 'climate' folk.

BURNOUT TIME

My first meditation class, more than twenty years ago, was an evening session for beginners at a local Buddhist meditation centre. The class consisted of a few short spells of guided 'metta', or 'loving-kindness' meditation, which is one of the basics for beginners as well as a core practice for the life-long meditator. It was a close summer evening, thick with pollen and traffic fumes. The stuffy, still room was packed. Our knees pressed together as those of us who couldn't yet kneel on a cushion sat cross-legged in rows on the floor. Almost as soon as I closed my eyes, I was afflicted by intense and multiple discomforts. Itching all over my body; a stabbing in my stomach. I was sweating, felt a tight discomfort around my neck; my eyes were on fire behind my closed lids. I didn't try again for several years.

'It's striking that when people come to a retreat to slow down and simply notice, often what arises is immense turmoil and emotion that their speediness is keeping out of awareness,' says my friend and collaborator, the systems thinker Sophy Banks. Stripped of some of its primary defences against feeling – action, busyness – our body–mind system throws out physical discomfort as distraction. A former engineer and then a psychotherapist, Banks was a co-founder of Transition Towns, an initiative that began in England and spread internationally, encouraging communities to work together to create resilience in the face of climate breakdown. Now she holds grief rituals and burnout retreats, and runs Healthy Human Culture, a collective of facilitators and teachers of which I am a part, sharing radical maps and understandings of what it will take to create better relational culture – interpersonally, in groups, and at scale.

What happens if we don't slow down? Urgency doesn't just affect our relational capacity or the chances of our message being heard; it affects our very ability to function. Many of us are in long-practised, unconscious patterns of urgency in how we act that, cumulatively, exhaust us. These patterns are held in our bodies, often from childhood, supported by a clock-watching culture that values speed, work, achievement and 'doing' over 'being'. Urgency patterns can get built into movements for change. One of the young protesters featured in Jonathon Porritt's 2025 book regarding Just Stop Oil – an otherwise largely positive account – went on the record to say what others have noted behind the scenes: that its 'urgency culture' results in a lot of broken activists.[28]

'It's not that urgency is bad itself,' Banks said. 'Some stress is good. And we like going fast! Then we need to slow down and integrate. If we don't have that, and just keep going, we collapse.'

My body did just that for a year in my mid-twenties. On good days I'd drag myself into work, but the screen would blur in front of me. Eventually I lost my job and bumped along for a while with part-time freelance work. I came to describe my condition as 'burnout' rather than the 'chronic fatigue' that my GP had settled on after some initial weeks of signing me off with 'post-viral fatigue'. That chronic-fatigue diagnosis left me feeling that something was doubly wrong: I was not only ill, but with something that couldn't properly be diagnosed. This umbrella term was applied to all the conditions that weren't something else, or didn't have symptoms people could see or understand, and the same diagnosis covered a whole range of experiences, including people far more ill than I was. I sometimes wished I had a leg in plaster so my limitations were more obvious.

For a while, 'burnout' felt like a label I could wear without having to explain myself so much. It made sense that it happens when we spend too much time with our bodies in stress mode. Until that shutdown, I always threw myself into work with far more intensity than it required. By the time I conked out in 2000, 'burnout' had become a recognised psychological diagnosis that could be applied to people in a wide variety of work settings. It took me longer to learn not to individualise something that is systemic. Burnout is inseparable from the context in which it occurs. My retrospective sense of my shutdown is that it was fuelled by growing up in a family and a wider culture shaped around hard work and the ability to continue without rest.

The literature on workplace burnout sees it in terms of two key imbalances. One is an obvious equation: too many demands backed up by too few resources results in loss of energy. The other relates to energy, but not in entirely material ways: when our personal values conflict with those of our employer, resulting in loss of motivation.[29] For those of us trying to change the world, that motivational imbalance might manifest differently: it can look like the insufficiency and thwarting of our own power when we're up against something so much bigger than ourselves.[30]

While it's not always reflected in the extensive psychological and occupational literature, produced in an academy still shaped by old power relations, burnout is also political. It can happen to anyone experiencing systemic oppression, always up against it, working to mitigate relentless harm and improve conditions for family and community on top of long work hours. It can happen to anyone in a job that is insufficiently valued by neoliberal capitalism. Many folks don't want to call it 'burnout' in this kind of context, because a term that has been so caught up in individualism does not fully recognise the source of the problem in politics and economics. A nursing-union organiser told me that nurses resist the word 'burnout', just as they resist the word 'resilience', because of the way these words get used to suggest that if nurses can't cope it might be their own failing, rather than the effects of insufficient pay and a savagely under-funded work environment. Nurses, like other frontline and first responders to the trauma of others, prefer the phrase 'compassion fatigue', which they see as encompassing more of the structural conditions in which they're working.

Many of the people I met whose work directly supports others in need had experienced some kind of burnout under the urgency pressures of their job. Several had been knocked out by it, sometimes more than once. One woman worked several stints in the Moria refugee camp on the Greek island of Lesbos, built for three thousand of the refugees fleeing Syria, Palestine, Afghanistan, Somalia and Eritrea, but in which – prior to its destruction in 2020 by a fire – thirteen thousand people were stranded by EU migration policies. A human rights lawyer had worked in Palestine for five years, and then, still supporting Palestinians, for another couple of years from Beirut. There was a public health worker who had completed a fraught assignment with Medécins sans Frontières in South Sudan. One former refugee camp worker said: 'There was never time and space to sit down and question: What are we doing here? We're never going to change how the camp in Lesbos looks, and I'm destroying myself in the process.'

In this kind of work you are there precisely to support people in the moment, rather than to change the structural problems that are putting them into such distressing situations. This is why many people cycle in and out of those jobs; it's hard to stay in them long term.

'You can talk all you like about the reality of burnout and having to put your own life vest on first,' said Ella Moore, who used to provide legal support for people seeking asylum in the UK. She now works at the Ulex Project, a centre that runs residential courses for (often exhausted) activists and humanitarian workers in the foothills of the Pyrenees in Catalunya. 'But people will overstep. All the time. In a situation where you are having to respond from your baseline human empathy, because there is little or no structural backup or resource, you're just going to keep giving. If you know that you making that phone call at nine o'clock at night or taking on one more case is going to be the difference for that person, potentially between life or death, or certainly between a really miserable time or [one] that you could have intervened in or made a bit better, it's just very hard from a human level of response to say no.'

We don't need to be in frontline work to succumb to urgency, however. I have lost count of how many people I've met who, driven by the drumbeat of climate news, have thrown themselves into campaigning for a few months or years then realised, as they crashed and burned or came close, that they cannot continue like that. Being on the receiving end of the problems I looked at earlier in the book can contribute to changing-the-world burnout, especially the purity tests (Chapter 3), the knowing-better (Chapter 4) and the saviour attitudes (Chapter 5). So, too, can being on the run from our own feelings of grief. Sometimes it is helpful to look them in the face.

STOP THE CLOCKS

It is Hackney Carnival and the streets are full as sound systems pump out of venues up and down the road. I am indoors at a grief ritual and can't help thinking for a moment that I might prefer to be out there dancing. I am in here, however, because on my own it is too much to hold the fear and grief for what is happening to the world.

'How can you bear to deal with that every day?' people would ask, when I told them about the human rights abuses I was working to stop. Not wanting to be in touch with the pain of the world is one reason why people don't even want to think about all that's wrong, let alone to try to change any of it. The late systems thinker Joanna Macy's insight was that in order for people to respond to the plight of the earth, they need to be able to process the impact on them of the truth of what is happening.[31] Whether the busyness of activist urgency has been keeping grief at bay and it is time to slow down, or whether we've been absorbing urgency messages about the state of the world and are feeling overwhelmed, we might need support in feeling our grief. And if we have not questioned society's messages about pushing pain and grief away, the very idea of attending a 'grief ritual' might seem ridiculous, regardless of whether we have taken on board the magnitude of the threat to the earth's living systems on which we depend.

As we sit in a circle waiting for everyone to arrive, I remember a recent conversation with my friend Emily after she backed away from Extinction Rebellion. When she left, her understanding was that she had been overwhelmed by how much there was to do. Now, a few years later, she could see that the movement's framing of grief for the earth[32] activated her grief for her mother, who had died a decade earlier just before her babies were born, triggering a postnatal depression that suppressed her until the kids began school. It was during those years that Extinction Rebellion took off. Desperately worried and sad about ecological breakdown, she had dived in, ended up running her local group – until she did herself in.

I said, 'Oh! So one kind of grief became the other.'

'They were the same thing,' she replied, after a pause. 'My mother, who created me and was everything. The earth…' She tailed off. She didn't need to repeat '…that created us all, and is everything.' We leaned in silence against her kitchen counter with our mugs of tea, hearing the pad of her lurcher's paws as he came in from the other room to see what was going on.

I had attended other grief workshops as part of climate-related gatherings, but this session during Hackney Carnival is an open one: bring whatever grief you carry. I was reassured by Sarah Pletts, one of the organisers, who says she tries to avoid the 'new age tyranny' of participants feeling they must visibly emote. About half, she says, come full of grief; others find it harder to access their feelings. She told me that Francis Weller, one of the teachers whose lineage this work is in, attended several grief ceremonies before tears fell.[33]

Another important source for this kind of 'grief tending' was a remarkable couple, Sobonfu and Malidoma Somé, from the Dagara people of Burkina Faso; both died too young. They spent much of their energy sharing ancestral teachings that they felt the West badly needed, including the regular expression of grief and pain and, specifically, doing it in community. Many of the growing constellation of grief tenders now working in the UK and US, including Sophy

Banks, learned from them.[34] We need the smaller regular griefs in order not to collapse completely; we need to witness and support one another's grief in order to remain in good relation with each other; not to build up towards war.

'Isn't that what funerals are for?' asked the friend I stayed with the night before the ritual. While not a religious person, he feels that the old rituals do something important and we boot them out at our peril. I'm often minded to agree. Yes, I said, trying not to be defensive – though I suppose it's good if our grief for the world, or our own pain, don't have to build up until the next death we need to mark.

Also, at funerals you're there to mourn the departed person, and while our tears may inevitably have other losses mixed up in them, it's bad form to be grieving too obviously for something else. Grief-tending ceremonies have no hierarchy of grief, no requirement to choose the most grief-worthy of your troubles or even to communicate explicitly what you're there for – and every encouragement to consider that it's all related anyway. Sometimes the grief for the world feels so huge that personal grief can be a doorway. And clearly, anything I say here might also be achieved through the rituals of an existing faith tradition. It's just that, like so many of us, I'm not in one.

We were fifteen: twelve grievers and three 'grief tenders': Sarah, her partner Tony Pletts, and Aama Sade Shepnekhi. After a morning of getting used to being there with each other and to the very idea of sharing grief together – and with a *lot* of tea breaks – there was a very affecting ritual, adapted from Joanna Macy, called the 'bowl of tears', where one by one we came into the middle of the circle to pour water into a bowl and say, if we wished, 'My tears are for…'

Some were silent, and some just wept here, not speaking. Everyone witnesses; you don't try to comfort anyone. I had signed up after several months during which my father, passed for nine long years, had been appearing in dreams. Furthermore, by the time the day came round, my regularly ebbing and surging distress at the violent misogynistic fuckery of the world was in its overwhelm phase. I had recently lost my shit and confronted a bunch of drunken young men on a train when they were shouting and singing at an obnoxious volume, then, when – predictably – I made no headway, I gathered my bags and stormed out of the carriage to ribald jeers.

They were arrogant in taking over a public space, but in losing my sense of humour and ripping off the scold's bridle what I was actually unleashing on them was my fury and grief about rape culture (the trial of Dominique Pelicot who drugged his wife so his neighbours could rape her was underway in France, and Mohamed Al Fayed abusing Harrods staff was in the news). Then there was the situation for women living under Taliban rule in Afghanistan, and the bombing of Gaza, and the butterflies and insects that I had just read that morning were disappearing at ever-faster rates. It was time to take all this somewhere so I could stop shouting at idiots. I said a bit of this, and wept, when it was my turn to pour the water.

After more tea there was a second ritual, where people could go, repeatedly if they wanted, to a grief altar: some crates draped in fabric with stones and other objects placed on top. Others could sit with them for support. Everyone else was singing. We repeated the same two verses for an hour, and they developed that incantatory power that anyone who has sung or played live music knows: a power with capacity to contain and channel the flow of huge feelings. It wasn't that the sadness and anger disappeared. But they moved.

'Growing up, I used to get really depressed and I couldn't understand why, until the word that I put to it was world-pain:

like I could feel the pain of the world,' said Aama Sade Shepnekhi when we spoke a few days later. She is a Sangoma celebrant: beginnings and endings of life; grief ceremonies. 'It would hit me a couple of times a year, I would just be engulfed with the sorrow: *If this is what the world is really like, why am I here?* And then as I grew, I overstood [a Rastafari term for understanding] that this thing I'm feeling, rather than take it in and hold it, I had to let it flow through me. When I learnt the practice of not holding but flowing, it became easier.'

I crawled through the next two days with a crushing headache (not unusual, I was told), then woke on the third, rain-washed, clearer, with energy to act – for the next while, at least. And it wasn't only what I was doing myself that felt good. It was that we were doing it together. I imagined what life could be like if society made space for us to share our vulnerability and pain regularly.

'I find that because grief tending has the element of village, and gives people a little snippet of what it is to be touched and held by community – village watches you at your most vulnerable moment – people come out uplifted,' said Aama Sade. 'What I like about grief tending is it gets a lot of crap out of the way! It allows us to get rid of all the fear of us communing – because community spirit is being eroded,' she added. So it's offering a felt experience of something that can be profoundly missing. It's easy to talk about the need for connection and community as part of political analysis, but harder to act from if we're not really living it.

PLAYING WITH TIME

It's autumn 2022, and we're in a corporate-vibes room on the tenth floor, albeit one with a bright view through full-height windows across the newly developed hinterland behind King's Cross station in London. The carpet is grey, there's a plate of biscuits, someone is trying to fire up Zoom on the big screen for those working at home. Normal office stuff. But the room is full of hubbub, and it's coming from twenty-six people who are time travelling. Half are regular twenty-first-century folk. The other half are from seven generations into the future. With prompts from Phoebe Tickell, the 'imagination activist' running the session, they are conversing earnestly across two centuries. The people from 2222 are grateful for what their ancestors managed to do, and are asking them what it felt like to imagine a better future and then actually to make it happen. No child went hungry after 2032. Green spaces were rewilded a few years later. 'How did you find the motivation?' the twenty-third century people want to know. 'How did you stick with it against the obstacles?'

The time travellers are staff at Camden Council from adult education, children's services, housing, social care and public health. Some work in direct contact with the community, some in back-office roles. They are on an 'imagination activism' programme called Camden Imagines devised by Tickell, formerly a research scientist, and her colleagues from Moral Imaginations, the community-interest company she founded.[35]

Ben Margolis and the other climate communicators I spoke to said that all the audience research points to 'future generations' approaches as the most effective way to fire up people's imaginations and desire to act, regardless of which audience segment you're talking to in the UK. As a frame it's a helpful way to sneak in some urgency: it carries a dose of 'We need to do this now for the children,' but without the nervous-system-overwhelm of 'We're all going to die tomorrow.'

Later, Tickell asks them to spend a few minutes journal-ling, before a discussion. I find myself unexpectedly moved by the soft sound of fervent collective scribbling. 'We hear so much from Greta talking about what we're getting wrong. It was so nice to hear something about what we can do right,' one of the 2022 team reports back. A member of the 2222 cohort is struck by the clarity of the present humans: how clearly they could see what was necessary, and that it was possible to do it.

Camden initially got involved to build a culture of 'psy-chological safety' among staff, so that they can develop the muscle of proposing bold new ideas – or responding to bold ideas from the community – without self-censoring or hiding behind policies and procedures to say no. Tickell, meanwhile, wanted to use imagination to bring care for the next seven generations and the non-human world right into the heart of local government decision-making, as part of a wider aim to reconnect people to values like intercon-nectedness that are under threat. Building on the work of Joanna Macy, her late mentor, she aims to catalyse climate action through the building of 'moral imagination', which she thinks of as 'imagination on behalf of the welfare of the whole.' Camden's is one of several experiments with future-generations thinking.

'We have a major problem with imagination… we can more easily imagine ecological apocalypse or technological advances than improvements in how our society works: better options for health, welfare or neighbourhoods a generation or two from now,' writes Geoff Mulgan, a social entrepreneur and researcher.[36] The Joseph Rowntree Foundation has been funding collective imagination projects and building a network of people and groups involved in many kinds of future-imagining work. Wales now has a Well-being of Future Generations Act which requires public policy to consider the needs of future generations.

When people have not yet stepped out of business-as-usual preoccupations, that 200-year time-travel exercise is a wake-up call, a way to get them seeing beyond the urgency of hamster-wheel earning-to-consume in a materialist system. 'By building an emotional connection with people who will be born who you won't ever meet, it creates a bigger purpose,' says Tickell. 'Your life is about more than just this life here right now; actually you are part of a chain of life, and that's a holy and sacred thing.'

And for people who are already in public service or some kind of change-creating work, connecting with future generations can make clear that things really need to change; that slightly greener capitalism is not going to cut it. 'We help people make sense of living in an "industrial growth system", and to feel, in an embodied way, what that is like. You move around the room in a way that embodies that paradigm for you. People rush around frantically, push each other: "Get out of my fucking way!" We make it funny, but they see it. Then we do the same for a "life-sustaining society"[37] – we invite people to imagine what that looks like. Where do they see it in their community, and in the world, what does it feel like if you embody that? People exhale, it's a relief! What if we had enough? What if we *were* enough?'

Imaginative practices like this can allow us to feel the built-in scarcity that animates our world view the rest of the time. Even if the urgency comes from our fears and hopes about the future, urgency's hijacking of our nervous system keeps us stuck in the tightness of *now*. Stress creates tunnel vision. Under that pressure, we can often only respond to the piece of it in front of us, choosing immediate wins and survival strategies from the same assumptions that have created the world we are in.

Chris Shaw, a climate-policy researcher, notes how extensively climate-related discourse – including the setting of political targets – is constrained within existing middle-class liberal (and thus capitalist) assumptions, such as, for example, that climate breakdown is not a challenge to individualism, or that the world we are aiming for is 'this world, minus emissions'. Such visions of net-zero futures still tend to feature capitalist economies providing everything we need and want, where the longed-for 'transformations' are anything but.[38] The narrowing of perspective wrought by urgency helps to trap us in this hall of mirrors.

Like Tickell, Ella Saltmarshe plays with multi-generation timescales. She also gets, as she puts it, geological. It was a sudden insight. Nearly a decade ago she was looking after her nephew at her mum's house. He was doing that toddler thing of bumbling around the room, and had settled for a while on the satisfying task of banging a cupboard door. She was keeping an eye while reading – as climate wonks tend to – an article about climate change. Like the other climate communicators I've spoken to, Saltmarshe knew on some level that what they were doing wasn't really working. Suddenly she realised the rhythmic banging had stopped, and looked up to see that the free-standing cupboard, a tall one, was tipping over.

She still doesn't know how she got there in time, but she leaped up, took its weight and levered it upright. As she cuddled the boy, her mind was alight: here she was, reading about terrifying outcomes for the biosphere and human civilisation by the end of this century if we don't act. And also here she was, rescuing this beloved child from immediate doom. By the end of the century, she realised, she wouldn't be around to rescue him or his generation from what is coming.

'It was quite a transformational experience – of feeling intergenerational empathy and feeling very different about the future even though I'd been working on climate futures for so long. *If this is so transformative for me,*' she thought, '*can building intergenerational empathy be helpful for others?*' There's a lot of fire in me to try and do my part in ensuring that life gets to continue for a long time,' she said. She co-founded the Long Time Project, a collaboration with artists, scientists, philosophers, policymakers and others, to call on people to act on behalf of future generations and become better ancestors. They do so by sharing felt experiences of timescales – geological, civilisational – that feel like the opposite of urgency.

'It's funny, I find it so hard to remember all the eras and get the names right, and I've never been that interested in rocks,' Saltmarshe said. 'But the more time I spend in geological time, the more I keep discovering these different moments that show how improbable life on earth is. It makes me realise the insane serendipity of our lives, of complex life at all. I think getting geologic helps people understand what's at stake, how many billions of years we are about to destroy – well, a small group of people are about to destroy, so quickly and so violently.'

She and her colleagues at the Long Time Project work with policymakers and culture-makers, though many of the practices they offer are on their website so anyone can use them in meetings in their workplaces or communities. A simple one is having an empty chair at meetings, to represent future generations. She gets people doing 'deep time' walks, and her Long Time Academy podcast series, co-produced with the Headspace meditation app (a cunning way, as I see it, of sneaking radical information into the culture via an accepted and not obviously 'activist' portal) includes a 'well of deep time' meditation.

A mellifluous voice takes listeners down into the planet's ancient past, through dinosaurs and ferns, single-celled organisms and bacteria, all the way to its formation 4.5 billion years ago, then brings us back up knowing that those first elements, crashing into the early earth on asteroids and comets, are now in our bodies; that our eyes have evolved from the visual apparatus of millions of years of creatures. It's a good antidote to the paralysing urgency induced by one of the most widely known deep time metaphors: the one with our geologic past as twenty-four-hour clock, humans emerging just over a second before midnight.

Saltmarshe agrees with the geologist Marcia Bjornerud's view that the geologic clock image denies us a future: 'It's such armageddon thinking that we are reaching midnight and have no long future in front of us. It also misrepresents the huge impact we've had as a species in those ninety seconds we've been around.'[39]

'Civilisational' ways of doing time, on the other hand, are an antidote to the problems presented by the idea of the anthropocene. That humans have begun to leave a record of our disruptions in the geologic record is not disputed.[40] But that term anthropocene suggests that humans are a problem, full stop. A more accurate suggestion is that we should call it the 'capitalocene'.[41] Looking at time on a civilisational scale, Saltmarshe says, reminds us that the current systems we live under are neither immutable nor eternal. Ways of ordering society come – and they go. The peril we're in is not the inevitable result of 'humans', but of a particular shape of civilisation and culture which it's easy, living within it, to equate with being human.

If we think this is what being human is — destruction, conflict, selfish accumulation, lack of mature leadership (and that is often all we see in the news) — we may get very stuck. I've been stuck here. It was around the time when I went up that mountain for the night (see Chapter 6). This felt different to what had happened when I burnt out a decade earlier. Less physical, less to do with having to figure out how my own self worked. I was living more healthily now: less booze, mostly sleeping enough, climbing and walking at weekends. I was no longer doorstepping celebrities for Rupert Murdoch but doing human rights work I cared about: producing investigations, meeting law-makers, trying to curtail the worst activities of companies and greedy individuals. But I was falling into the chasm between practical-tasks-to-meet-achievable-aims and my realisation of what was actually needed.

Wildlife numbers were collapsing within my lifetime; birds were falling silent; violence was spreading. Moving from a culture of extraction to one based on cooperation felt impossible at any scale beyond the micro. I felt over-whelmed by the devastations of modernity.

This is common in our time, although it is not a new experience.[42] I was seeing, as others had before me, that capitalism is not fixable on its own terms; that it has been extracting and destroying (even while creating wealth for some) since its beginnings; that the extractive mindset goes back further, to the beginnings of empires and patriarchy. And for a while, I was flattened. Though I always knew, rationally, that what I was doing wasn't enough on its own, it had felt like reducing harm in the short term was 'worth it'. But now my will for trying to 'fix' this flawed system was diminishing.

This, for Saltmarshe, is where 'civilisational' timescales come in. There will be worlds in the future without capitalism, racism or misogyny, and thinking on a civilisational scale helps us to be able to imagine this. adrienne maree brown, the Detroit-based activist whose teaching, writing and social media presence shares generative images towards changing the world, offered Saltmarshe an image of the history of our species as the geology of the Grand Canyon: one day capitalism and white supremacy will just be rock strata, artefacts. Layers of generative systems will be built on top.

This kind of imagination is what science fiction writers can help us with. brown draws her inspiration from Octavia Butler; others from Ursula K. Le Guin. We can also educate ourselves about how some indigenous cultures have carefully stewarded the ecosystems they live in for millennia,[43] and found ways to deliberately maintain peace with each other despite the difficulties.[44]

What this means, however, is that we have to be prepared to do work whose outcomes we may not see in our lifetime. This was perhaps the insight I hadn't realised I was looking for when I spent that despairing night on the mountain. And it has been the biggest change in me since those very low years. I have started to know and accept in my bones that we might not 'win' in my lifetime.

You could say, 'But how ridiculous ever to have thought that you might! Look back through history; look how long it took to achieve the rights that we do have; look how many reversals there have been.' But for those of us who have thus far benefitted from current power structures, who are raised to aim for status, who are used to more immediate gratifications, it can feel hard, at first, to be such a small part in something.

Maybe we can engage our imaginations to connect with future generations and thus inspire useful work. And maybe we can acknowledge 'movement ecology', the helpful idea that everyone is playing their part in different ways (see Chapter 3). But it's next-level, for relatively privileged modern citizens, to consider that we might not live to get what we want *and* that that is still no reason not to try.

In the language of philosophy, this is a kind of virtue ethics, where a course of action is chosen based on it being the moral thing to do, rather than consequentialism, where it is based on the likely outcome. We can talk about being 'good ancestors' all we like, but we're less likely to become good ancestors if we're always striving to pin our names to what we're doing while we're still here. We need to get over ourselves, and our unacknowledged feelings of entitlement to easy fixes and instant results.[45]

People who've been fighting for a long time are already painfully familiar with the reality of apocalypse – the colonised have been living in its wake for five hundred years[46] – and of not-winning. Yet they keep going because there is no choice. Resmaa Menakem, a therapist and anti-racist educator in the US who focuses on the bodily, nervous-system reactions that reproduce and uphold racism, says it may take nine generations of work to shift cultures of white supremacy that are transmitted intergenerationally. He does his work of teaching, anyway – and asks white people to start getting their practice in.

In the meantime, treating each other with the care that we wish would enliven the whole world may make joining our change efforts a more attractive prospect for those who are currently not feeling it. Rushing for the urgent result pushes the 'how' we do it to the margins, as we have seen in every chapter.

'Rehearsing freedoms' is a frame used by Healing Justice Ldn, an organisation which supports healing and justice for

marginalised communities affected by structural and interpersonal violence. Inspired by the American abolitionist
scholar Ruth Wilson Gilmore,[47] that phrase 'rehearsing
freedoms' is a potent image suggesting living as if already
free, in the world we want to create, even while experiencing and surviving the problems of this one.

I don't think this phrase can be lifted wholesale for
people not experiencing marginalisation, because the tasks
may be different. Some of us may need to acknowledge *constraints* on our freedom to consume endlessly, or to occupy
space without considering our impact on others or questioning who is not present. But 'rehearsing freedoms' does
convey the importance, for everyone, of creating the world
we want through each of our daily actions, and not just
holding out for the big moment over the horizon in which
we manage to 'save' the world.[48]

By contrast, that phrase 'saving the world' risks encouraging us to think that the task is to fix the world – back
to what it was, for those of us who have largely benefitted
from the way things have been. It's the delusion both of
industrial modernity and of the patriarchal hero we met
in the previous chapter: the delusion that everything can
be brought under control, and that the kind of systems and
technologies that might achieve this will be benevolent to
everyone – or, indeed, much of a change from where we
are now.

WALKING NEW PATHS

Saltmarshe uses the phrase 'long-timism' for these geologic
and civilisational kinds of deep-time perspectives that cultivate care for the future, because she wants to distinguish

them from some of the other kinds of big-timescale thinking going on that have already grabbed the handle 'longtermism'.

Lots of people want a say in what the future looks like, and the billionaires are no exception. The longtermism in the public eye in the first half of the 2020s has been the version that grew out of 'effective altruism' (EA), a movement founded in 2009 by two young Oxford philosophy scholars, Toby Ord and William MacAskill. They wanted to encourage everyone to tithe ten percent of their income to charity, an ambitious and moral idea in itself, and one with long religious roots. If we can save a human life at little cost to ourselves, then it is unethical not to do so. They also wanted people to focus on maximising earnings to give them away, and assess hyper-rationally where to give charitable donations.[49]

Both of these ideas generated many followers and many objections.[50] The obvious problem was their de-prioritisation of critical questions about climate change and political economy: the highest-earning jobs are in the financial sector, those that, in their effects elsewhere, are destroying the biosphere and creating poverty.[51] By 2020, with Silicon Valley tech money flooding in to support EA causes (much more would come the following year from the now-jailed crypto fraudster Sam Bankman-Fried), the founders pivoted their concern. Their utilitarian interest in maximising the greatest good for the greatest number led to an interest in preventing human extinction so that the many billions of potential future humans, who outnumber all the humans living and already passed, can live good lives.

As they see it, the greatest risk here is not climate breakdown – which, they argue, a hugely reduced population of humans will probably survive – but artificial intelligence and engineered biohazards. The urgent importance of getting humanity into a far future in which many billions of lives might be lived outweighed, in some of the more extreme arguments, both the suffering of a billion currently living people and the preservation of a liveable biosphere in the face of climate and ecological breakdown. This techno-utopian view chimed with tech bros; Elon Musk tweeted that MacAskill's book on longtermism, *What We Owe the Future*, 'was a close match for [his] philosophy'. (I should add for transparency that MacAskill and I share a publisher.[52])

It's true that artificial general intelligence and engineered biohazards may present grave threats to future genera-tions, and while I object profoundly to the reduction of life to calculated 'value', I don't doubt MacAskill's sin-cerity in wanting better futures. Yet to many of us outside the Effective Altruism and longtermist movements, this is a colossal, multi-billion-dollar case of getting things arse-about-face.

If you apply a wider thinking that takes into account the role of neoliberal capitalism in creating both poverty and climate breakdown there is still plenty of logic to follow, but it goes the other way. It's that curtailing the power and resources of the super-wealthy would increase the likeli-hood of winning back democratic control of politics from fossil fuel interests, thus allowing collective decision-making towards both current and future humans being able to live with dignity and in accordance with the earth's planetary boundaries (and, indeed, managing artificial intelligence wisely and on the basis of the precautionary principle).

Many of us are working on the basis that this is what might actually maximise the chances of more humans making it into the future with good lives. Kate Raworth's Doughnut Economics, for example, embeds precisely these principles – a floor of dignity, and a ceiling that's commensurate with ecological boundaries. But unless there's something Raworth isn't telling us, it isn't Doughnut Economics that's been getting billions from tech foundations. Nor is it the campaigns to get money out of politics, or the many efforts towards citizens assemblies. I occasionally wonder what might have happened to longtermism had William MacAskill not been hanging out with consequentialist philosophers as an earnest Oxford grad student in search of big ideas, but with Raworth, who at that time was a couple of miles up the road at Oxfam's head office developing the ideas that became the Doughnut.

The critiques of both effective altruism and longtermism took a sharper tone after FTX, Bankman-Fried's crypto fund, went bankrupt in November 2022 and when he was subsequently convicted.[53] 'I suspect that the tech billionaires didn't want to be heroes merely by saving individual lives', wrote the philosopher Leif Wenar. 'That's just what firemen do; that's just what Spider-Man does. The billionaires wanted to be heroes who saved the whole human race.'[54] Reading some of the commentary on Bankman-Fried's fall and its effects on the effective-altruism movement, I found myself, I confess, enjoying a little schadenfreude.

It is not only the charity folk and woolly-jumpered climate campaigners who end up with cultish atmospheres, righteous fervour, purity tests, hero vibes and assumptions that we know better than the people we're trying to help, these behaviours on the save-the-world script. Look, the garlanded philosophers and our tech overlords do it too.

That's how cultural scripts work: they're in the culture. Yet in that recognition of shared pitfalls lies something interesting. It is easy to have a go at a mistaken idea, especially when over-entitled rich people throw heaps of (stolen) money at it. But as William James pointed out 125 years ago in his study of the psychology of religion, 'it always leads to a better understanding of a thing's significance to consider its exaggerations and perversions.'[55] The longtermists are doing an extreme version of something that I think many of us do, which is to see the task of saving the world through the frame of the dominant culture's urgency/collapse polarity – the addict's all-or-bust, the Protestant's work-hard-to-show-you're-saved-else-you're-damned – which operates at every scale we can perceive.

'Burnout' is where we feel this polarity in our bodies. As individuals we run, run, until we collapse. Capitalism, which turned time into money, tells us we must do this: align our survival and success with running, running, to grow the economy. At the societal level the economy must grow, grow, or we collapse into recession. Climate breakdown and ecological collapse will be the planetary level consequence of urgently growing the economy until it destroys the biosphere that makes life possible.

So we see some of these problems, and we try to intervene to save the world. But we don't see that, for most of us in industrialised modernity, the urgency/collapse pattern is in us too. And at every level where we're trying to change things, we can flip from one to the other. Individually, we throw ourselves at it... until we're done in. Groups getting together to make change are pushed into urgency by the founders' way of being, especially if they're action-only people, as founders often are. People who are like them will feel that they belong. Those who don't may not come back, or there may be conflict that leads to burnout. The group collapses.

At the societal level of attempted change, 'green growth' ideas tell us that we can substitute renewables and continue consuming, growing the economy and exploiting workers. But even if that does reduce carbon emissions, we will cross other boundaries for the health of soil, water and air with catastrophic implications for other species and our own food security.[56] And at the interplanetary scale of the long-termists' techno-utopian fantasies, they are pursuing an abstract future for abstract lives at the expense of current suffering and at the risk of climate and ecological break-down, both of which they have the resources to do so much to mitigate.

I see scarcity at the heart of this urgency–collapse pattern. Even those of us not building rockets are often running on unacknowledged scarcity feelings – of the sort that also drive capitalism. Nick Anim often talks about 'learning to die', using the American philosopher Cornel West's lovely phrase that both is, and isn't, literal.

Not-literal, here, because when it comes to our scarcity-mentality, we need to 'learn to die' so that we can act from a sense of abundance that is always, to some extent, accessible, even when material life is scary and difficult. That abundance is found through community and connection: to each other, to our own hearts, to the web of life and, for those so inclined, to higher powers. And literal, because what are we really talking about when we talk about 'collapse'? It is death. Here we are trying to escape annihilation, but in our typically Western and modern way: avoiding the prospect of mortality by keeping urgently running and growing.

Death-denial is inevitably human, an aspect of our singular consciousness and of being the only creature with the knowledge that we are mortal.[57] But it runs strong in the foundations of a linear, extractive culture that has turned us away from the cycles of life, death and compost – and, dare I say it, from the old divine feminine in her

death-dealing crone aspect, surplus to patriarchal requirements and long since diabolised and turned into the witch.
We try to break the circle of life and death by insisting
that our economic system's linear waste-creating produc-
tion lines and unending growth can persist forever. The
painful irony is that by not thinking clearly enough about
our individual mortality, we are creating the conditions for
extinction.

The undeniable urgency of mitigating existing and future
breakdown makes it hard to discern that, at each scale, there
are paths we can take *between* the poles of urgency and
collapse, even if we have to walk them into existence ourselves. I have learned to articulate these, and am still learning
to put them into practice, through working with Sophy
Banks and her profound vision for creating 'return paths' to
'healthy human culture'. At each level of scale, we are re-
joining aspects of life that have been artificially sundered by
the ruling culture of extraction. These mistaken separations
are driven by the ultimate separation of modernity – of
ourselves from the rest of life, with the foundational feeling
of scarcity that such a break brings.[58]

On our own, we can learn that we are not our thoughts
or feelings, and start to notice when we're being pushed
into action by stories from the outside world (Consume!
Achieve! Save!) or stories from inside ourselves (Be good!
Don't feel! Gain approval! Be liked!). We can break up our
action with periods of rest; learn where our internalised
voices saying 'no rest' are coming from and choose whether
to listen to them.[59] We can slow down and create space to
notice and connect with non-human kin: in the urgency
of our work to save it we can end up further disconnecting
from the natural world. We can look for collective support in
feeling our grief to help dissolve our own urgency/collapse

polarity, and can experiment with what it feels like to work on an urgent issue, yet without so much urgency in our bodies. This is one cutting edge of the growing field of somatic work at the moment.[60] Within ourselves, then, we put *action* and *rest* back into relationship. Perhaps I should remember to take a breath, here. Perhaps you might, too.

In our groups, we can build cultures where reflection, repair and relationship have a legitimate space alongside tasks, thus resourcing ourselves in a more circular economy of care and action. From the very first meeting, the people calling a new venture into being can create a certain body feeling, a set of norms about how to be. Do we listen to everybody in the room? Do we put care as well as task at the centre of meetings? A healthy relationship between *task* and *relationship* reflects the natural outwards–then–inwards cycle known by the tides, the seasons, and anybody who's ever had a menstrual cycle. We can build in feedback loops like regular check-ins so that there is opportunity, amid the urgency, to recognise when our group 'system' is heading for conflict or burnout.[61] In our strategies for change, we can connect with others who have a stake, and listen to what they have to say, and ensure the people with experience lead if they wish to. In our groups and organisations, then, we put *action* and *time-for-connection* back into relationship.[62]

In our aims for the world and the necessary transformations of economy and society, we can recognise that there are many more options than those two polarised tales of business-as-usual versus apocalypse. There are an infinite number of potential stories where we accept that the task is not to return some of us to the blind state of enjoyment of modernity's boons that prevailed for a while before we realised the truth about climate and ecological breakdown. It is to create a world where we put life and the relationships that support it and make it worth living at the centre of whatever we do. When we do this, we put *economy* back into relationship with *care*.

Many of you are already working towards these stories, and many more of you, I hope, might be inspired to join if you don't have to be bound by the save-the-world script. All that tech money, meanwhile, could go towards creating these just and sustainable futures on our own, still lovely, green-and-blue planet.

AFTERWORD

I frequently felt almost overwhelmed by the wisdom, joy, energy, commitment and generosity of everyone I interviewed for this book, and it thrills me to share some of these conversations. Trying to make change is never just about the campaigning, or community-building, or activism, or service, or organising, or volunteering, or being a good citizen, or whatever you call what you do. It's about meaning, survival, friendship, purpose, identity, togetherness, joy and having a laugh; it's about conflict, disruption, trauma, grief, recovery and holding; it's about politics, psychology, sociology, philosophy, history, theology and, sometimes, poetry.

Likewise, the ill-effects of the save-the-world script are not just problems for change-making but help illustrate the wider crisis, since the script emerges from the culture around us. So the do-gooder's desire to be both 'good' and 'pure' drives – and is driven by – the ancient human dynamics of projection and group-bonding that create the 'other'. The protester's habit of identifying with their own viewpoint and giving people a hard time for not already knowing what they know – let alone for not agreeing with them – fuels resentment against those who look like they're still benefitting from the economic system, resentment exploited by the far right. The knowing-better habits of political activists, politicians and charity, 'development' and

NGO professionals emerge from class and racial hierarchies – and are also a reflection of the delusions of liberalism that its ways of knowing and seeing, and its information-provision habits, are the only game in town.

The heroic-saving habit says something about what we are not willing to relinquish. If we are in a saving relation to *other people*, we don't want to give up the perception of our own power or exceptionalism, nor admit that we, too – and possibly the culture that we are from – might need some work.

And if we think we need to save *the world*, then I suspect that underneath might lie our unwillingness to accept we must change how we live. We don't want to give up the fantasy that the earth's complex biophysical systems are subject to human control, no matter how much we misuse them, and that if we could only find the right political, technological or legal intervention everything would work out.

Conversely, then, the antidotes to the save-the-world script that interviewees have shared are potential offerings not just to change-makers, but to everyone. Taming the desire for 'goodness' and 'purity' in ourselves makes us better collaborators and potentially leads to better communication, but more widely it reduces othering, and points to the priority of developing social media models that don't profit from this evolved aspect of human psychology.

Giving people the opportunity to reach their own understanding and not just to absorb what we already know: this is certainly the basis of effective communication. But it could also underpin a refreshed political system rooted in more grassroots, local and deliberative democracy.

Organising to build people power is the only way to win when we have no or little access to real power (an old lesson that may be new to those who previously assumed some access to power). But it is also the only way our communities might adapt to and survive already-baked-in climate breakdown.

Finally, contributing 'in service' rather than as saviour, and metabolising our hero desires so we don the hero's cape only when it supports us to stand up against the odds, will, yes, help to prevent us from re-enacting existing power dynamics and burning ourselves out. But these moves are also the foundations for a political and social economy that puts care for life and its cycles at the centre of everything, and that is no longer dominated by heroic fantasies of endless linear growth.

Look, we can't fix ourselves entirely. We can care mightily about our neighbours, and about those suffering nearby or far away. We can move mountains to help them or to prevent worse things happening, to protect the natural world and mitigate climate breakdown. Yet we will remain troubled, blinkered, prone to avoiding our own dark side, sometimes overreaching and sometimes wishing we didn't have to do anything. Indeed, we may be working on precisely the problem-in-the-world that reflects our own not-so-good side. We are unconsciously drawn towards the very knot we haven't yet resolved in ourselves: the wound that seeks expression and healing. So we may end up focusing on the very thing that embodies a vulnerability of our own.

This is the more subtle aspect of what I meant in Chapter 4 when I said that many change-makers have 'lived experience' of a problem even if it is not at all obvious. People who have experienced a lack of accountability from adults in their early life may demand justice and account-ability from corporations and people in power... and baulk at being accountable to their own colleagues. People compensating for never quite feeling 'enough' might work passionately towards new paradigms of post-capitalist sufficiency... and get stuck in their own scarcity stories. This isn't saying that campaigns derive only from our blind spots – just that some of us can be drawn towards particular issues, and that these dynamics intersect with those arising from our positionality.

What is seeking resolution in me? In campaigning for justice, it used to be a version of that accountability example. I have become more aware of it over the last decade, and in consequence it has less hold over me. It is a subtle shift: I feel freer to go after things simply because they matter for the world. Most authors would say that something *really* has to bother them to justify the long labour of writing a book, however. I suspect the unresolved (and maybe lifelong) tension in me now is that I hold so passionately a vision of a more cooperative and peaceful world, and yet I know how easily the activation of my own nervous system can still elicit my fight-or-flight response and tip me towards control or dominance. I know how I can become not-good.

You could argue that each of the instructions on the save-the-world script derives, in effect, from a trauma reaction. And if the script comes from the culture, then I'm saying that trauma reaction pervades the culture, too. By 'trauma' I don't only mean the occurrence of serious harm or fear in the moment that it happens, but the failure of subsequent holding that, individually, leaves us prone to dysregulation, and societally, over many generations, leaves us misunderstanding the true nature of what it is to be human. A failure of holding-after-trauma leaves us thinking we are on our own. And by 'reaction' I mean not just our personal experiences of this feeling of isolation, but the way – as the author and anti-racist educator Resmaa Menakem so brilliantly describes – that the coping patterns become locked down over time as personality, family style and, inter-generationally, as culture.[1]

I think the save-the-world script draws strongly on such patterns, modelling a way of being and acting that dashes into urgency because our bodies are so often in fight-or-flight mode. The script also implicitly suggests its opposite, numbness, if we are repelled by or can't see an alternative to the frantic urgency. Both urgency and numbness are embodied habits, more than literal or conscious beliefs. But such embodied habits, passed on across generations, create culture through a reinforcing feedback loop between self and society.[2]

What the antidotes to the save-the-world script have in common, as illustrated by so many of the stories I am sharing, is their emphasis on relationship. I did not plan this aspect of the book as I did not know exactly what I would find when I followed my curiosity to see how some campaigners are managing to subvert the script. Yet it was no surprise to see it. The current excess of power in the hands of rich men who happen to be good at tech and growing money is the inevitable product of a culture that for centuries has conflated narrowly defined intellectual, technological and financial prowess with 'progress', 'advancement' and 'development'.

Sidelined and devalued by this focus have been intuitive and relational skills, lifelong support for the development of emotional maturity, and the maintenance of social practices by which together we support people who have experienced harm to metabolise their pain and return to a regulated state so that they are less likely to discharge it repeatedly over others in order to feel better. Seeking to avoid pain and vulnerability is very human, but one of the hallmarks of the dominator approach to life – and thus of any group whose identity is built on feeling superior to others – is to make culture out of the avoidance of pain and the projection of these unwanted feelings onto scapegoated others.

It's one thing to observe these dynamics among those whose justifiable economic resentment is being manipulated for divide-and-rule purposes – but it applies also to those who wield the power to manipulate. What might collective grief and healing look like, in communities harmed by exploitation and deindustrialisation?[3] What might it look like for everyone? What might well-held discussion and digestion of interlocking and shared histories look like, at scale and in different locations in mainstream culture? It's true that some of the social tools we need are rusty. Old shared 'return paths' from pain and trauma – like communal grief, dance, music and carnival – have not thrived in the Protestant lands.[4] And more widely, holding and healing have long been individualised and confined to the private and women's domains, and to religion and spirituality. They re-emerged in Western modernity in the form of individualised psychotherapy and, collectively, late in the twentieth century, in rave culture.

Yet we evolved to regulate each other. The pushback against social media's weaponisable capacities focuses on its power to hook our nervous systems to a global tumult of dysregulation: a boon for far-right strongmen and manosphere influencers who promise simplistic comfort in the form of dominance. As defence, we're encouraged to switch ourselves and our kids off from the social media mayhem. But even if we could abstain, that will not disrupt our underlying isolation within the individualised self unless we rebuild relationships of interdependency and care, become more skilled at relating to each other, and create public spaces in which to do it – perhaps starting in our hollowed-out high streets.

Love is not all we need, but we do need more of it, and change-making is a great place to practise together: both in the shared action, and when we reflect on what we're doing and what we're bringing to it. Even if we don't think we are working for dramatic political goals, we may yet be doing something huge if we start to rebuild webs of relationship. This is why I think there was something quietly radical, and that inevitably escaped notice, in what Martin Forde KC was saying about the Labour Party in his 2022 report into its antisemitism and racism problems. He wasn't only making the obvious and sadly necessary point about preventing bullying, racism, antisemitism and other forms of discrimination and hate. He was saying, as I read it, that the forming of good relational culture should be at the heart of everything, even in environments where there is inevitable political difference.

I was finishing writing as Donald Trump began his second term, and as Israel's genocide in Gaza continued. It can be hard to keep going when every week there is some new assault on morality or good sense. There are troubles this book cannot solve. And yet the antidotes to the script might support us to line up coalitions of resistance against authoritarian threats to everyone's freedom and survival. The antidotes to the script might help us to see that even if we cannot ourselves 'save the world' – politically, ecologically – there is still, and always, value in offering service, solidarity, resistance, resilience and care. In fact, these may come to be the things that matter most. The idea of saving the world carries a great danger: that when we realise we cannot, we don't try anything at all. But in any given moment, so long as we are here, things can be made better.

FURTHER READING

I am one thread in a vast intergenerational web of thinking and action. The sources I draw on directly are cited in the endnotes. What follows is a selected list of works that have shaped my thinking or that attend to aspects of change-making beyond the scope of this book. I have omitted most subtitles for ease of reading.

The last few years have seen some excellent how-to and why-to books about campaigning, including Mikaela Loach's *It's Not That Radical* (DK, 2023), Joshua Virasami's *How to Change It* (#Merky Books, 2020), Kajal Odedra's *Do Something* (Hodder & Stoughton, 2019), Jane Holgate and John Page's *Changemakers* (Policy Press, 2025), and Deepak Bhargava and Stephanie Luce's *Practical Radicals* (The New Press, 2023) There are also many resources online offering ways to think about roles and strategy, like the Sheila McKechnie Foundation's Changemakers' Toolkit, the Ayni Institute's Five Foundational Theories of Change, and Bill Moyer's Movement Action Plan.

Change-making is also about the power to imagine that things can be different, as exemplified by New York abolitionist organiser Mariame Kaba in *We Do This 'Til We Free Us* (Haymarket Books, 2021). Rebecca Solnit's *Hope in the Dark* (Canongate, 2004/2016) pushes back against the idea that we have to succeed straightaway for our action to 'count'. Jon Alexander's *Citizens*, with Ariane Conrad (Canbury Press, 2023), is about the shift from 'consumer' to 'citizen'; Rob Hopkins' *Falling in Love with the Future* and *From What Is to What If* (Chelsea Green, 2020 and 2025) are about using imagination more boldly. Leticia Neto's *Beyond Inclusion, Beyond Empowerment* (Cuetzpalin, 2010) is helpful in navigating identity, oppression and privilege, from multiple perspectives.

My growing sense over years of campaigning that we were recreating some of the problems we were trying to solve first found words in Audre Lorde's essay 'The Master's Tools Will Never Dismantle the Master's House' in *Sister Outsider* (The Crossing Press, 1984). My instinct that the healing, psychological and spiritual aspects of trying to change the world needed attention was first given voice by Alastair McIntosh's *Soil and Soul* (Aurum, 2004) and Joanna Macy's idea of 'Work that Reconnects', which she set out in several books including, with Molly Young Brown, *Coming Back to Life* (New Society, 2014) and, with Chris Johnstone, *Active Hope* (New World Library, 2012). Alastair McIntosh's *Spiritual Activism*, with Matt Carmichael (Green Books, 2016) sets out what a spiritual foundation to activism might look like. Over the past decade adrienne maree brown's writing on change-making has been sympathetic and insightful, including *Emergent Strategy*, *We Will Not Cancel Us* and *Loving Corrections* (all AK Press, 2017, 2020 and 2024) – and let's just say that online, her presence and memes are life-giving.

Work from the field of 'political somatics' brings together healing, justice and change-making and busts any illusions that 'inner' and 'outer' aspects of change, politics – and, indeed, reality – are separate: Prentis Hemphill's *What It Takes To Heal* (Cornerstone Press, 2024), Resmaa Menakem's

My Grandmother's Hands (Penguin, 2021), Staci Haines' *The Politics of Trauma* (North Atlantic Books, 2019) and Susan Raffo's *Liberated to the Bone* (AK Press, 2023). Work from climate psychology also dissolves the inner/outer duality, like Steffi Bednarek's edited collection *Climate, Psychology and Change* (North Atlantic Books, 2024). Camille Sapara Barton's *Tending Grief* (North Atlantic Books, 2024) argues for attending to grief as part of change-making work and offers practices. *Sustaining the Climate Justice Movement: A Psychosocial Resilience and Regenerative Activism Training Manual* (Ulex, 2022, online), compiled by activist training groups the Ulex Project and Transformative Education, offers theory and practical exercises.

On saviourism's manifestations in the UK, Darren McGarvey's *Poverty Safari: Understanding the Anger of Britain's Underclass* (Luath Press, 2017) and D. Hunter's *Chav Solidarity* (The Class Work Project, 2018) contain first-hand evidence. McGarvey's later book *Trauma Industrial Complex* (Ebury, 2025) reflects on the effects of exposing personal trauma, with implications for questions about the role of lived experience in change-making. Jordan Flaherty's *No More Heroes* (AK Press, 2017) is an account of saviourism in US social action. Themrise Khan, Kanakulya Dickson and Maïka Sondarjee's *White Saviorism in International Development* (Daraja Press, 2023) is a wide-ranging entry point to the literature on that topic. Anand Giridharadas' *Winners Take All* (Alfred A. Knopf, 2018) exposes the hollowness of philanthropic saviourism; Alnoor Ladha and Lynn Murphy's *Post Capitalist Philanthropy* makes radical proposals for a rethinking of philanthropy (Daraja Press, 2022). Barbara Ehrenreich's *Fear of Falling: The Inner Lives of the Middle Class* (Pantheon, 1989) and Betsy Leondar-Wright's *Missing Class* are US-specific but have wider resonance.

Jason Hickel's *The Divide* (Heinemann, 2017), Kojo Koram's *Uncommon Wealth* (John Murray, 2022), Nicholas Shaxson's *Treasure Islands* (Vintage, 2016) and *The Finance Curse* (Bodley Head, 2018) and Oliver Bullough's *Butler to the World* (Profile, 2022) introduce the real economic picture behind the story that rich nations are helping to 'develop' poorer ones with aid, showing instead the systematic extraction of wealth that has persisted since the end of formal empire.

Grappling with 'I know better' also invites the question (to paraphrase Donna Haraway): what kind of thinking do we use to think *with*? And how do we value different kinds of knowledge? Minna Salami's *Sensuous Knowledge* (Zed Books, 2020) makes these questions tangible, as did, a generation ago, Patricia Hill Collins' *Black Feminist Thought* (Routledge, 1990/2000).

I wrote about the implications of psychodynamic thinking for the construction of activist identity in *The Entangled Activist* (Perspectiva Press, 2021), and gained confidence in the legitimacy of looking at change-making through this lens from Andrew Samuels' work on psychology and politics, including *A New Therapy for Politics?* (Routledge, 2015). Samuels' *Jung and the Post-Jungians* (Routledge, 1985) is a useful complement to Jung's thought. Naomi Klein's *Doppelganger* (Penguin, 2023) examines the shadow-double, that evil twin of mythology and psychoanalysis, as it plays out in right-populism, in whiteness and empire, in fascism, and in Israel's settler colonialism. From a decolonial perspective, Vanessa Machado de Oliveira (also known as Vanessa Andreotti)'s bracing *Hospicing Modernity* and its sequel *Outgrowing Modernity* (2021 and 2025, both North Atlantic Books), invite us to 'compost' all of the assumptions most of us will ever have held about saving the world.

ACKNOWLEDGEMENTS

This has been a collaborative work. My immense gratitude goes to the hundreds of change-makers I've spoken to since 2018, who have shared, with great generosity, their time, interest, enthusiasm, experience, analysis, contacts, hope and spirit. You have all influenced the course of the book – regardless of which stories ended up in it – and strengthened my faith in people. I don't want to hold any of you up as individual heroes for all the reasons I unpack in Chapter 6, but at the same time, you are all courageous and loving and some of you have been keeping at it for a long time, and it needs saying how amazing you are.

Gratitude, too, to all those with whom I've campaigned, investigated, organised, strategised, written, marched, grumbled, ranted and sat down in the road, about whom I could say the same thing. Gratitude to the wisdom of other writers on the subject of making change, and to the many generations who have fought before us. Gratitude to all those alive at this time who are surviving and opposing empire, extraction and dominance while imagining, modelling and arguing for more just, collaborative and ecologically sane ways to live. Many do so at far greater personal cost than I may ever know. Gratitude to the wider intelligence that is always at work whenever someone decides not to comply or to accept how things are, or, indeed, whenever a writer sits down to put one word after another. Gratitude for wisdom and laughter to my friend Elise Bean, former Chief Counsel to the US Senate Permanent Subcommittee on Investigations, who died too young at the beginning of 2025 after decades of chasing down the corrupt.

Immense thanks to all those who were willing for their stories and views to appear here, and for your patience as I found a way to write about them. Thanks also to Amy Barry, Ben Sills, Caroline Sugg, Chris Shaw, Colin Davis, Ella Moore, Indra Adnan, Isabel de Bruin Cardoso, James Cook, Jane Stavert, Jeremy Kidwell, John Christensen, Jon Moses, Leonie Hicks, Liam Barrington-Bush, Natasha Adams, Nick Anim, Oliver Courtney, Sarah Pletts, Sarah Stein Lubrano and Sophy Banks for reading and commenting on drafts of sections, chapters or the whole manuscript. Any errors or misrepresentations are mine.

Thanks to my agent Charlotte Merritt for her vision, encouragement and steadfast practical support, and to my editor Cecilia Stein at Oneworld for seeing what I was trying to do, for her clear eye and wise interventions. Thanks to the rest of the team at Oneworld: Hannah Haseloff, Rida Vaquas, Tom Feltham, Jon Walker, Paul Nash and Hayley Warnham. Thanks to Darius Cuplinskas and Ayisha Osori at the Open Society Foundation's Ideas Workshop for financial support during the year in which I was writing, and to Ivan March, Romy Kraemer and Teresa Lorena Machado at Guerrilla Foundation in Berlin whose financial support and enthusiasm made possible the initial research and experiments to workshop the 'script'. Thanks to Phoebe Tickell who helped to make things happen, to Leina Schiffrin for searching questions and top gossip, and to Ivo Mensch on a long-outstanding matter. Thanks to those readers of *The Entangled Activist* whose enthusiastic responses inspired me to keep the enquiry going, and to Jonathan Rowson, its publisher, for encouraging me to write that book in the first place. My thanks as always to the staff and volunteers at the public libraries where I often write.

Thanks to my mum for love, fieriness and putting up with the annoying activist at the table. Thanks to the wise friends whose confidence in the work sustained me when I had mislaid my own, and offered hospitality when I needed to concentrate for longer than the daily domestic cycle permits. Speaking of which, bottomless thanks to my beloved husband for unconditional love, support, integrity and good humour, and doing more than his share of the childcare over many months. And thanks to our kids for tolerating me being exceptionally boring, remaining at my desk through too many evenings, weekends and holidays. I'm desperately sorry about the state of things, but I promise you that so many of us are working on it.

NOTES

Introduction: The Save-the-World Script

1. The word 'activist' can be polarising. Sometimes people I have interviewed use it. If I do, it is, unless indicated, a synonym for campaigning in its broad sense, not an indicator of the most hardcore direct action, which is how it is sometimes taken.

2. The Police, Crime, Sentencing and Courts Act of 2022 lowered the threshold for police to determine if a protest is disruptive. The Public Order Act 2023 created new criminal offences of locking on or being equipped to do so, causing 'serious disruption' by tunnelling, obstructing major transport works or interfering with key national infrastructure.

3. For example, Helen Lewis, 'The Church of Social Justice', *BBC Radio 4*, 2022.

4. Scripts are a helpful concept in psychosocial thinking, bridging psychological or cognitive processes, and cultural transmission. Guilaine Kinouani, *White Minds, Everyday Performance, Violence and Resistance*, Bristol University Press, 2023, p. 27 (of eBook).

5. 'Treasury Reopens the Floodgates to Dirty Money in the U.S.', Financial Accountability and Corporate Transparency Coalition, press release, 3 March 2025.

6. Richard Partington, 'One in six UK workers skipping meals to make ends meet, says TUC', *Guardian*, 13 January 2025.

7. Eleanor Lawrie, 'UK child poverty numbers reach a record high', *BBC*, 27 March 2025; 'Child poverty statistics – new record high and further breakdowns', Child Poverty Action Group, press release, 27 March 2025.

8. Mark Poynting, Erwan Rivault and Becky Dale, '2024 first year to pass 1.5C global warming limit', *BBC*, 10 January 2025; Dr Zeke Hausfather, Prof. Pierre Friedlingstein, 'Analysis: Global CO2 emissions will reach new high in 2024 despite slower growth', *Carbon Brief*, 13 November 2024.

9. Banking on Climate Chaos, *Fossil Fuel Finance Report 2025*, pp. 4–5.

10. 'Tipping point' describes the flipping of an earth system like the climate out of its equilibrium and into an irreversible new state. Potential tipping points include loss of the Amazon rainforest, collapse of major ice sheets, permafrost melting and breakdown of the Atlantic Meridional Overturning Circulation (AMOC). Jakob Deutloff, Hermann Held and Timothy M. Lenton, 'High probability of triggering climate tipping points under current policies modestly amplified by Amazon dieback and permafrost thaw', *Earth System Dynamics*, vol. 16, 2025, pp. 565–83.

11. This framing is from the Wealth Hackers Collective and I wish we had thought of it when I was investigating their activities. We called them the 'pinstripe army'; the journalist Oliver Bullough describes Britain's wealth industry as 'butler to the world' in his book of that name (Profile Books, 2022).

12. Credit to the founders of the Tax Justice Network, John Christensen and Richard Murphy, who taught so many of us how the offshore system works.

13. This is the latest stage of the 'imperial boomerang' identified by Aimé Césaire, the Martinique writer and politician: repressive tactics tried out in colonised lands would eventually be used in the heartlands of empire – as the racism developed in Europe's colonies was brought home to Europe by the Nazis. Kojo Koram's *Uncommon Wealth: Britain and the Aftermath of Empire*, John Murray, 2022, shows how wealth extraction from Britain's colonies is now replicated in the stripping of wealth from the public realm within the UK.

14. Scholars of the far right distinguish between the 'radical right', operating within democratic norms, and the 'extreme right', which does not. Cas Mudde, *The Far Right Today*, Polity Press, 2019.

15. This was the suggestion in 1989 by Francis Fukuyama, then a US State Department official, that Western liberalism had won the day. 'The End of History?', *The National Interest*, no. 16, Summer 1989, pp. 3–18.

16. Class identity in these islands is contested: is it based on employment status, occupation, income, education, cultural pursuits, connections? Some insist on a strict Marxist approach: if you're paid a wage to make money for someone else, you're working class; others point out the difficulty of well-paid folk with cultural capital claiming to be in the same boat as those struggling to get by. In 2013 the BBC's Great British Class Survey produced seven categories. Further reading: Mike Savage, *Social Class in the 21st Century*, Penguin, 2015; Dan Evans, *A Nation of Shopkeepers: The Unstoppable Rise of the Petty Bourgeoisie*, Repeater Books, 2023; Daniel Lavelle, 'My life in class limbo: am I working class or insufferably bourgeois?', *Guardian*, 2 April 2025.

17. 'Every generation must fight the same battles again and again. There's no final victory and there's no final defeat and therefore a little bit of history may help.' Tony Benn said this repeatedly in similar ways, in speeches, writings and interviews in the years before his death in 2014. For example, Tony Benn, *Letters To My Grandchildren, Thoughts on the Future*, Arrow Books, 2009, p. 4; and 'We Don't Really Have a Democracy', *New Internationalist*, 1 October 2010.

1: 'I Am Good'

1. Aleksandr Solzhenitsyn, *The Gulag Archipelago 1918–1956: An Experiment in Literary Investigation*, III–IV, translated by Thomas P. Whitney, Harper & Row, 1975, p. 615.

2. Ursula K. Le Guin, *The Lathe of Heaven*, Gollancz, 2021 (originally published 1971), p. 82.

3. See Daniel O'Mahony, 'Croydon's riots five years on: The story of the night the streets burned', *Sutton & Croydon Guardian*, 8 August 2016.

4. Charity Commission for England and Wales, *Inquiry Report: Summary Findings and Conclusions: Oxfam*, 11 June 2019; Charity Commission

for England and Wales, *Statement of the Results of an Inquiry: The Save the Children Fund (Save the Children UK)*, 5 March 2020.

5. The KonTerra Group, *Amnesty International Staff Wellbeing Review*, 2019.

6. Karen McVeigh, 'Amnesty "failed to support and value" Paris worker who killed himself', *Guardian*, 19 November 2018; Karen McVeigh, 'Amnesty International has toxic working culture, report finds', *Guardian*, 6 February 2019.

7. Howlett Brown, *Amnesty International Focus Group Report*, 12 October 2020, pp. 8–10; Global HPO, *'Good people doing good things, who cannot do bad things': An Inquiry into institutional racism at Amnesty International UK*, June 2022, pp. 16, 21.

8. Simon Murphy, 'Alzheimer's Society "paid out £750,000" to staff amid bullying claims', *Guardian*, 21 February 2020; Simon Murphy, 'Samaritans drop new chief executive after bullying claims', *Guardian*, 26 February 2020.

9. 'Regulator concludes regulatory case involving Alzheimer's Society', Charity Commission, press release, 4 May 2020.

10. Simon Murphy and Ben Quinn, 'Anger as watchdog clears Alzheimer's Society of wrongdoing', *Guardian*, 4 May 2020.

11. James Beal, 'Harassment row at fundraising body', *The Times*, 15 October 2022. An external inquiry subsequently concluded that CIOF and its former chief executive were 'more likely than not' aware of allegations of sexual assault and harassment and thus failed to act. JEDI Consultancy, *Chartered Institute of Fundraising: Independent Review of past processes and procedures in relation to allegations of sexual harassment/assault, Summary Findings*, September 2024.

12. Department for Culture, Media and Sport, *Independent Inquiry on the National Lottery Community Fund: summary of findings and recommendations*, 11 November 2021.

13. Rebecca Cooney, 'Bullying and harassment took place "with impunity" at all levels of the NCVO, report concludes', *Third Sector*, 5 February 2021.

14. Rebecca Cooney, 'Investigation upheld complaints of harassment and race discrimination against former NCVO chief and deputy', *Third Sector*, 25 January 2022.

15. This pattern of behaviour by abusers is given the acronym
    DARVO: deny, attack, and reverse victim and offender.

16. 'Oxfam: UK halts funding over new sexual exploitation claims',
    BBC News, 7 April 2021; Karen McVeigh, 'Save the Children can
    resume funding bids following sexual abuse scandal', *Guardian*, 11
    September 2020.

17. Whiteness is not a characteristic of those racialised as white, but, as
    the psychoanalyst Guilaine Kinouani puts it, 'the ways the struc-
    ture of white supremacy (or white racism) becomes embedded,
    normalised and inscribed within modes of feeling, thinking,
    being... so as to maintain the illusion of white superiority.' *White
    Minds*, p. 49 (of eBook).

18. The Forde Inquiry Panel, *The Forde Report*, 19 July 2022, pp. 84,
    108. Report commissioned and published by the Labour Party's
    National Executive Committee.

19. The context was the leaking of an explosive report, initially
    intended for submission to the Equality and Human Rights
    Commission, which began as an investigation into Labour's
    handling of antisemitism complaints and grew into a wide criti-
    cism of factionalism by senior Labour Party staff towards Jeremy
    Corbyn's leadership team and his supporters. *Forde Report*, p. 10.

20. An open letter from Black party members calling for action on
    the culture of racism that Forde had detailed gathered hundreds of
    signatories from constituency Labour parties across the country.

21. Phil Burton-Cartledge, 'The Forde Report's Villains Now Control
    the Labour Party', *Tribune*, 21 July 2022.

22. *The Forde Report*, pp. 8, 108.

23. See Owen Jones, *This Land: The Story of a Movement*, Allen Lane,
    2020; Gabriel Pogrund and Patrick Maguire, *Left Out: The
    Inside Story of Labour Under Corbyn*, Bodley Head, 2020; Michael
    Chessum, *This Is Only the Beginning: The Making of a New Left, From
    Anti-Austerity to the Fall of Corbyn*, Bloomsbury Academic, 2022.

24. Nadine White, 'Labour tried to gag Black lawyer who wrote
    party's own racism report', *Independent*, 19 June 2024.

25. Isabel de Bruin Cardoso, Allison R. Russell, Muel Kaptein, *et al.*,
    'How Moral Goodness Drives Unethical Behavior: Empirical

Evidence for the NGO Halo Effect', *Nonprofit and Voluntary Sector Quarterly*, vol. 53(3), 2024, pp. 589–614.

26. Several noted a desperation during the Corbyn years that led to extreme behaviour: from the Corbyn side, a feeling that this was the best chance in decades for a more socialist vision to prevail; and from the right of the party, a keenness to shut that down for fear of destroying electoral chances.

27. Isabel de Bruin Cardoso, Marco Meyer and Muel Kaptein, 'Exploring the Dark Side of the NGO Halo: Relating NGO Mission, Morals, and People to NGO Unethical Behavior', *Journal of Philanthropy*, vol. 30(3), 2025.

28. Isabel de Bruin Cardoso, 'The NGO Halo effect: The internal glorification of moral goodness and its relationship to NGO unethical behavior', *European Research Network on Philanthropy*, undated.

29. Cardoso, Russell, Kaptein, *et al.,* 'How moral goodness drives unethical behavior'.

30. Adding a halo to the mission leads to an ends-over-means problem of *moral justification* for bad behaviour. Adding a halo to people's morals leads to a *moral superiority* problem where accountability is lacking because they feel better than others. Adding a halo to people's goodness so that they are perceived as less likely to do wrong leads to a *moral naivety* problem where accountability and restraints on power are seen as less necessary. See Cardoso, Russell, Kaptein, *et al.*, 'How moral goodness drives ethical behavior'.

31. One incident was in 1902, when tensions in the Russian Social Democratic Workers' Party were brewing into what would become the Bolshevik and Menshevik split. A party activist, Claudia Prikhodko, committed suicide after another activist drew a malicious cartoon questioning whether the father of her unborn baby was himself, or another man to whom she was understood to be married. Her suicide note appealed to the party to consider the private morals of senior figures; some members wanted the cartoonist to face investigation. Lenin did not, assessing it a personal matter and against the interests of a revolutionary organisation to adjudicate. Abigail B. Bakan and Paul Kellogg, 'Sexism and the left: case studies in an epistemology of ignorance', *Socialist Studies*, vol. 16(1), 2022.

32. The Charity Commission told Oxfam: 'being a charity is more than just about *what* you do, it is also about the way in which you do it.' Charity Commission, *Inquiry Report: Summary Findings and Conclusions: Oxfam*, 11 June 2019.

33. Julia A. Minson and Benoît Monin, 'Do-Gooder Derogation: Disparaging Morally Motivated Minorities to Defuse Anticipated Reproach', *Social Psychological and Personality Science*, vol. 3(2), 2012, pp. 200–7.

34. Isabel de Bruin Cardoso, Allison R. Russell, Muel Kaptein and Lucas Meijs, 'How moral goodness drives unethical behavior', op cit, has references.

35. Guy Shrubsole, *The Lost Rainforests of Britain*, William Collins, 2022.

36. The repressed shadow, and how we project it onto others, is a mainstay of Jungian psychology.

37. I wrote about this in Chapter 4 of *The Entangled Activist*, Perspectiva Press, 2021.

38. Office for National Statistics, 'More than 1 in 10 addresses used as holiday homes in some areas of England and Wales', 20 June 2023; South Hams & West Devon [Councils], *Better Homes, Better Lives Housing Strategy 2021–2026, Review 2022–2023*.

39. Helena Horton, 'Dartmoor landowner who won wild camping ban may be putting rare beetle at risk', *Guardian*, 21 January 2023.

40. Miles Davis and Jonathan Morris, 'Supreme Court backs wild camping on Dartmoor', *BBC News*, 21 May 2025.

41. Saul D. Alinsky, *Rules for Radicals: A Pragmatic Primer for Realistic Radicals*, Vintage, 1971, pp. 130–4.

42. Jane Holgate and John Page suggest that while Alinsky's thirteen rules are useful, his title 'has encouraged it to be mistakenly read as if it were a proscriptive, universal blueprint for organisers.' *Changemakers: Radical Strategies for Social Movement Organising*, Policy Press, 2025, p. 2.

43. Carmen Aguilar García, Anna Leach and Sandra Laville, 'Water firms use up to 28% of bill payments to service debt in areas of England', *Guardian*, 18 December 2023; Professor Prem Sikka, 'We are currently witnessing the re-privatisation of water', *Left Foot Forward*, 20 September 2024.

44. Luke Barr, 'UK water firms drowning in £65bn of debt with cost of repayments set to soar due to inflation (but they're still paying shareholders huge dividends)', *Daily Mail*, 28 June 2023.

45. Sandra Laville, 'Water companies in England "use greenwashing playbook to hide environmental harm"', *Guardian*, 27 January 2025.

46. Alistair Osborne, 'Davy may find water savings a struggle', *The Times*, 11 January 2024.

47. Robert Miller, 'South West Water owner pays dividend despite pre-tax loss and fine', *The Times*, 2 June 2023.

48. 'South West Water boss gives up £450k bonus amid public anger over sewage pollution', *ITV News*, 9 May 2023.

49. *Pennon Annual Report 2023*, p. 136.

50. Jonathan Morris and PA Media, 'Boss of water firm in parasite scare drops bonus', *BBC News*, 10 June 2024.

51. 'Full Year Results 2023/24', Pennon, press release, 21 May 2024.

52. Applications are decided by DEFRA, the Department for the Environment, Food and Rural Affairs. New applications for bathing water status were closed during 2024 because so many had been received from across the country; the regulations and application guidance were being reviewed.

53. D. Hunter, *Chav Solidarity*, Lumpen/The Class Work Project, 2020, p. 129.

2: 'I Protest'

1. Kamila Shamsie, *Best of Friends*, Bloomsbury, 2022, p. 271.

2. Renée Lertzman, 'Taming the Righting Reflex', *Becoming Guides, Substack*, 17 January 2025.

3. Of course, the shock was part of the point; part of the idea behind Extinction Rebellion's strategy was that the sight of citizens putting themselves in this jeopardy would create a kind of moral shock.

4. The figure is from the Met Police, provided to the Mayor of London's office for Mayor's Question Time in the London Assembly on 15 September 2022.

5. There are many ways to break this down. Bill Moyer, an American trainer of activists, described four roles. His 'rebel' is the typical 'activist' or protester. The 'citizen' can communicate with ordinary people. The 'advocate/reformer' gets closer to power to influence things. The 'change agent' works in communities, spending time with people who suffer most from the political and economic system as it is. Each role has its strengths and is needed; each has blind spots and can fail to see the importance of the others. Seeing these distinct roles is helpful (a) for people already involved in change-making who struggle to see the value of different approaches and (b) for anyone who wants to change things but fears having to be the typical rebellious protester. Another approach is to focus not on being a hero activist, but on being a citizen who gets involved in your community; see Jon Alexander with Ariane Conrad, *Citizens: Why the Key to Fixing Everything is All of Us*, Canbury Press, 2022 – and see also Chapter 6 of this book. A further model that maps different kinds of change-making activity is the 'social change grid', easy to find online, from the Sheila McKechnie Foundation, an organisation that supports change-makers. (McKechnie was a trade unionist, housing campaigner and 'fully paid-up member of the awkward squad.')

6. Jonathan Haidt, *The Righteous Mind: Why Good People Are Divided by Politics and Religion*, Penguin, 2012, pp. 52–6, 79–83.

7. Quoted as an epigraph to Chapter 1 of Thich Nhat Hanh and the Plum Village Community, *Planting Seeds: Practicing Mindfulness with Children*, Parallax Press, 2011, p. 10.

8. Influenced by Richard H. Thaler and Cass R. Sunstein, *Nudge: Improving Decisions About Health, Wealth, and Happiness* (Penguin, 2008), Cameron's and Obama's governments both set up a nudge unit and others proliferated around the world. Nudging is attractive to politicians, noted Carolyn Pedwell, a professor of cultural studies, because 'it promotes the fantasy that we do not have to wade into the murky abyss of psychic ambivalence or socio-political relations to transform individual or collective behaviour.' ('Habit and the Politics of Social Change: A comparison of nudge

theory and pragmatist philosophy', *Body and Society*, vol. 23(4), 2017, pp. 59–94.) Some of the psychologists behind nudging have issued a *mea culpa*, acknowledging the limitations of trying to address 'some of society's most pressing problems' at the level of the individual without also looking at wider systems. (Nick Chater and George Loewenstein, 'The i-frame and the s-frame: How focusing on individual-level solutions has led behavioral public policy astray', *Behavioral and Brain Sciences*, vol. 46, 2023, p. e147.)

9. Adam Phillips, *On Wanting to Change*, Penguin, 2022, p. xiii.

10. Ibid., pp. 22–5.

11. Diarmaid MacCulloch, *A History of Christianity*, Allen Lane, 2009, pp. 586–7.

12. Nancy Farriss, 'Sacred Power in Colonial Mexico: The Case of Sixteenth Century Yucatan', *Proceedings of the British Academy*, vol. 81 (1993), pp. 145–162.

13. My undergraduate thesis, unpublished, analysed the missionaries' journals recording their intellectual encounters with Hindu pandits in the holy city of Benares (now Varanasi) in the mid-nineteenth century.

14. There are other problems with leaning too hard on psychology, when its institutions can be part of harmful systems of racism and classism.

15. Vitalie Duporge, 'Without water there is no life', *New Internationalist*, 18 October 2021.

16. Dr Sally-Anne Huxtable, Professor Corinne Fowler, Dr Christo Kefalas, *et al.* (eds), *Interim Report on the Connections between Colonialism and Properties now in the Care of the National Trust, Including Links with Historic Slavery*, September 2020.

17. Madge Dresser and Andrew Han (eds), *Slavery and the British Country House*, English Heritage, 31 July 2013.

18. Corinne Fowler, 'Red walls, green walls: British identity, rural racism and British colonial history', *Renewal*, vol. 29(3), 2021.

19. Aamna Mohdin, Glenn Swann and Caroline Bannock, 'How George Floyd's death sparked a wave of UK anti-racism protests', *Guardian*, 29 July 2020.

20. 'I've declined most invitations to adult events over the past year due to the abuse,' wrote Sathnam Sanghera in *The Times* when *Empireworld*, his sequel to *Empireland*, came out. Sathnam Sanghera, 'Why I'm taking on the racist trolls again', *The Times*, 12 January 2024.

21. Corinne Fowler, *Our Island Stories: Ten Walks through Rural Britain and Its Hidden History of Empire*, Penguin, 2024.

22 Octavia Butler, *Parable of the Sower*, Headline, 1993.

23. Sarah Stein Lubrano, *Don't Talk About Politics: How to Change 21st-Century Minds*, Bloomsbury, 2025.

24. This is 'social contact theory', developed by Gordon Allport in the 1950s and extensively tested since. Thomas F. Pettigrew and Linda R. Tropp. 'A meta-analytic test of intergroup contact theory.' *Journal of Personality and Social Psychology*, vol. 90(5), 2006, pp. 751–83 at p. 751. See also Stein Lubrano, *Don't Talk About Politics*, Chapter 4.

25. She is talking about demonstrations here rather than blockades or strikes.

26. Stein Lubrano and other researchers I spoke to agree that the more robust evidence for the impact of protest is on its participants. One survey of evidence from the US suggests that demonstrations on their own have limited effect on public opinion: Amory Gethin and Vincent Pons, 'Social Movements and Public Opinion in the United States', *National Bureau of Economic Research Working Paper No. 32342*, April 2024.

    Other research suggests the effect of protest can depend on existing political views and, in the case of climate change, understandings of it; Dylan Bugden, 'Does Climate Protest Work? Partisanship, Protest, and Sentiment Pools', *Socius: Sociological Research for a Dynamic World*, vol. 6, 2020, pp. 1–13. See also Dana R. Fisher, Oscar Berglund and Colin J. Davis, 'How effective are climate protests at swaying policy – and what could make a difference?' *Nature*, vol. 623, pp. 910–13, 28 November 2023.

27. Sara Vestergren, John Drury and Eva Hammar Chiriac, 'The biographical consequences of protest and activism: A systematic review and a new typology', *Social Movement Studies*, vol. 16(3), 2017, pp. 203–21. Stein Lubrano, *Don't Talk About Politics*, Chapter 3.

28. Madalina Vlasceanu, Kimberley C. Doell, Joseph B. Bak-Coleman, *et al.*, 'Addressing climate change with behavioral science: A global intervention tournament in 63 countries', *Science Advances*, vol. 10(6), 2024. Another review in twenty-three countries found that the most persuasive reason to offer for the necessity of new policies was 'protecting the planet for future generations'; it was twelve times more effective than 'increasing jobs, opportunities and economic growth' or 'reducing social inequality': Potential Energy, *Later is Too Late: A comprehensive analysis of the messaging that accelerates climate action in the G20 and beyond*, November 2023, p. 7.

   Other research has found that people who believe in climate change and express concern will nevertheless express resistance to policies where the cost is framed as something they have to pay: this was dubbed the NOMBA – Not Out of My Bank Account – effect. Janet K. Swim, Nathaniel Geiger and Joseph G. Guerriero, 'Not out of MY bank account! Science messaging when climate change policies carry personal financial costs', *Thinking & Reasoning*, vol. 28(3), 2022, pp. 346–74.

29. It does, however, he added, increase people's punitive attitudes towards disruptive protest: 'people favour slightly harsher sentencing after they've read about a disruptive protest.'

30. Dale T. Miller, 'A century of pluralistic ignorance: what we have learned about its origins, forms, and consequences', *Frontiers in Social Psychology*, vol. 1, 2023.

31. Peter Andre, Teodora Boneva, Felix Chopra, *et al.*, 'Globally representative evidence on the actual and perceived support for climate action', *Nature Climate Change*, vol. 14, 2024, pp. 253–59. The 89% Project, a collaboration by media and climate organisations to reduce pluralistic ignorance, uses these figures. The People's Climate Vote 2024, a public opinion survey of 77,000 people representing more than 87% of the world's population, by the United Nations Development Programme and Oxford University, found that 53% of people globally were more worried about climate change than they were the previous year, and over 56% of people globally think about climate change daily or weekly.

32. Andre, Boneva, Chopra, *et al.*, 'Globally representative evidence', p. 257.

33. Research into deep canvassing's effect on equal marriage opinions in California was retracted after discovery of fraud; the whistleblowers then conducted their own research on its effects on attitudes to transgender people in south Florida, and found that ten-minute doorstep conversations 'substantially reduced transphobia' for at least three months. David Broockman and Joshua Kalla, 'Durably reducing transphobia: A field experiment on door-to-door canvassing', *Science*, vol. 352(6282), pp. 220–4 at p. 220. Anand Giridharadas's *The Persuaders: Winning Hearts and Minds in a Divided Age*, Penguin, 2023, covers deep canvassing in support of undocumented immigrants' rights in Arizona.

34. Danielle F. Lawson, Kathryn Stevenson, M. Nils Peterson, *et al.*, 'Children can foster climate change concern among their parents', *Nature Climate Change*, vol. 9, June 2019, pp. 458–62.

35. George Lakoff, *Don't Think of an Elephant! Know Your Values and Frame the Debate*, Chelsea Green, 2004.

36. Daniel M. Wegner, David J. Schneider, Samuel R. Carter, *et al.*, 'Paradoxical Effects of Thought Suppression', *Journal of Social Psychology*, vol. 53(1), pp. 5–13 at p. 5. Wegner and Schneider later noted that Tolstoy 'wrote about how difficult it is to avoid thinking about a white bear,' and Freud 'thought of all this long ago and developed it into a grand theory.' Daniel M. Wegner and David J. Schneider, 'The White Bear Story', *Psychological Inquiry*, vol. 14(3–4), 2003, pp. 326–9.

37. George Lakoff and Mark Johnson, *Metaphors We Live By*, University of Chicago Press, 1980, p. 3.

38. Nadine Andrews offers another definition: 'Cognitive frames are bundles of strongly linked concepts and associated, emotions and values, learnt through experience and stored in memory.' 'How Cognitive Frames about Nature May Affect Felt Sense of Nature Connectedness', *Ecopsychology*, March 2018, pp. 61–71 at p. 63.

39. This work was initially done for a group of environmental and aid organisations including WWF, Oxfam and Friends of the Earth who sensed that the multiple issues they were grappling with were

connected by the same underlying world views. Tom Crompton set up the Common Cause Foundation in 2015, which has continued to publish applied research on values and frames.

40. Tom Crompton, *Common Cause: The Case for Working with Our Cultural Values*, September 2010; see previous note. Tim Holmes, Elena Blackmore, Richard Hawkins, *et al.*, *The Common Cause Handbook: A Guide to Values and Frames for Campaigners, Community Organisers, Civil Servants, Fundraisers, Educators, Social Entrepreneurs, Activists, Funders, Politicians, and Everyone in Between*, Public Research Centre, 2011. Further resources are on the PIRC and Common Cause Foundation websites.

41. Using a metaphor of the family, Lakoff called these frames 'strict father' and 'nurturant parent'.

42. George Lakoff, 'Why it Matters How We Frame the Environment', *Environmental Communication*, vol. 4(1), 2010, pp. 70–81. See also his essay from 2006, 'Simple Framing', available online.

43. A study by political scientists of seventy elections across western European countries found that 'voters are on average more likely to defect to the radical right when mainstream parties adopt anti-immigration positions.' Werner Krause, Denis Cohen and Tarik Abou-Chadi, 'Does accommodation work? Mainstream party strategies and the success of radical right parties', *Political Science Research and Methods* vol. 11(1), 2023, pp. 172–9.

44. Stephan Lewandowsky, John Cook, Ullrich Ecker, *et al.*, *The Debunking Handbook*, 2020. Subsequent research suggested that the order of presentation of myth and fact did not matter: Briony Swire-Thompson, John Cook, Lucy H. Butler, *et al.*, 'Correction format has a limited role when debunking misinformation', *Cognitive Research: Principles and Implications*, vol. 6, article number 83, 2021. I asked Prof. Lewandowsky if he would update the advice about the 'truth sandwich' based on this finding; he said no; what's important is to provide the correction, and the repetition of facts is still useful.

45. Ellie Mae O'Hagan, 'Lessons From the Anti-Austerity Movement', *Jacobin*, February 2017.

46. NEON, NEF, Frameworks Institute and PIRC, *Framing the Economy: How to win the case for a better system*, February 2018.

47. See the resources on her website at ASO Communications. Anand
    Giridharadas interviewed her in *The Persuaders*.

3: 'I Am Pure'

1. From Timothy Snyder, 'How to Stop Fascism', Thinking about...,
   Substack, 5 July 2024; updated 23 November 2024.
2. This is especially true of some approaches: abolitionism, for
   example, puts visionary thinking at the centre. Mariame Kaba,
   a New York organiser, says that when she talks about abolishing
   prisons and police, people think it's a negative project. But 'abolition is a vision of a restructured society in a world where we have
   everything we need: food, shelter, education, health, art, beauty,
   clean water, and more things that are foundational to our personal
   and community safety.' *We Do This 'Til We Free Us: Abolitionist
   Organizing and Transforming Justice*, Haymarket Books, 2021, p. 2.
3. The Arms Trade Treaty has also failed to prevent the UK arming
   Saudi Arabia against the people of Yemen. The cluster-bomb ban
   has, to date, not been signed by seventeen countries that produce
   cluster munitions. Cluster Munition Coalition, *Cluster Munition
   Monitor 2024*, ICBL-CMC, September 2024, p. 3.
4. The advertising firm Ogilvy & Mather helped BP to come up
   with the idea of individual carbon footprints. Rebecca Solnit, 'Big
   oil coined "carbon footprints" to blame us for their greed. Keep
   them on the hook', *Guardian*, 23 August 2021.
5. Karen Horney, *Neurosis and Human Growth: The Struggle Toward
   Self-Realization*, Routledge & Kegan Paul, 1951, p. 65.
6. Marion Woodman, *Conscious Femininity: Interviews with Marion
   Woodman*, Inner City Books, 1993, pp. 14, 154.
7. Thanks to Ella Moore (see Chapter 7) for this observation.
8. Susan Raffo, 'The Language of the Land', *Dark Mountain,* Issue 25,
   2024, p. 14.
9. Jerald C. Brauer, 'Reflections on the Nature of English Puritanism',
   Church History, vol. 23(2), June 1954, pp. 99–108. See also Chapter 5.
10. In its older meaning – of or belonging to letters or writing –
    being literal was precisely the Puritan project. The Reformation
    they were defending jettisoned the ritual, image and bodily

participation of Catholic ceremony in favour of direct connection with God through his Word, given in the Bible. In its modern meaning, literalism connects, as we saw in Chapter 2, to the leftish habit of focusing on the literal *facts* of economic justice at the cost of telling compelling stories that appeal to people's emotions – as the right finds it easier to do. See Alex Evans, *The Myth Gap*, Eden Project Books, 2017.

11. This argument was put forward by the anthropologist Mary Douglas in her celebrated 1966 study of cross-cultural views on pollution, *Purity and Danger*, Routledge, 1966.

12. Since Adorno's 1950 research in *The Authoritarian Personality*, one of the psychological substrates for authoritarianism has been seen as a preference for certainty and order. For child-development theorists, beginning with Jean Piaget, a focus on rules is a particular developmental stage. On this basis, puritanical insistence on conformity can look like a kind of arrested development, where we are still reassured by a rules-based world and want it to apply universally. There are extensive literatures on both topics.

13. Alexis Shotwell, a philosopher, observes that in our awareness of living in the anthropocene, we 'worry that we have lost a natural state of purity or decide that purity is something we ought to pursue and defend.' Alexis Shotwell, 'Against Purity', *Differens Magazine*, Winter 2022–23, pp. 50–60.

14. More in Common, *Britain's Choice: Common Ground and Division in 2020s Britain*, October 2020. In 2024 the National Centre for Social Research also developed a new scheme of British voters with six types that take account of cross-cutting views on economic and social questions.

15. Climate Outreach used it for its *Britain Talks Climate* toolkit for engaging people in conversations about climate change, first published in 2020 and updated in 2024.

16. Ed Hodgson and Luke Tryl, *Progressive Activists*, More In Common, 2025.

17. Luke Tryl, Conleth Burns, Tim Dixon, *Dousing the Flames*, More in Common, 2021, pp. 69, 76.

18. adrienne maree brown, *We Will Not Cancel Us, And Other Dreams of Transformative Justice*, AK Press, 2020, p. 26.

19. Loretta J. Ross's 2021 TED talk was titled 'Don't call people out – call them in'.

20. Bobby Duffy, Paul Stoneman, Kirstie Hewlett, *et al.*, *Woke, cancel culture and white privilege – the shifting terms of the UK's 'culture war'*, The Policy Institute, Kings College and Ipsos, May 2022. Bobby Duffy and Gideon Skinner, *Woke vs anti-woke culture war divisions and politics*, The Policy Institute, Kings College and Ipsos, October 2023.

21. Duffy and Skinner, *Woke vs anti-woke?*, pp. 15–20.

22. Sunder Katwala, *Culture Clash: Bridging Our Divides*, British Future, September 2023.

23. *Counter Culture: How to Resist the Culture Wars and Build 21st Century Solidarity*, Fabian Society, July 2021, was authored by Kirsty McNeill, now a Scottish Labour MP, and Roger Harding (see Chapter 4).

24. This is the view of Bart Cammaerts, a politics professor at the London School of Economics. Those in power are 'abnormalising' those arguing for justice into the 'other', closing ranks against what is impure, and using the traditional method of moral panic – this time over 'wokeness' and having their views shut down – as a tool. Bart Cammaerts, 'The abnormalisation of social justice: The "anti-woke culture war" discourse in the UK', *Discourse & Society*, vol. 33(6), 2022, pp. 730–43.

25. For a pithy summary, see George Monbiot and Peter Hutchison, *The Invisible Doctrine: The Secret History of Neoliberalism (& How it Came to Control Your Life)*, Allen Lane, 2024.

26. Marianna Spring, 'Marianna in Conspiracyland', *BBC Radio 4* and online, June 2023. Naomi Klein's *Doppelganger: A Trip into the Mirror World*, Allen Lane, 2023, analyses these tendencies.

27. Ryan Grim, 'Elephant in the Zoom: Meltdowns Have Brought Progressive Advocacy Groups to a Standstill at a Critical Moment in World History', *The Intercept*, 13 June 2022; Ellen Barry, 'How

Russian Trolls Helped Keep the Women's March Out of Lock Step', *New York Times*, 18 September 2022.

28. john a. powell and Sara Grossman, 'Countering Authoritarianism: Forging a Progressive Response to Fragmentation', *NonProfit Quarterly*, 16 March 2023; see also Maurice Mitchell, 'Building Resilient Organizations', *The Forge*, 29 November 2022.

29. A request to 'bridge' can easily sound like a call to meet in the middle. 'For radicalised people, the moderate sort of talk just does not cut it,' says Nick Anim. 'The moderate talk means you don't really want to change the system. You want green capitalism, with the same exploitation.'

30. john a. powell, 'Overcoming Toxic Polarization: Lessons in Effective Bridging', *Minnesota Journal of Law and Inequality*, vol. 40(2), June 2022.

31. See Fatima Ibrahim's comments later in this chapter.

32. 'Bridging work is not for everyone, and we appreciate and value other approaches [...] that are more confrontational in order to raise awareness, disrupt complacency, or urgently address harms', acknowledges the Democracy and Belonging Forum in its sign-up agreement for members.

33. Nella Van Dyke and Brian Amos, 'Social movement coalitions: Formation, longevity, and success', *Sociology Compass*, vol. 11(7), 2017; Michelle I. Gawerc, 'Diverse social movement coalitions: Prospects and challenges', *Sociology Compass*, vol. 14(1), 2020.

34. Individualism and digital communication have made the political space competitive rather than collaborative, suggested another interviewee.

35. It isn't new, firstly, as Farrell was speaking a few years after these events, and secondly because such divisive criticism is an old pattern. The late cultural theorist and blogger Mark Fisher described this phenomenon on the left as the 'Vampires' Castle': 'driven by a *priest's desire* to excommunicate and condemn, an *academic-pedant's desire* to be the first to be seen to spot a mistake, and a *hipster's desire* to be one of the in-crowd.' 'Exiting the Vampires' Castle', *openDemocracy*, 24 November 2013.

36. Open Spaces for Dialogue and Enquiry Methodology, shared on a Creative Commons licence by Vanessa Andreotti, Linda Barker, Katy Newell-Jones and the Centre for the Study of Social and Global Justice.

37. This echoes the Sermon on the Mount: 'Judge not, that ye be not judged…' Matthew 7:1–3 (King James Version).

38. The veteran environmentalist Jonathon Porritt reflects on the 1980s disjunct between environmentalism and social justice – a mutual incomprehension – in *Love, Anger and Betrayal: Just Stop Oil's Young Climate Campaigners*, Anthony Eyre/Mount House Press, 2025, pp. 233–7.

39. They become, in Sara Ahmed's words, the 'killjoy', getting in the way of what might otherwise be harmonious. *The Feminist Killjoy Handbook: The Radical Potential of Getting in the Way*, Penguin, 2024.

40. Adam Barnett and Sam Bright, 'Anti-ULEZ Protest Group Promotes Conspiracy Theories and Climate Science Denial', *DeSmog*, 2 September 2023.

41. The campaign group Platform collaborated with North Sea oil workers to demand a 'just energy transition' away from oil. Platform, Friends of the Earth Scotland, *Our Power: Offshore Workers' Demands for a Just Energy Transition*, 2023.

42. Drawing on the scholarship of Jacques Rossiaud, the historian Silvia Federici describes the near-decriminalisation of rape by medieval French authorities and in fourteenth-century Venice as a means of defusing class antagonism by turning it 'into an antagonism against proletarian women.' *Caliban and the Witch: Women, the Body and Primitive Accumulation*, Autonomedia, 2004, pp. 47–9.

43. Emma Dabiri summarises the creation of 'white' identity in the American colonies to split the European poor from enslaved Africans, in *What White People Can Do Next*, Penguin, 2021, pp. 51–7.

44. Andreas Malm and the Zetkin Collective, *White Skin, Black Fuel: On the Danger of Fossil Fascism*, Verso, 2021.

45. Adam Greenfield, 'Behind the Knife: The Intellectual Roots of Ecofascism', *The Ideas Letter*, 28 November 2024.

46. In 2023 it splintered and produced an equally hate-filled gathering called Homeland.

47. Hope not Hate, *Patriotic Alternative: Britain's Fascist Threat*, 26 November 2021.

48. Hilary A. Moore, *Burning Earth, Changing Europe: How the Racist Right Exploits the Climate Crisis and What We Can Do About It*, Rosa Luxemburg Stiftung, 2020.

49. The three key principles are: (1) open with a shared value and be explicit about who shares it; (2) explain the problem and locate it with key powerful actors who are worsening/causing it; (3) communicate an aspirational vision of what can be achieved if we join together. Raquel Jesse, *The UK Race Class Narrative Report*, CLASS UK and ASO Communications, May 2022.

50. Farina Sultana, 'Critical climate justice', *The Geographical Journal*, vol. 188(1), March 2022; Kathryn Yusoff's *A Billion Black Anthropocenes or None*, University of Minnesota Press, 2018.

51. Research in 2021 showed that the majority of Britons did not understand the connections between racial justice and climate change. PIRC, 350.org and NEON, *Framing Climate Justice*, 2021.

52. National Trust members took part in a 'Restore Nature Now' march of sixty thousand people in June 2024, alongside other established environmental charities as well as direct-action groups.

53. This kind of slowing-down practice is at the heart of somatic-based approaches to change. See Resmaa Menakem, *My Grandmother's Hands: Racialised Trauma and the Pathway to Mending Our Hearts and Bodies*, Central Recovery Press, 2017; Staci K. Haines, *The Politics of Trauma: Somatics, Healing and Social Justice*, North Atlantic Books, 2019.

54. Susan Raffo, *Liberated To The Bone: Histories, Bodies, Futures*, AK Press, 2022, p. 103.

55. Representative Alexandria Ocasio-Cortez and Senator Ed Markey introduced a Green New Deal congressional resolution in 2019, containing a ten-year vision for a just transition. It was defeated in the Senate, although some of its principles informed Biden's Inflation Reduction Act of 2022.

56. Rupert Read and Rosie Bell: 'Come as you are: towards a new wave of citizen climate action', in Rupert Read, Liam Kavanagh and Rose Bell (eds), *The Climate Majority Project: Setting the Stage for a Mainstream, Urgent Climate Movement*, London Publishing Partnership, 2023, pp. 27–31.

57. Jonathan Haidt, *The Righteous Mind: Why Good People are Divided by Politics and Religion*, Penguin, 2012.

4: 'I Know Better Than You'

1. Minna Salami, *Sensuous Knowledge: A Black Feminist Approach for Everyone*, Zed Books, 2020, p. 17.

2. George Orwell, *The Road to Wigan Pier*, Penguin, 2001 (originally published 1937), p. 167.

3. Reclaim, *Missing Experts*, September 2022.

4. 'It is common for internal conversations to reveal that people assume that people from working-class backgrounds are not in the room,' noted *Missing Experts*, pp. 10, 28.

5. Ibid., pp. 30–4.

6. For example, the Settlement House Movement of the late nineteenth and early twentieth centuries, which began at Toynbee Hall in East London and then spread to the US, saw middle-class people move to shared houses in working-class and immigrant neighbourhoods to help alleviate poverty while sharing knowledge both ways.

7. Baljeet Sandu interviewed social-sector leaders and funders a decade ago to find out how they worked together with 'experts by experience'. The majority of social-sector leaders, she reported, 'pushed back against this inquiry'. She found widespread awareness of the value of lived experience, but patchy actual commitments. *The Value of Lived Experience in Social Change: The Need for Leadership and Organisational Development in the Social Sector*, July 2017, pp. 6–9.

8. The Sutton Trust, *Elitist Britain*, 2025, 18 September 2025.

9. 'Do-er and done-to' is from the psychoanalyst Jessica Benjamin. I discussed this theory in *The Entangled Activist*, pp. 143–4.

10. The philosophers Kristie Dotson and Miranda Fricker write about epistemic injustice. The term 'epistemic violence' is from Gayatri Chakravorty Spivak, 'Can the Subaltern Speak?', in Cary Nelson and Lawrence Grossberg (eds), *Marxism and the Interpretation of Culture*, University of Illinois Press, 1988, pp. 66–111.

11. D. Hunter, *Chav Solidarity*, The Class Work Project, 2018; D. Hunter, *Tracksuits, Traumas and Class Traitors*, Lumpen, 2020.

12. Indeed, when middle-class writers who have worked in NGOs write about change-making they may miss important points about grassroots and working-class activism, even after speaking to many people involved in them.

13. See for example INCITE!, *The Revolution Will Not Be Funded*, 2007; Nina Luo, 'Left Organizing Is in Crisis. Philanthropy Is a Major Reason Why', *The Nation*, 16 January 2025; in the UK, the annual Uncharitable Festival run online by Martha Awojobi and her company JMB Consultancy is an excellent place to learn about the limitations of current funding models and emerging alternatives.

14. Research since the 1950s has shown links between the desire for certainty and preference for both right-wing and authoritarian political choices. Some of it is reviewed in Christopher M. Federico and Ariel Malka, 'The Contingent, Contextual Nature of the Relationship Between Needs for Security and Certainty and Political Preferences: Evidence and Implications,' *Political Psychology* vol. 39, 2018, pp. 3–48.

15. The theory and practice of 'politicised somatics' suggests that our embodied self carries habitual conditioning and reactions that might make us behave in ways that conflict with our chosen values – and that there is something we can do about it. Haines, *The Politics of Trauma*, p. 35; Prentis Hemphill, *What it Takes to Heal: How Transforming Ourselves Can Change the World*, Cornerstone Press, 2024; Susan Raffo, *Liberated to the Bone*.

16. On the need to recognise the pain that may be hiding behind the dominance-strategies of the more privileged, Susan Raffo warns that attending to this pain without being in 'response and

relationship' to the harmful impact your prior unawareness of it may have had 'will be just another way of justifying and evading the truth of your own supremacy.' *Liberated to the Bone*, p. 74.

17. Benjamin Y. Fong and Melissa Naschek in 'NGOism: The Politics of the Third Sector', *Catalyst*, vol. 5(1), Spring 2021, pp. 92–131. (They write about the US, though there has been a similar pattern in the UK.) As NGOs took on advocacy for their own issue agendas as well as being commissioned to provide welfare-state functions, they became part of the status quo. The full article is paywalled; see Cale Brooks and Jen Pan, 'NGOism Serves the Status Quo', *Jacobin*, 14 June 2021.

18. 'Target' (as opposed to 'agent') is a term from Leticia Nieto and Margot Boyer's framework for thinking about privilege and oppression with respect to the various ways that society still ranks us. Their 2006 articles from *ColorsNW* magazine can be found online.

19. See Akram Salhab and Neha Shah, 'Building the migrant justice movement', Migrants Organise, 30 November 2020.

20. Elizabeth Jones, 'The Bristol Bus Boycott of 1963', available online at blackhistorymonth.org.uk/article/section/civil-rights-movement/the-bristol-bus-boycott-of-1963/.

21. Chris H. Glasgow, 'Tradition of Resisting the Home Office', *New Socialist*, 19 May 2021.

22. See interview with Dami Makinde further on.

23. Hahrie Han, *How Organizations Develop Activists: Civic Associations and Leadership in the 21st Century*, Oxford University Press, 2014.

24. Citizens UK's founder, the late Neil Jameson, who died in 2023, was a social worker from Somerset who studied Saul Alinsky's methods in Chicago from the 1930s to the 1960s, and wanted to try something similar in the UK. Heather Stewart, 'Neil Jameson obituary', *Guardian*, 14 May 2023; 'Marking the legacy of Neil Jameson, Citizens UK's Founder', Citizens UK, 2023.

25. Everyone I spoke to about community organising in this country mentioned Citizens UK. Some had trained or worked there or had worked in partnership with it. The more critical comments concerned its insistence on particular methods, a tendency to

preachiness, and the limitations of focusing on institutions – often faith-based ones – when religious attendance is declining. It is undeniable, however, that Citizens UK has trained up a new generation of community organisers in the UK.

26. According to the 2014 Immigration Act, unaccompanied children could only be detained, under strict conditions, for up to twenty-four hours; children with their families, for up to seventy-two hours. This was undone by the 2023 Illegal Migration Act, which contains powers to detain children.

27. Even at the height of David Cameron's commitment to end the detention of children, the Home Office was still locking up unaccompanied minors on the grounds of age dispute, Bralo said.

28. Jon Cracknell and Eliza Baring, *Funding Justice 2: An analysis of social justice grantmaking in the UK in 2021–2022*, Civic Power Fund and The Hour is Late, October 2023.

29. Jon Cracknell and Eliza Baring, *Funding Justice 3: An analysis of social justice grant making in the UK in 2022–2023*, Civic Power Fund and The Hour is Late, February 2025. Across more than twenty thousand grants worth £935.7 million from eighty-four funders, only 4.5% of funding from the UK's largest grant makers is for social justice. Nearly half of this portion goes to 'service delivery'; more than a quarter goes to 'inside game' approaches, i.e. advocacy work in 'elite settings'.

30. Civic Power Fund, *Growing the Grassroots: How we can strengthen our movements through the power of place*, May 2022; Civic Power Fund, *Power Up: Community Organising and Big Charities*, December 2022. Natasha Adams' blog 'Can grassroots groups genuinely partner with NGOs?', October 2022, on thinkingdoingchanging. com (https://thinkingdoingchanging.com/2022/10/12/ can-grassroots-groups-genuinely-partner-with-ngos/).

31. This has happened, for example, with the concept of intersectionality, resulting in the irony of organisations who most embody it being excluded from funding for not using the right language. This was reported at the online Uncharitable Festival in October 2024.

32. Some organisers argue for dues-based models, so that by paying collectively to cover the cost of employing an organiser, communities can have full ownership of the process. Charlotte Fischer and Stephanie Wong, *Collecting Our Dues*, Love & Power and Act Build Change, June 2023.

33. As the quote attributed to Lilla Watson and an Aboriginal women's group goes, 'If you have come here to help me, you are wasting your time. But if you have come because your liberation is bound up with mine, then let us work together.'

34. Shelter analysis, March 2025, using ONS Census by tenure data (2021), and Department of Work and Pensions Stat-Xplore data on Universal Credit and Housing Benefit claimants (November 2024).

35. Figure provided by Shelter, based on Department for Levelling Up, Housing & Communities, English Housing Survey: local authority housing stock condition modelling, 2020. (This government department has since been renamed the Ministry of Housing, Communities & Local Government.)

36. Neil Demause, 'The Gentrifier's Guide to Not Being an Asshole', *The Village Voice*, 25 August 2015.

37. The Supreme Court ruled in 2015 that student loans could be made to people with limited leave to remain. R (on the application of Tigere (Appellant) v Secretary of State for Business, Innovation and Skills (Respondent); [2015] UKSC 57, 29 July 2015.

38. Feminist-standpoint epistemology in the 1970s argued that women can see their own oppression – and therefore the world which creates that oppression – more clearly, through their experience of being marginalised; more marginalised women, for example Black women, can see more. They weren't making ethnocentric claims about their own knowledge, nor claiming greater moral validity for certain groups. The claim was solely epistemological: that those experiences were a better place to begin knowledge projects. Sandra Harding, 'Rethinking Standpoint Epistemology: "What is Strong Objectivity"?', pp. 54–9 and Bat-Ami Bar On, 'Marginality and Epistemic Privilege', p. 85, both in Linda Alcoff and Elizabeth Potter (eds), *Feminist Epistemologies*, Routledge, 1993; Patricia Hill

Collins, *Black Feminist Thought: Knowledge, Consciousness, and the Politics of Empowerment*, Routledge, 1990/2000, p. 11.

39. Emerging in the US as a principle from the Black feminist activism of the Combahee River Collective, intersectionality was named by the legal scholar Kimberlé Crenshaw in 'Demarginalizing the Intersection of Race and Sex: A Black Feminist Critique of Antidiscrimination Doctrine', *University of Chicago Legal Forum*, vol. 1989(1), 1989, pp. 139–68.

40. Olúfémi O. Táíwò, 'In-the-Room-Privilege and Epistemic Deference', *The Philosopher*, vol. 108(4), Autumn 2020. He expanded on the argument in *Elite Capture: How the Powerful Took Over Identity Politics (And Everything Else)*, Pluto Press, 2022.

41. Daniel Denvir, 'Olúfémi O. Táíwò : "Oppression Is Not a Prep School": Interview With Olúfémi O. Táíwò', *Jacobin*, 25 August 2022.

5: 'I Save People'

1. Emma Dabiri, *What White People Can Do Next: From Allyship to Coalition*, Penguin, 2021, p. 81.

2. Stefano Harney and Fred Moten, *The Undercommons: Fugitive Planning and Black Study*, Minor Compositions, 2013, p. 10.

3. Themrise Khan, Kanakulya Dickson and Maïka Sondarjee, *White Saviorism in International Development: Theories, Practices and Lived Experiences*, Daraja Press, 2023, p. 4.

4. Humanitarian workers in the early 2000s were passing around battered copies of Tony Vaux's *The Selfish Altruist*, Earthscan, 2001, which, commendably, encouraged us to question our motivations and assumptions in the complex situations we were in. A former Oxfam emergencies specialist, Vaux examined racism, the risk of creating policy based on subjective reactions to suffering, aid agencies caught up in their own governments' military aims, and the abuses of power that are more likely when 'the issue of power is swept under the carpet'. While much of what he discussed is at the core of the critique of white saviourism he didn't frame it as such.

5. See Binyavanga Wainaina, 'How To Write About Africa', *Granta*, 92, 2019.

6. Daniella Medeiros Cavalcanti, Lucas de Oliveira Ferreira de Sales, Andrea Ferreira da Silva, *et al.*, 'Evaluating the impact of two decades of USAID interventions and projecting the effects of defunding on mortality up to 2030: a retrospective impact evaluation and forecasting analysis', *The Lancet*, 19 July 2025.

7. Larry Elliott and Ashley Seager, '£30bn debts write-off agreed', *Guardian*, 11 June 2005.

8. It's less, in practice, calculates the Centre for Global Development: in 2023, 28% of the aid budget went to housing for asylum seekers in the UK. Patrick Wintour, Rowena Mason and Peter Walker, 'Keir Starmer to carry out largest cut to UK overseas aid in history', *Guardian*, 28 February 2025.

9. John Keats, 'The Fall of Hyperion: A Dream', 1819.

10. Nurith Aizenman, 'U.S. Missionary With No Medical Training Settles Suit Over Child Deaths At Her Center', *NPR*, 31 July 2020.

11. Illich's speech now gets used by some volunteer organisations as part of their pre-trip training.

12. Teju Cole, 'The White-Savior Industrial Complex', *The Atlantic*, 21 March 2012.

13. Sathnam Sanghera's *Empireworld: How British Imperialism Has Shaped the Globe*, Viking, 2024, includes the story of Britain's 'disproportionate number' of international charities and their connections with empire. See also Khan, Dickson and Sondarjee, *White Saviorism*.

14. Campaigning networks of staff and former staff were set up, like Decolonise MSF (Médecins Sans Frontières), Charity So White and No More White Saviours.

15. The 1990s version of this was 'participatory' projects, with more local 'buy-in'. 'Localisation' became the thing from the mid-2000s and through the 2010s.

16. INCITE! (eds), *The Revolution Will Not Be Funded: Beyond the Non-Profit Industrial Complex*, Duke University Press, 2017; Alnoor Ladha and Lynn Murphy, *Post-Capitalist Philanthropy: Healing Wealth in the Time of Collapse*, Daraja Press, 2023. The Uncharitable Festival, an annual online event hosted by Martha Awojobi, a

British fundraising consultant, features discussion by industry insiders on racism in the funding and charitable sectors and the emerging possibilities to decolonise how it works.

17. 'We view the traditional philanthropy model as so entangled with Colonial Capitalism that it inevitably continues the harms of the past into the present', statement on Lankelly Chase website, accessed 8 January 2025.

18. The Baobab Foundation supports Black and global-majority communities in the UK; Kwanda is a diaspora membership platform where monthly donations support local entrepreneurs across Africa.

19. Sky News online report, 'Comic Relief to stop sending celebrities to Africa after "white saviour" criticism', 28 October 2020.

20. Jason Hickel, *The Divide: A Brief Guide to Global Inequality and its Solutions*, Penguin, 2018, pp. 9–11.

21. *The Sustainable Development Goals Report 2025*, United Nations, p. 8.

22 Two classics: Walter Rodney, *How Europe Underdeveloped Africa*, Verso, 2018 (originally published 1972) and Eduardo Galeano, *The Open Veins of Latin America: Five Centuries of the Pillage of a Continent*, Serpent's Tail, 2009 (originally published 1971).

23. Action Aid, Education International and Public Services International, *The Public vs Austerity: Why public sector wage bill constraints must end*, 2021, p. 6.

24. Global Inequality Project, based on World Bank International Debt Statistics, https://globalinequality.org/debt-financial-outflows/.

25. OECD Policy Brief, *Cuts in official development assistance: OECD projections for 2025 and the near term*, 26 June 2025, p. 3.

26. War on Want, *Towards Trade Justice: Changing trade for a just and sustainable planet*, September 2023.

27. Gastón Nievas and Alice Sodano, 'Has the US exorbitant privilege become a rich world privilege? Rates of return and foreign assets from a global perspective 1970–2022', World Inequality Lab Working Paper, no. 2024/14.

28. Jason Hickel, Dylan Sullivan and Huzaifa Zoomkawala, 'Plunder in the Post-Colonial Era: Quantifying Drain from the Global South

Through Unequal Exchange, 1960–2018', *New Political Economy*, vol. 26(6), 2021, pp. 1030–47.

29. Jason Hickel, Morena Hanbury Lemos and Felix Barbour, 'Unequal exchange of labour in the world economy', *Nature Communications*, vol. 15, article 6298, 2024.

30. Some conceptual and measurement difficulties are summarised in Joras Ferwerda and Brigitte Unger, 'How Big Are Illicit Financial Flows? The Hot Phase of IFF Estimations', in Brigitte Unger, Lucia Rossel, and Joras Ferwerda (eds), *Combating Fiscal Fraud and Empowering Regulators: Bringing tax money back into the COFFERS*, Oxford University Press, 2021.

31. Tax Justice Network, *State of Tax Justice 2024*, pp. 8, 23, 25.

32. House of Commons International Development Committee, *Racism in the Aid Sector*, First Report of Session 2022–23. One witness was Themrise Khan, a consultant in the aid industry and editor of a 2023 anthology on white saviourism (see note 3 in this chapter). Pushed to answer a question about what should be in the UK government's 'development strategy', Khan said, 'I'm done – no more answers!... I am not denying that there is poverty and that we need economic growth across the board in all countries of the world, but if you frame a development strategy in that way, you are getting off on the wrong foot all over again. What we need to talk about is what other countries want.' She had already set out the colonial history of aid relationships and the need to transcend them. International Development Committee, *Oral Evidence: The Philosophy and Culture of Aid*, 9 November 2021.

33. Development Finance International, *Tackling Inequality at its Epicentre: Eastern and Southern Africa*, April 2025.

34. One of the scholar Vanessa Andreotti's definitions of modernity is 'a single story of progress'. Vanessa Machado de Oliveira, *Hospicing Modernity: Facing Humanity's Wrongs and the Implications for Social Activism*, North Atlantic Books, 2021, pp. 65–85.

35. For example Global Witness, *Undue Diligence: How banks do business with corrupt regimes*, 2009.

36. Khan, Dickson and Sondarjee, *White Saviorism*, p. 4.

37. 'The words we heard most in describing the organisation during the testimony and focus group discussions were "white saviour and colonialist"', Global HPO, *Good People Doing Good Things, Who Cannot Do Bad Things: An Inquiry Into Institutional Racism at Amnesty International UK*, 2022, p. 20.

38. The word *ubuntu* comes from the Zulu and Xhosa languages; there are related terms in other Bantu languages.

39. This phrase is from Stephen Hopgood, *Keepers of the Flame: Understanding Amnesty International*, Cornell University Press, 2006, p. 6.

40. Tyler Wigg-Stevenson, *The World Is Not Ours To Save*, InterVarsity Press, 2013.

41. The Vatican repudiated it five hundred years later, in 2023. Bill Chappell, 'The Vatican repudiates "Doctrine of Discovery," which was used to justify colonialism', *NPR*, 30 March 2023.

42. C. B. Leupolt, *Recollections of an Indian Missionary*, London, 1843.

43. Kidwell observes a saviour pattern in climate activism in the UK: a particular version of the Christian concept of salvation, 'probably one of the worst possible ones. A hyper-individualist, late modern, Protestant' one. 'We need to save everyone, but when we say everyone, we mean a horde of individuals, and every single one of them needs to be reached and spoken to.' See Chapter 7.

44. Rowan Williams, *Being Christian*, Society for Promoting Christian Knowledge, 2014, p. 6.

45. The Patriotic Millionaires group and Tax Justice UK suggest that a 2% tax on assets over £10 million would raise £24 billion; reforming capital gains tax would produce another £12 billion (from Patriotic Millionaires website). The campaigner and political economist Professor Richard Murphy's *Taxing Wealth Report* 2024 proposed changes to the taxation of wealth and property income that would raise £90 billion a year; he adjusted to £75 billion following Labour's autumn budget in 2024. Personal correspondence in March 2025.

46. Seeing problems as rooted in the individual or their family could potentially result in social workers trying to 'save' them. Part of the

antidote to saviourism in social work is awareness of the bigger context – that family and parenting difficulties are often rooted in poverty. This awareness creates the classic dissonance that humanitarian workers also experience: they know that their work, by mitigating the worst impact of unjust and inequitable political and economic systems, is keeping a lid on things and thus potentially perpetuating those systems, yet compassion keeps them in the work.

47. John McWhorter uses 'elect' to describe the new 'religion' of anti-racism in the US in *Woke Racism: How a New Religion Has Betrayed Black America*, Swift Books, 2022. He uses 'elect' as a metaphor for various aspects of fundamentalist religion, rather than in its sense relating to predestination.

48. Cynthia Bourgeault, *Wisdom Jesus*, Shambhala, 2009, pp. 19–20. This influence is in some Western strands too.

49. Diarmaid MacCulloch, *A History of Christianity*, Allen Lane, 2009, pp. 606–11.

50. Christopher Hill, *The English Bible and the Seventeenth Century Revolution*, Penguin, 1993, pp. 433–4.

51. Indigenous observers might go further: the profound sense of scarcity in Western culture comes from our separation from the web of life. Machado de Oliveira, *Hospicing Modernity*, pp. 20, 56.

52. Caroline Lucas, *Another England: How to Reclaim Our National Story,* Penguin, 2024, p. 24.

53. Caroline Lucas discusses the consequences of this feeling for the UK's response to Covid in *Another England*, p. 48.

54. MacCulloch, *A History of Christianity*, p. 607.

55. There is also, mostly separately from the idea of the elect, the 'prosperity Gospel', which originated in the twentieth century in American charismatic Christian movements, teaching that financial success is God's plan and can be increased through faith and good works.

56. Michael Sandel, *The Tyranny of Merit*, Penguin, 2020, Chapter 2, especially pp. 41–2. The term 'meritocracy' was coined by the British social reformer Michael Young, who published his satire *The Rise of the Meritocracy* with Thames & Hudson in 1958.

57. The drama triangle was developed by Stephen Karpman, and emerged from a psychoanalytic model called transactional analysis now widely used in management training courses.

58. According to Rape Crisis England and Wales, 1 in 6 children have been sexually abused, 1 in 4 women have been raped or sexually assaulted since the age of sixteen, and 1 in 18 men have been raped or sexually assaulted since the age of sixteen.

59. Satya Robyn, 'Daily Prayer For The Earth': https://www.satyarobyn.com/earthprayer/.

60. Richard Schwartz, *No Bad Parts: Healing Trauma and Restoring Wholeness*, Sounds True, 2021, pp. 14–16.

61. 'Richard Schwartz has had lots of stick from Buddhists saying there's no such thing,' said Robyn. 'So, if you're Buddhist, you might want to think of it as "non-self".'

62. This is a Winnicottian idea: that the witnessing can be 'good enough'.

63. A useful online resource on the links between trauma and activism is a pamphlet by the Jane Addams Collective, *Mutual Aid, Trauma and Resiliency*.

64. My thanks to Liam Barrington-Bush for an insightful conversation on this topic.

6: 'I Am a Hero'

1. Bertolt Brecht, *Life of Galileo*, ed. Eric Bentley and trans. Charles Laughton, Grove Books, 1994 (originally performed in this version in 1947).

2. Damien Gayle, '"You can be happy in prison": climate protester reflects on punishment,' *Guardian*, 2 January 2024.

3. See Chapter 2 for a discussion of the effectiveness of such protest tactics.

4. At the time, these were the longest sentences given to peaceful protesters in the UK (in 2024 a group of Just Stop Oil protesters received sentences of four or five years, later reduced on appeal). Trowland was released after serving thirteen months; Decker after sixteen. Gayle, '"You can be happy in prison"'; George Monbiot, 'Victimise people who raise a voice in Britain? Then destroy their families? Not in my

name', *Guardian*, 19 April 2024. Decker, who has a partner and step-children in the UK, was facing deportation to his native Germany as a result of his conviction, but won his appeal in 2025.

5. There are many accounts of the experiment. Useful reflections from a distance are Philip G. Zimbardo, Christina Maslach and Craig Haney, 'Reflections on the Stanford Prison Experiment: Genesis, Transformations, Consequences', in Thomas Blass (ed), *Obedience to Authority: Current Perspectives on the Milgram Paradigm*, Psychology Press, 1999, pp. 207–52 and Philip Zimbardo, *The Lucifer Effect: How Good People Turn Evil*, Rider Books, 2007.

6. Zimbardo and Milgram were at school together in the Bronx.

7. Hannah Arendt, *Eichmann in Jerusalem: A Report on the Banality of Evil*, Penguin, 2022 / Viking, 1963.

8. More recent social psychology work suggests that our willingness to obey an authority figure depends on the extent to which we identify with what they represent, and on whether they can present 'vicious acts as virtuous'. S. Alexander Haslam and Stephen D. Reicher, 'Contesting the "Nature" Of Conformity: What Milgram and Zimbardo's Studies Really Show', *PLoS Biology*, 10(11), November 2012.

9. Elizabeth Heathcote, 'Maverick academic Philip Zimbardo says we are all capable of evil. Is he right?', *Independent*, 2 March 2008.

10. Zimbardo, *The Lucifer Effect*, p. 373.

11. Kathy Blau, Zeno Franco and Philip Zimbardo, 'Fostering the Heroic Imagination: An Ancient Ideal and a Modern Vision', *Eye on Psi Chi Magazine*, 13, 2009, pp. 18–21.

12. He had noticed it earlier: writing in 1999, he said that he and Milgram 'discussed but did not act on the need for psychologists to study the dissidents, the rebels, the whistleblowing heroes. Demonstrating the power of the situation to make good people do evil deeds somehow held more appeal to us than the more difficult reverse process of showing how ordinary people could be induced to do heroic deeds within a Milgram-like paradigm.' Zimbardo, Maslach and Haney, 'Reflections on the Stanford Prison Experiment'.

13. Zeno E. Franco, Kathy Blau and Philip G. Zimbardo, 'Heroism: A Conceptual Analysis and Differentiation Between Heroic Action and Altruism', *Review of General Psychology*, vol. 15(2), 2011, pp. 99–113.

14. Ibid.

15. See Crisis Action's *Creative Coalitions: A Handbook for Change*, available online.

16. Joseph L. Badaracco, Jr, 'We Don't Need Another Hero, in Leadership Insights', *Harvard Business Review*, vol. 79(8), September 2001.

17. Daniel Goleman, 'Leadership That Gets Results', *Harvard Business Review*, vol. (78)2, 2000.

18. Hortense le Gentil, 'Leaders, Stop Trying to Be Heroes', *Harvard Business Review*, 25 October 2021.

19. Jon Alexander with Ariane Conrad, *Citizens*, pp. 214–18.

20. Scott T. Allison, 'The Initiation of Heroism Science', *Heroism Science*, vol. 1(1), 2016.

21. Kristian Frisk, 'What Makes a Hero? Theorising the Social Structuring of Heroism', *Sociology*, vol. 53(1), 2019, pp. 87–103 at p. 99, citing G. L. Mosse, *Fallen Soldiers: Reshaping the Memory of the World Wars*, Oxford University Press, 1991.

22. Or from Nietzsche's sister Elisabeth's mangling of his work after his death.

23. My informal quest to ban military metaphor from the human rights groups I worked in was influenced by Carol Cohn's feminist study of the language of nuclear defence. 'Sex and Death in the Rational World of Defense Intellectuals', *Signs*, vol. 12(4), Summer 1987.

24. Deference to my-thing-ism also means that we hold back from pushing a message because so-and-so is 'already working on that'. (See Chapter 2.)

25. Franco, Blau and Zimbardo, 'Heroism: A Conceptual Analysis'.

26. From a 2021 online conversation hosted by the Sophia Center with Andrew Samuels, Vorris Nunley and Betty Sue Flowers: 'After the Hero – What The F**k? Testing the Claims of Anti-heroic Narratives in Psyche, Culture and Politics'.

27. Sylvia Schweiger, Barbara Müller and Wolfgang H Güttel, 'Barriers to leadership development: Why is it so difficult to abandon the hero?', *Leadership*, vol. 16(4), 2020, pp. 411–33.

28. Ursula K. Le Guin, 'The Carrier Bag Theory of Fiction', in *Dancing At The Edge of the World: Thoughts on Words, Women, Places*, Harper and Row, 1990, pp. 165–70.

29. As citizens did in the town of Frome in Somerset in 2015, taking over the council; see Peter Macfadyen, *Flatpack Democracy: A DIY Guide to Creating Independent Politics*, Eco-logic Books, 2017.

30. Amitav Ghosh, *The Great Derangement*, University of Chicago Press, 2016, p. 25.

31. Attempts to regulate the weather with technology place earth as the 'monster' and humans as the heroes who must tame her, writes Sophie Strand in *The Flowering Wand: Rewilding the Sacred Masculine*, Inner Traditions, 2022, p. 27.

32. It was longer. Adam Weymouth, author of *Lone Wolf: Walking the Faultlines of Europe*, Penguin, 2025, tells me that wolves had largely disappeared from Wales by the end of the first millennium.

33. Kathleen Jamie, 'A Lone Enraptured Male', *London Review of Books*, 6 March 2008.

34. The anthropologist Ernest Becker suggested that many aspects of our behaviour and culture – including our attachment to the hero – come from our species' painful consciousness of life's finitude. Ernest Becker, *Denial of Death*, Free Press, 1973, p. 11.

35. See Martin Shaw, *Wolf Milk: Chthonic Memory in the Deep,* Wild, Cista Mystic Press, 2019. He has been leading wilderness vigils in the UK for twenty years, and prefers the word 'vigil', to limit the expectations of instant shattering enlightenment that can be raised by the term 'quest'.

36. Joseph Campbell, *The Hero with A Thousand Faces*, Paladin, 1988 (originally published 1949).

37. Andrew Samuels, *Jung and the Post-Jungians*, Routledge, 1985, p. 66.

38. Giovanni V. R. Sorge, 'The construct of the "mana personality" in Jung's works: a historic-hermeneutic perspective. Part II', *Journal of Analytical Psychology*, vol. 65(3), 2020, pp. 519–37.

39. The myth-teller Martin Shaw regularly makes this point. Carl Jung said that archetypes – shared images held in the collective unconscious – can be easier to understand esoterically, via myth and fairy tale, than psychologically. Carl Jung, *The Archetypes and the Collective Unconscious*, Collected Works, vol. 9, Princeton University Press, 2014.

40. 'It seems to me that the ultimate cause of environmental degradation is that almost all of us, whatever we do and wherever we do it, regard ourselves as sympathetic central characters,' wrote the novelist Toby Litt in *How to Tell A Story to Save the World*, Extinction Rebellion Writers Rebel, available online.

41. His blog can be read at dwightturnercounselling.co.uk/library/blog/.

42. Carl Jung, 'On the Psychology of the Unconscious', in *Two Essays on Analytical Psychology*, *Collected Works*, vol. 7, Princeton University Press, 2014.

43. Andrew Samuels, 'Appraising the Role of the Individual in Political and Social Change Processes: Jung, Camus, and the Question of Personal Responsibility–Possibilities and Impossibilities of "Making a Difference"', *Psychotherapy and Politics International*, vol. 12(2), 2014, pp. 99–110.

44. Campbell, *The Hero with a Thousand Faces*, pp. 97–8, 105–8.

45. Sarah Nicholson, 'The Problem of Woman as Hero in the Work of Joseph Campbell', *Feminist Theology*, vol. 19(2), 2011, pp. 182–93; Kristian Frisk, 'What Makes a Hero? Theorising the Social Structuring of Heroism', *Sociology*, vol. 53(1), 2019, pp. 87–103.

46. Carol Gilligan's *In A Different Voice: Psychological Theory and Women's Development*, Harvard University Press, 1983, criticised psychological models that ranked the 'male' pattern of disconnecting from community to grow into independence as more developed than the 'female' pattern of prioritising relationality. Ursula K. Le Guin's 1986 essay 'The Carrier Bag Theory of Fiction' takes issue with the straight lines of the male hero's story. Sharon Blackie's *If Women Rose Rooted: The Journey to Authenticity and Belonging*, September Publishing, 2016, proposes a 'Heroine's Journey'. Maria Tatar's *The Heroine with 1001 Faces*, Liveright, 2021, finds the overlooked heroism in the women of the mythological and literary canons.

47. 'Ideal Androgyne' in Marina Warner's *Joan of Arc: The Image of Female Heroism*, Vintage, 1981, pp. 139–58, discusses the evidence for Joan's commitment to male dress.

48. Once men were being killed in the First World War, this self-sacrifice looked less appealing, 'and the language of female purity suffered a swift devaluation as well.' Susan Pedersen, 'A Knife To the Heart', *London Review of Books*, 30 August 2018.

49. Luise Eichenbaum and Susie Orbach, *What Do Women Want?*, Fontana, 1984, is useful here.

50. Strand, *The Flowering Wand*. See also Riane Eisler, *The Chalice and the Blade*, Thorsons, 1987.

51. The Rewilding Cinderella project celebrated versions of the story from around the world: wildstorycommons.org/rewilding-cinderella. Joanna Gilar, 'The Rewilding Cinderella Project: Exploring the Ecological Multiplicities of the Cinderella Cycle', *Marvels & Tales*, vol. 38(1), 2024, pp. 98–114.

52. This reminded me of Dougald Hine's four suggested tasks in a time of endings: salvage the good we can take with us; mourn the good that we can't; discern and notice the things that were never as good as we told ourselves about the way we live; and look for the skills and practices we thought were obsolete. Dougald Hine, *At Work in the Ruins: Finding Our Place in the Time of Climate Crises and Other Emergencies*, Chelsea Green, 2023.

53. According to Corporate Watch, Elbit supplies 85% of Israel's military drones and land-based equipment.

54. This is a term from the Brazilian playwright and activist Augusto Boal's Theatre of the Oppressed, in which theatre is a tool for transformation and political education.

55. R (on the application of Ammori) v Secretary of State for the Home Department & Others [2026], EWHC 292 (Admin).

7: 'I Must Save the World *Now*'

1. Greta Thunberg, speech to the World Economic Forum, January 2019.

2. Bayo Akomolafe says this in many of his lectures. See his blogpost at https://www.bayoakomolafe.net/post/a-slower-urgency.

3. The treaty in question was the UN Convention Against Corruption, adopted in 2003.

4. This coalition was called the Global Campaign for Climate Action.

5. Also, Simms noted, the strategy seemed to make sense in 2008: with a financial crisis, sky-high oil prices and harvest failures around the world, the purpose of '100 months' was to launch the Green New Deal, which he co-created. (See Chapter 3.)

6. Andrew Jordan Wilson and Ben Orlove, *What do we mean when we say climate change is urgent?* Center for Research on Environmental Decisions, Earth Institute/Columbia University, 2019.

7. Mark Poynting, Erwan Rivault and Becky Dale, '2024 first year to pass 1.5C global warming limit', *BBC News*, 10 January 2025.

8. United Nations Office for the Coordination of Humanitarian Affairs, *Revised Pakistan 2022 Floods Response Plan Final Report*, 15 December 2023.

9. Fiona Harvey, 'Droughts worldwide pushing tens of millions towards starvation, says report', *Guardian*, 2 July 2025.

10. UK Climate Change Committee, *Progress in adapting to climate change: 2025 report to Parliament*, April 2025.

11. A 2021 review of behavioural psychology research suggested a 'Goldilocks' degree of urgency for climate communications: too little and it won't register; too much and attention, decision-making and effectiveness are impaired. Andrew J. S. Wilson and Ben Orlove, 'Climate urgency: evidence of its effects on decision making in the laboratory and the field', *Current Opinion in Environmental Sustainability*, vol. 51, 2021, pp. 65–76.

   Eco-linguistics researchers, who study the 'deep frames' that verbal metaphors evoke in us (see last section of Chapter 2), are also wary of urgency framing. Elisabetta Zurru, 'Communicating the Urgency of the Climate Emergency through Verbal and Non-verbal Metaphors', in Maria Bortoluzzi and Elisabetta Zurru, *Ecological Communication and Ecoliteracy: Discourses of Awareness and Action for the Lifescape*, Bloomsbury, 2024, pp. 88–111.

12. Thanks to Dougald Hine whom I have heard describe this realisation in a similar way.

13. This was a tactical mistake, but there were strategic ones too. See Nafeez Ahmed, 'The flawed social science behind Extinction Rebellion's change strategy', INSURGE intelligence, *Medium*, 28 October 2019.

14. The time taken to build solidarity and belonging could be named 'political time'; it is excluded by emergency framings. Graeme Hayes and Sherilyn McGregor, 'Taking Political Time: Thinking Past the Emergency Timescapes of the New Climate Movements', *South Atlantic Quarterly*, vol. 122(1), 2023, pp. 181–91; Sarah Amsler, 'Bringing Hope to "Crisis": Crisis Thinking, Ethical Action and Social Change', in Stefan Skrimshire (ed.), *Future Ethics: Climate Change and Apocalyptic Imagination*, Bloomsbury, 2010, pp. 129–52.

15. A 'carbon bomb' is a fossil fuel extraction project that will generate more than one gigatonne of carbon dioxide over its remaining lifetime. See https://carbonbombs.org.

16. Kate Beaton's graphic memoir *Ducks: Two Years in the Tar Sands*, Jonathan Cape, 2022, depicts a young woman's experiences working there.

17. Shell sold most of its stake in an oil sands mining company in 2017 (Karolin Schaps, 'Shell sells Canadian oil sands, ties bonuses to emissions cuts', *Reuters*, 10 March 2017); BP sold its stake in the oil sands in 2022 (Laura Hurst, 'BP Sells Out of Oil Sands, Snaps Up Canada Offshore Project', *Bloomberg News*, 13 June 2022).

18. According to Banking on Climate Chaos, *Fossil Fuel Finance Report 2024*, pp. 60–1, from 2016 to 2023 Barclays invested $5.313 billion and HSBC $2.533 billion in companies extracting tar sands oil. Barclays said it did 'not recognise the classification or attribution of some transactions' in the report. ('Barclays responds to Rainforest Action Network, "Banking on Climate Chaos" report', Barclays Bank, press release, 13 May 2024.) A few months earlier, Barclays had announced it was pulling out of oil sands financing. (Barclays *Climate Change Statement*, February 2024). A campaigner from Share Action – which pressures banks over their investment policies – pointed out the detail to me: while Barclays ceased direct project financing for tar sands, its policies permit corporate financing to companies with less than 10% of their revenue from tar sands, or where they have a

minority stake. HSBC said in 2025 that it had 'no direct exposure to oil sands following the completion of the sale of HSBC Bank Canada' (HSBC Energy Policy February 2025). Canadian banks have dominated in the tar sands industry in recent years. Banking on Climate Chaos, *Fossil Fuel Finance Report 2025*, p. 43.

19. Nearly two million acres of boreal forest were destroyed from 2000 to 2014. Rachael Petersen and Nigel Sizer, 'Tar Sands Threaten World's Largest Boreal Forest', World Resources Institute, 15 July 2014.

20. Jon Fennell, Tim K. Arciszewski, 'Current knowledge of seepage from oil sands tailings ponds and its environmental influence in north-eastern Alberta', *Science of The Total Environment*, vol. 686(10), October 2019, pp. 968–85; Ruth Kamnitzer, 'A year after toxic tar sands spill, questions remain for affected First Nation', *Mongabay*, 16 July 2024.

21. Matthew Taylor, 'Canadian tar sands pollution is up to 6,300% higher than reported, study finds', *Guardian*, 25 January 2024.

22. See Greenpeace Canada, 'Everything you need to know about the tar sands and how they impact you', 17 May 2021.

23. When I spoke about this to Gail Bradbrook, one of Extinction Rebellion's co-founders, she said that in the two-year run up to launching Extinction Rebellion she and her collaborators organised several open meetings with other campaign groups and took part in shared campaigning with some of them. She agreed however that there was something in this critique, and said that Extinction Rebellion ground to a halt internally as it attempted to respond to all of the criticisms that were received.

24. One casualty of urgency is learning from previous generations. Lola Olufemi presented her doctoral archival research and interviews with older Black activists in the UK in a non-chronological format, allowing readers to find their own connections with and between these histories. See lolaolufemi.co.uk/this-is-a-temporal-landscape.

25. Some climate-communications researchers now use More in Common's political taxonomy (see Chapter 3) to target messaging, like Climate Outreach's *Britain Talks Climate: A toolkit for engaging the British public on climate change (2024)*. The risk here, however, is

that by meeting people exactly where they are, we may reinforce their existing values.

26. See Rupert Read and Morgan Phillips, *Transformative Adaptation: Another world is still just possible*, Permanent Publications, 2024.

27. Maggie Nelson, *On Freedom*, Jonathan Cape, 2021, p. 180. Thanks to Vita Sleigh for noticing this.

28. Jonathon Porritt, *Love, Anger and Betrayal: Just Stop Oil's Young Climate Campaigners*, Anthony Eyre/Mount House Press, 2025, p. 40.

29. Wilmar B. Schaufeli, Michael P. Leiter and Christina Maslach, 'Burnout: 35 years of research and practice', *Career development international*, vol. 14(3), 2009, pp. 204–20.

30. Lucas B. Mazur, 'The desire for power within activist burnout. An illustration of the value of interpretive social science', *Sociology Compass 2024*, vol. 18(2).

31. Allowing space for grief was at the core of her work. Joanna Macy and Chris Johnstone, *Active Hope: How to Face the Mess We're in without Going Crazy*, New World Library, 2012.

32. Extinction Rebellion's explicit framing of grief in 2018 and 2019 was fairly new in climate activism. Anthea Lawson, 'Hyde Park to Wembley', *Dark Mountain*, Issue 16: Refuge, 2019.

33. See Francis Weller, *The Wild Edge of Sorrow: Rituals of Renewal and the Sacred Work of Grief*, North Atlantic Books, 2015.

34. Camille Sapara Barton, *Tending Grief: Embodied Rituals for Holding Our Sorrow and Growing Cultures of Care in Community*, North Atlantic Books, 2024. Sophy Banks, 'Tending Grief, Together', in Steffi Bednarek (ed.), *Climate, Psychology and Change: Reimagining Psychotherapy in an Era of Global Disruption and Climate Anxiety*, North Atlantic Books, 2024.

35. I have done a small piece of freelance work for Moral Imaginations.

36. Geoff Mulgan, 'Four ways we can use our collective imagination to improve how society works', Joseph Rowntree Foundation, 18 April 2022.

37. 'Industrial growth system' is a term from Joanna Macy, who envisaged a 'great turning' to a 'life sustaining society'.

38. Christopher Shaw, *Liberalism and the Challenge of Climate Change*, Routledge, 2024.

39. Marcia Bjornerud, *Timefulness: How Thinking Like a Geologist Can Help Save the World*, Princeton University Press, 2018.

40. Simon L. Lewis and Mark A. Maslin, 'Defining the Anthropocene', *Nature*, vol. 519, 12 March 2015.

41. Benjamin Kunkel, 'The Capitalocene', *London Review of Books*, vol. 39(5), 2 March 2017.

42. Anna Schaffner observes that writers on exhaustion and what we now call burnout have long blamed the ills of modernity, albeit through the lens of their own age. The Romantics lamented a pre-industrial past. Freud thought modernity's complexity led us to expend energy repressing our instinctual drives. 'Exhaustion and the Pathologization of Modernity', *Journal of Medical Humanities*, vol. 37(3), 2016, pp. 327–41.

43. Lyla June Johnston's research into Indigenous management of ecosystems across the Americas shows how they created food systems that were stable for millennia. *Architects of abundance: indigenous regenerative food and land management systems and the excavation of hidden history*, Doctoral Dissertation, University of Alaska Fairbanks, 2022 (available via her website lylajune.com/).

44. The best known is the Haudenosaunee Peacemaker story from the founding of the Haudenosaunee (sometimes known as the Iroquois) Confederacy. There are plenty of versions online, including on the Haudenosaunee Confederacy's own website.

45. See Vanessa Andreotti (writing as Vanessa Machado de Oliveira), *Hospicing Modernity*, p. 81.

46. Kyle Powys Whyte, 'Our Ancestors' Dystopia Now: Indigenous Conservation and the Anthropocene', in Ursula Heise, Jon Christensen and Michelle Niemann (eds), *The Routledge Companion to the Environmental Humanities*, Routledge, 2017. The image of the wake is from Christina Sharpe, *In the Wake: On Blackness and Being*, Duke University Press, 2016.

47. Ruth Wilson Gilmore describes abolition as 'life in rehearsal'. See note 2 of Chapter 3.

48. adrienne maree brown's concept of 'emergent strategy' in her book of that name (AK Press, 2017) is about (among many things) the transformed ways of being that shift how we act at small and everyday scales and which, if everyone was doing them, would be transformative more widely.

49. Measuring outcomes by value, they calculated the most efficient way to save a human. Early on it was de-worming; later, anti-malarial bed nets.

50. For example, Rupert Read, 'Must Do Better', *Radical Philosophy*, no. 201, February 2018, pp. 106–9; Alice Crary, 'Against "Effective Altruism"', *Radical Philosophy*, no. 210, Summer 2021, pp. 33–43.

51. For example, by driving profit-gouging: Nick Shaxson, 'Rural America Doesn't Have to Starve to Death', *The Nation*, 18 February 2020; by driving land grabs: War on Want, *Profiting from Hunger: Popular Resistance to Corporate Food Systems*, 2023, pp. 29–33; by driving defor-estation: 'British financiers funnelled over £1 billion into "forest-risk" companies despite COP26 pledges', Global Witness, press release, 16 October 2024; by facilitating corporate profit-shifting: Tax Justice Network, *State of Tax Justice 2024*, November 2024.

52. William MacAskill, *What We Owe the Future*, Oneworld, 2022.

53. Linda Kinstler, 'The good delusion: has effective altruism broken bad?', *Economist*, 15 November 2022; Dylan Matthews, 'How effective altruism let Sam Bankman-Fried happen', *Vox*, 13 December 2022.

54. Leif Wenar, 'The Deaths of Effective Altruism', *Wired*, 27 March 2024.

55. William James, *The Varieties of Religious Experience: A Study in Human Nature*, Barnes & Noble Classics, 2004 (originally pub-lished 1902), p. 31.

56. We have already crossed seven of the nine 'planetary boundaries' calculated by the Stockholm Resilience Centre, including climate change, biosphere integrity, freshwater and ocean acidification.

57. Ernest Becker, *The Denial of Death*.

58. See the 'house of modernity', a visual teaching tool developed by Vanessa Machado de Oliveira and the Gesturing Towards Decolonial Futures collective, in *Hospicing Modernity*, p. 106.

59. See Tricia Hersey, *Rest Is Resistance: Free yourself from grind culture and reclaim your life*, Aster, 2022.
60. Haines, *The Politics of Trauma*; Hemphill, *What It Takes To Heal.*
61. Sophy Banks shares ways to do this on her Healthy Human Culture substack and online courses.
62. This mirrors what happens at the intrapersonal level, where rest creates space for relationship with all aspects of ourselves.

Afterword

1. Menakem, *My Grandmother's Hands*, p. 39. See also Raffo, *Liberated to the Bone.*
2. This book focuses on how these patterns of thought and behaviour manifest in change-making, but they go deeper and there are other ways to describe them. Urgency, perfectionism and knowing-better feature in some accounts of the culture of white supremacy. Resmaa Menakem's view of how a conditioned nervous-system response perpetuates racist culture, for example (see previous note), is an embodied linking of 'urgency' and white supremacy. Another lens is 'coloniality/modernity', an analytical frame from decolonial studies that sees the link between colonial violence and the extractive, subject–object ways of seeing that characterise Western modernity. Chapters 8 and 9 of my book *The Entangled Activist* contain references. Vanessa Machado de Oliveira sees desires for control, urgency, knowledge, purity and innocence as symptoms of modernity, bolstering us against the existential anxiety that proceeds from our feeling of separation from the rest of life, and each of which we must 'compost' if anything is to change. Vanessa Machado de Oliveira, *Hospicing Modernity.*
3. See Amahra Spence, 'Who Is Organising Poor White Folks Towards Liberation?', *Substack*, 14 September 2025.
4. Barbara Ehrenreich, *Dancing in the Streets: A History of Collective Joy*, Granta, 2007.